Confessions of a
Wee Poison PGA Golf Pro

JOHN GROSHELL

Agio
PUBLISHING HOUSE

PUBLISHING HOUSE

Gabriola, BC Canada V0R 1X4

Confessions of a
Wee Poison PGA Golf Pro
ISBN 978-1-990335-17-4 (paperback)
ISBN 978-1-990335-18-1 (ebook)

Printed on acid-free paper. Agio Publishing House is a socially and environmentally responsible company, measuring success on a triple-bottom-line basis.

10 9 8 7 6 5 4 3 2 1 b

DEDICATION

Dedicated to our loyal members at
Snoqualmie Falls Golf Course who brought
their own rakes and shovels to help us
recover from the five disastrous floods. Their
help made the course recover physically, but
bigger than that, it helped me hang in there
mentally, knowing they would always help
save me and their home-away-from-home.

I would also like to dedicate this book to
my former students—both high school and
eighth grade—who have made me believe
that I was instrumental in preparing them for
success in life.

And, of course, to my wife Liz, sons Willie
and Jeff and their families. And to our dear
puppies who remind us that life is about love,
kindness, belonging, and sharing joy.

TABLE OF CONTENTS

Confessions of a
Wee Poison PGA Golf Pro

CHAPTER 1

Introduction

My name is John Groshell but I have gone by at least 10 different names during my life. As my story goes on many of them along with their origins will be mentioned. A few were Jumbo, Dairy Queen, Cassius, Punkin, Captain G Spot, Tiny Wood and Cupcake. Once I became a golf pro Johnny G has been used more than any. At Snoqualmie Falls Golf Course there has been a tournament for over 30 years named "The Johnny G." There is another tournament where you get one foot of string per stroke in handicap. That one is called "The Johnny G. String." A horse named Johnny G also kept me from starving on a College Team golf trip.

My favorite is Cupcake, I pinned that on myself the first year I was teaching school in 1967. I was trying to be funny while lecturing my class of 8th graders. A year ago, I went to the 50th reunion of one of my classes I taught at Tolt High and was greeted by all with a *"Hi, Cupcake!"* The name had followed me from Snoqualmie Middle School to Tolt High School. Cupcake travels well. Three years ago, in 2019, a new neighbor of ours here at Ocean Shores yelled, *"Hi, Cupcake,"* to me as I was walking my dog. A guy he knew was married to one of my ex-students.

❦

THIS BOOK IS SIMPLY THE story of my life as I experienced it; it is way more happy than sad. Many of my problems were self-inflicted but no matter the source I have fortunately been able to survive and thrive through them all. In this introductory chapter, I'll give you a hint of the tales to come in this memoir....

❖

MY MOTHER (THE BEST ONE of those that ever was) gave me caring and love for others and a love for dogs. She was an author of nine books and a graduate from Wellesley College. You will be reading more about her in this story. Her name was Charlotte Groshell.

My father (Ed) gave me a work ethic and a drive to succeed. He also helped give me a twisted sense of humor that I have used continually, sometimes to my detriment but more often positively. He also introduced me to betting. Most of the bets have been in regard to things taking place around me. In one of them I rigged a bet concerning which fly strip in the kitchen of my golf course would capture the most flies. Once the bet was made, I pointed a fan at that fly strip.

Both Mom and Dad tried to make me understand that okay was not good enough, that average didn't cut it. But I didn't care about school. I only cared about sports. If the activity didn't include a ball to hit, throw, shoot or catch, I didn't care. I came close to failing 5th and 7th grades. I hated Thanksgiving because it came just after the first report cards came out. We always went to Mom's parents' place for Thanksgiving and the topic was always, *"What are we going to do with Johnny?"*

We were never poor, and I never wanted for anything. If I did want something Dad made me earn it. When "Rock 'n' Roll" jackets came out I had to earn mine by pulling ferns. Dad paid me 1 cent each and I came up with $20 worth.

❖

MY FIRST CHALLENGE IN LIFE was following my brother in school by one year. Hiram had two fabulous talents. The first was getting Dad pissed off, the second was to make teachers look stupid. Almost every year I would have the same teacher he would have had the year before. It would take several months for them to realize this Groshell was not a threat. Goofball yes, threat no. The worst was when he alienated the high school baseball coach who was also his biology teacher. That ruined my freshman baseball year. Thankfully that coach left before my sophomore year.

The next challenge I have had is being short. When I entered high school, I was 4'8" tall and looked like I was 12 years old. Most every coach eliminates the really short kids without even giving them a chance. Sadly, sports were the only thing I cared about. I actually made the freshman basketball team and did finally play in several varsity baseball games my freshman year in spite of my brother.

❧

MY BROTHER GOT INTERESTED IN politics and was a page in the Washington State Senate in Olympia in 1959. I followed and was a page in the House in Olympia in 1961. At election time, we worked at doorbelling and putting up posters for candidates. We also attended the Washington State Democratic Convention in 1960. There I met JFK and Lyndon Johnson.

There was no big challenge to being a page. In Olympia I even figured out how to smuggle the occasional piece of pie out of the legislators' personal cafeteria.

We did have a much bigger challenge surviving in Washington, DC. Hiram was there for six months before I arrived. I took over his Senate page position and he went to work in the office of a representative from Illinois.

The challenge was living! We were in a four-storey apartment building. Each floor had ten rooms on it. There was one bathroom for all ten rooms. The basement had a kitchen that nobody used. I would sit there because it was cooler and polish my brown shoes black. Pages were required to wear black shoes and I couldn't afford to buy a pair. I did have a daily assignment (off the record) to steal a *New York Times* and a *Wall Street Journal* from the Senate library and put them on Senator Henry Jackson's desk in his office. At the end of the summer his office threw me a sendoff party.

❧

SPEAKING OF CHALLENGES AND BETS, there was a swimming hole in the

Snoqualmie River about one mile out of North Bend. It was called the "Blue Hole." That is where high school kids went swimming in the summer.

You had to get across the river to get to it as it was at the base of Mount Si. It was upstream from the trail to the river so one had to swim across, while being swept downstream, to the other side. Then walk over rocks and some brush to get to it.

I bet anyone there that I could swim straight to it. Read on to see how that went.

❧

ON FATHER'S DAY JUST AFTER high school graduation, when I was 17, an event happened that changed my life. Hiram was traveling to Europe but Mom, Dad and I had Father's Day dinner then I went off to water the greens at Mount Si Golf course.

I knew Mom was returning to an apartment she had in Olympia. At that time, she was on the State Parole Board.

When I came home at about midnight, I found Dad in the driveway with a shotgun beside him and part of his face blown away. He did live through it—so did I—but it made me realize that I was the only one in this world that would always take care of me. The next day I found out that Mom and Dad were getting divorced.

❧

THAT FALL WHEN I REGISTERED at WSU, my instructor told me I was going to fail, then he signed me up for 21½ hours. He explained that I would fail because I couldn't read. It was based on his interpretation of my SAT test results.

Since I couldn't read, I didn't buy books but never missed a class. I showed him when I got a 2.6 grade point average that semester. My sophomore year I bought books and dropped to a 2.2 GPA. Go figure.

My reading comprehension is fine, but I have always been a slow reader. I did best when I took excellent notes in class and used them for studying purposes.

❈

MORE CHALLENGES CAME WHEN I turned out for the WSU golf team. I hadn't gotten serious about golf until my junior year in high school. I had also missed playing golf the summer before when I was a page in the U.S. Senate. I had only played in one junior golf tournament. In spite of competing with others who had played for years, I was the top player for WSU my freshman year and for all three varsity years. In my junior year I finished second place individually in the Pac 8 Northern Division Championship, then took the state car without permission and my two team buddies to Portland Meadows racetrack where we almost lost all our meal money. You will get to read the happy ending to that fiasco later.

I managed to keep from getting kicked out of WSU even though I made social probation. Had I been booted I would have been drafted and sent to Vietnam. Looking back, I think most of the dumb stuff I did was in rebellion to finding Dad that night.

When the dean of men, the head resident, and some other officials were meeting to discuss my future at WSU I threw a snowball that went through the exhaust fan and sprayed them. My room was next to the conference room and on the 9th floor. I had explained to them that I was too short to have torn down a loudspeaker across from my room. I also explained that I had to stand on a chair to brush my teeth daily.

❈

MY FIRST TEACHING JOB WAS challenging but I even made it more challenging. After the first semester I got the principal to let me switch classes with the lady in the next room over. She was having a tough time handling them. There were six classes ability grouped 1 through 6. She had #1 in the morning and #6 in the afternoon. I had #3 and #4, the so-called average kids.

The #1 group was easily bored and had the ability to think up ways to be a problem once bored. I spoiled them by saying, "Let's learn together and have fun." The #6 group was 90% boys who didn't want to be in school, let alone learn. It was basically a classroom of Johnnys.

The fourth quarter I inspired them by giving them a chance to give me swats. I had them for English, Reading, Spelling and History and whoever got the best grade in each got to give me a swat on the front lawn of the school on the final day of school. Two of them wanted to give their rights to bigger, stronger kids. I said NO!!

Going to teach at Tolt High School two years later was a challenge with 35 to 42 students in every class and not even half enough books. I printed out material daily and the kids appreciated it. Those two years were absolutely fabulous. I left due to politics, it's all in this book.

✦

MY LAST YEAR AT MOUNT Si High really sucked—you will read why.

✦

MY FIRST JOB AS A golf pro at the Yakima Elks was fun but I went from making about $16,000 a year to $5,400. Thankfully part of the deal included a one-room apartment at the clubhouse but it had no A.C. and eastern Washington is hot!!

That year was a real challenge to Liz as she was pregnant with #1 son, Jeff.

Fortunately, at the end of the year I got the opportunity to buy in at Snoqualmie Falls golf course. I had the chance to buy 20% for $20,000. I only had to borrow $19,900 to pull it off. Over the next 25 years I bought my partner's shares, but at a significantly higher amount.

The opportunity came thanks to Jan Sorenson. She was the secretary at the middle school who I played jokes on and tormented for years following with prank phone calls. Each one of them ending in "John, you son of a bitch!" when she realized it was me.

I didn't know what a challenge was until I went there. I did get a raise in pay to $10,000 a year but to start with we lived in a small apartment in Fall City. We only had one car which Liz needed, so I walked back and forth to work daily rain or shine. It was a one-mile walk each way. After several months of that I bought a car for $70.

The golf course had been poorly maintained, had rubber mats for tee areas, no sand traps, and virtually no trees. The water system was only for the greens and required plugging in hoses at each one and moving the sprinkler head around. The place was a goat ranch. I only went there because we couldn't survive on what I made in Yakima.

My work was from opening to close six days a week. On Sundays I started mowing greens at 3:30 AM and would still be there at 10 PM cleaning the grill. I cooked, gave lessons, mowed, took greens fees, etc.

The biggest challenge came with floods. We had devastating floods in 1990, 1995, 1996, 2006 and 2009. Each shut us down for over two months and took close to a year for full recovery.

If it weren't for our loyal members who came out with their own shovels and rakes, we never could have made it. Their physical labor helped the golf course. The mental lift and emotional support from them got me through it. With my goofball style and friendly manner, I built a following that looked at Sno Falls golf course as being theirs.

Speaking of bets, one busy Sunday I bet I could hit a golf ball from one side of the clubhouse through it and out the door opening toward the river. Picture about 25 hollering men, all peering over the lunch counter and from behind turned over tables watching as I swung away with my 3 iron. Read on to see how that turned out.

❋

ANOTHER INCIDENT TOOK PLACE WHEN a sea plane got hung up on the rocks in the river by our clubhouse. My partner Chris and I had to wade in and push him off. Read on, like Paul Harvey used to say, "And that's the rest of the story."

❋

THERE IS A CAST OF characters, many of whom became sons to me. Amongst them are Spanky, Mutt, Pruggy and Side Show. Fortunately, I still see them all. Pruggy and our son Jeff (*aka* Radar) are both PGA professionals and are operating the golf course. There are also accounts of those who taught me lessons along the way. Some were verbal, others were through my observation.

I could keep rambling on but it's all in here. There are many goofy bets, the struggle to get a permit to build a new maintenance building, and my failure to prevent the "fugitive particulate matter" from being airborne. FYI—that is dust.

I managed, along with the help of many, to turn a cow pasture into a beautiful and busy public golf course. More importantly Liz and I have raised two great sons and now have four wonderful grandchildren.

On top of everything, I now have Dani Girl. She is the rescue pup I got almost 11 years ago from People United for Pets (PUP) in Issaquah. Without her my life would not be the same!

❊

HOPE YOU ENJOY THE STORIES!

CHAPTER 2

Pre-School Pain

My father and mother both worked for *The Chicago Times*. Dad was an editor, Mom worked as a writer, columnist and correspondent. When it merged with the *Chicago Sun* to become the *Chicago Sun Times*, my father, along with many others, was let go. My mother, who grew up in Washington State, wanted to go west where her father and stepmother lived in Seattle. So, at age 4, I packed up my older brother, mother and father who bought a weekly newspaper in Snoqualmie, Washington. We headed across country in 1949 to take over *The Snoqualmie Valley Record* and Falls Printing Company.

When we arrived in Snoqualmie Valley our first residence was a motel room in a small motel in North Bend. It must have been winter because it was cold, even in the room. I only have one memory from staying there. My mother had given me a bath and I was cold and shivering. I backed up by the heater to get warm. Before I realized it, I got a burn on my rear end about the size of a baseball. I did learn to be more careful with where I put my bare rear end from then on. I don't remember how long we stayed there but it couldn't have been very long.

Next, we rented a big old house only about a quarter-mile east of that motel. At that time Highway 90 went right through the middle of North Bend. It was the main road in North Bend and most all of the businesses were along both sides of it. At the time it was said that the one traffic light in North Bend was the only one on all of I-90 from Seattle to New York. The house was situated next to the real estate office of the realtor that we rented from. His office had a good-sized window facing our rental house.

One day my brother Hiram and I came up with a great game. Around this window the side of the office was like stucco, or cement. We started throwing rocks to hit the cement under the window. I am sure there was very little thought put into the creation of this

Beautiful Mom who taught me kindness.

activity—for instance, the inevitable conclusion thereof. Without a doubt the number of throws before the sound of breaking glass would have been a single digit. At that time, I wasn't familiar with the wager called an over/under. Had I been, I would have set the number at probably 2½. We took off running and hid in a small barn/big shed behind our house. Finally, when we hoped we were safe from blame, maybe 15 minutes later, we went into the house. Mom and the realtor were there waiting—what a surprise.

I don't remember the punishment, so Dad must not have been told about it. Dad's policy, at least once we got into school, was always, *"Whatever you get in school, you will get twice that when you get home."*

Dad sharing his McNaughtons and water with my parakeet.

So I NEVER ran home and said, "My teacher gave me two swats to-day"—I only said, "I had a great day at school today."

I only have two other memories from our stay in that house. We had a dog named "Teddy." Teddy looked a lot like a collie but was a mix of some kind. He was the first dog of my life—we had an Airedale in Illinois, but he wasn't a pet. He had been used in the military and wasn't really friendly. He never hurt anyone, but I was afraid of him. Anyways, one day Teddy wandered too close to I-90 and got clipped by a car. He survived but had a broken leg or hip. From then on Teddy mainly used three legs—but for at least the next 10 years Teddy was my best friend. I could hug him and sit on the back porch with him and tell him all my troubles. Teddy always took my side and told me I deserved better. Teddy also went fishing with me all the time.

The only other memory involved me, Hiram, a hammer, rocks and a concrete sidewalk. I was instructed to put rocks on the concrete that Hiram would then smash with the hammer. This was going along just fine until the index finger on my left hand got caught between the hammer and a rock and/or the concrete. Fortunately, all the damage was below the knuckle. The area between the knuckle and the end of the finger basically became hamburger—no nail—very little bone remaining. Apparently, Hiram thought he was a faith healer because he forced me out to the shed/barn and wouldn't let me go into the house. I guess he believed it would heal itself in under an hour. I did manage to get away after a while—Mom took me to the doctor—and I did eventually end up with a finger with a nail and the ability to grip a golf club.

So, this sums up the highlights of my pre-kindergarten years. Within a year my parents, Ed and Charlotte Groshell, would have a house built about one mile out of North Bend on the North Fork Road. That is where we lived for 12 or 13 years until the family went KABOOM!!

CHAPTER 3

Grade School Adventures

The house is a modest sized one with one medium-sized and two small bedrooms. It has a living/dining room, one bathroom, and a kitchen. It faces Mount Si but has virtually no windows facing the beautiful view of a mountain that isn't more than a half mile away. Within a couple years Mom and Dad have a huge front room with huge windows facing Mount Si added on. The windows were at least 5 foot x 8 foot and were thermo pane (two pieces). Also, there was a big bedroom (theirs), a nice bathroom (theirs), a small workshop, and a main entryway to the house that had a slate floor that was thermally heated.

The design was engineered so that their bedroom was at one end of the house and our bedrooms were as far away as possible while still being under the same roof. Mom and Dad were no dummies—proven to me by this separation in space more than by their accomplishments or education.

Dad had several degrees and had been the night editor at the *Chicago Times*. Mom graduated from Wellesley and at this point, had several magazine articles published and one book published. She went on to have eight more books published. As my efforts at writing go on, I will be mentioning the books and her other accomplishments. Most of all, her literary success paled to her success in raising Hiram and me. On top of everything she cared about people and spent her life trying to help others.

I really lucked out in the "Mom" department. That doesn't mean I couldn't work her over by saying, "Other kids' moms do ------." I even used that to get her to bake cookies and mail them to me at Washington State University. At the time she was living in Arlington, Virginia. How could such a nice mother have raised such a manipulating kid?

Anyways, back to the house. Being located one mile out of North

Bend (pop. 600+) there were few other houses. On one side of us was a dairy farm of several hundred acres. The farmhouse and barn were at the far end of the property. They couldn't even be seen from our house and were probably close to a mile away "as the crow flies". We had 2½ acres and on the other side was a house that was situated on about 5 acres. There were a few houses across the street (the North Fork Road) but they were mainly older couples with no kids to play with. Consequently, my brother would mainly read books and I would stay outside kicking a football, shooting a basketball, shooting my BB gun, or fishing. Mom tried to get me to read but I said I couldn't because reading made me dizzy. But I am getting ahead of myself now. Let's go back to my beginning in school.

When it was finally time for "Little Johnny" to go to school, apparently he wasn't up to it. I do remember my first couple of days at kindergarten. Actually, it was only close to kindergarten. I cried and bawled and screamed to be with my brother who was in first grade. I was absolutely terrified to be placed in a room with no one I knew. Why did I insist that I be with the guy who bullied me, smashed my finger, and consistently treated me poorly? As I remember, I finally succumbed to attending kindergarten on the second day. Basically, I was a shy little guy who was afraid to be without anyone I knew. Even at home when Mom and Dad had guests, Hiram would visit with everyone, and I would stay in my bedroom. As time went on though, I actually had lots of friends in school, on sports teams, at summer camp, and any activities involving other kids.

I guess our family was a bit old fashioned. Maybe we were more like other families at that time but looking back I'm thinking old fashioned. Nonetheless we always sat down for dinner together. In the first grade I made friends and there was one girl who would walk home with me occasionally. She lived about a half-mile from North Bend while I had to go one mile, but it was in the same direction. Nowadays I'm sure parents don't let first graders walk one mile alone to get home, but that was in 1951 in North Bend, WA. We would, of course, go to her house first then after playing for a while I would go on home. On one occasion she had me go into the bathroom with her while she peed. (She said we were playing "F**k"—it was the first time I ever heard that word). As a first grader I was kind of shocked or surprised or who knows what I was—but not really alarmed. I wasn't particularly interested in the different plumbing, but I would rather have been playing in the dirt outside, or digging worms to fish, or just about anything else. Eventually I headed home.

That night at dinner Dad asked, "Johnny, how was your day at school?"

I said "Fine, and when Carol and I walked home, she wanted to show me 'F**k' but I didn't look."

Dad rarely had a hard time thinking of something to say, I guess this was a tough one to answer because all he could come up with was, "That's nice."

I didn't walk home every day, although I wasn't told I couldn't. Mom and Dad also didn't tell me that I had to stay away from Carol or to not play that game anymore. I guess they could sense that even at age 6 I had high moral standards. Sometimes one of them would pick me up after school, or I would ride the school bus home, or I would ride a school bus to Snoqualmie. Snoqualmie was about four miles away and that is where the print shop was. Being only six, there wasn't much I could do to help, but sometimes I cleaned up ink off the floor or sorted leads and slugs (spacers used to make up a form for printing). If there wasn't something I could help with, I would just hang out or draw pictures or visit with employees. Just watching the presses running was fun.

On one of these school bus rides to Snoqualmie I was pushed into one of the back seats by an older boy who was probably a seventh or eighth grader. Back then the Snoqualmie Valley was almost entirely Caucasian. The only exception was a couple Native American families, then referred to as Indians. The boy who forced me into the corner of this back seat happened to be one of them. Once the bus was in motion, he took out his jack knife and threatened to cut my throat if I yelled or said anything. He also said that if I told my parents or anybody about this that he would kill me later.

Needless to say, I was quite shaken. By the time I got to the shop I was crying but I wouldn't tell Mom or Dad why. Finally, I gave in and told them. I know Dad did something about it but I have no idea what. After that I refused to take the bus to Snoqualmie again; I don't remember if I ever gave in and rode again.

A happy time with brother Hiram and the basset hounds. Image from my 70th birthday slide show.

Back to work at the print shop, once I became a seventh grader, I handled jobs that would be considered as dangerous nowadays. Both Hiram and I would cast pigs for the Linotype machine. This meant pouring molten metal into molds that were about 3 feet long. The ingots that were formed must have weighed at least 30 pounds. Picture a 12-year-old working with molten metal.

We also operated the press that was called a "hand snapper." This press was used to print smaller items like business cards or small invoices or other items not bigger than 4 inches by 6 inches. The paper was placed on one side, the press would close over it and print. It would then open up so the operator would remove the printed copy with one hand and put a new blank piece into the press to get printed. The press was like a big clam that would slam shut, then open, then slam shut again. It didn't care if your hand was still there or not. What you learned quickly was if you failed to grab the paper, get your hand out anyway. If you failed to put the new piece in properly, get your hand out anyway. These presses are the reason that many old-time printers were missing fingers. Hiram and I survived, and both still have eight fingers and two thumbs each, not total between us.

I liked school because that's where I could play with other kids. I never equated school with learning, it was just something I had to do. It wasn't until I was in my sophomore year at Washington State University that I figured out that school was for learning—maybe even to prepare for one's future.

Our neighbors on the 5-acre section to our south were Joe and Bonnie Lewis. They had two sons, Larry who was in his early 20's and Jim who was slightly younger. Larry worked rodeos as a trick rider, calf roper, and bronco rider. He had various calves to practice roping. He had a big coral and a chute for the calves to come out of. Joe owned the movie theater in Meadowbrook. Meadowbrook was a thriving community bordering Snoqualmie and close to the Weyerhaeuser Mill homes. Once the mill shut down, the houses were moved to another part of Snoqualmie and Meadowbrook became a ghost town. Before then the theater thrived.

As often as I thought I could get away with it I would fake that I was sick. This was during first, second and third grade. Since both Mom and Dad worked at the paper, they would send me next door to

Joe and Bonnie's. They would usually dress me up with chaps, cowboy boots— sometimes spurs added, and a cowboy hat. I would bring my own cap gun and holster. If son Larry was out of town, Joe and I would head out to put up movie posters or go to the theater where I would help clean up things. Sometimes Joe would even run a cartoon or more for me. As a kid it is fun to do work, like sweep or mow grass or whatever if it is not at home.

If Larry was home, he would take me to the coral where I would watch him practice trick riding. One of the tricks involved him going all the way under the horse and back up in the saddle from the other side while the horse was at a gallop. When it came time to practice calf roping, I got to help. When he signaled, I would open the chute with one hand and twist the calf's tail with the other. That would make them take off faster. It was amazing that a day next door always seemed to cure my illness.

Mom insisted that Hiram and I needed to have musical skills. Hiram took right to it by playing the accordion then the clarinet and then onto a saxophone. It actually was cool when he would play the accordion outside and the cows from the neighboring farm would gather along the fence to listen. They obviously enjoyed music more than I did.

But little Johnny was another story. Mom started me off with singing lessons (private) when I was in first grade. The lessons, including standing with hands cupped together in front, lasted into my second grade year. At that point my teacher, Mrs. Shanihan, recommended that they end. Both Mrs. Shanihan and I felt joy when Mom agreed.

The next step was piano lessons from Mrs. Gardner. I would walk to her house at least once a week for a one-hour session. These lessons lasted about two years, my third and fourth grade, until Mrs. Gardner came to the same conclusion that Mrs. Shanihan had. Mom accepted this decision but still insisted that I do something musical.

Because I wanted to please Mom I joined the school band in the fifth grade and chose drums. This lasted one year until Dad decided that was enough. Even though I didn't have a drum I had tables, chair backs and counters to practice on at home.

I give Mom credit for sticking to her guns. So, sixth grade year I took up the cornet. I hate to admit but I almost liked it. I played my

My buddy Roger Baker and me. He didn't seem thrilled to be in the picture.

sixth, seventh and eighth grade years. I wasn't wild about it since I preferred sports to music. I wanted to run, kick, throw, bat, or anything athletic over playing an instrument. Mom still insisted that I join the high school band as I entered my freshman year. The band just so happened to be without a tuba player, my lucky day! I thought that was nifty as the tuba was almost bigger than me and played just like a cornet. I even had my picture in both the *Seattle Times* and *Seattle PI* when we marched and played in the annual Santa Claus parade in Seattle. Even though I'll admit I liked playing the tuba, I really wanted to concentrate on golf, basketball and baseball. Mom finally folded and said OK.

Mom and Dad either thought Hiram and I were responsible and able to take care of ourselves or were training us to become so. The summer between my third and fourth grade years we were put on a train in Seattle to go to Chicago. We were in a "Pullman car" that had bunk beds that a curtain was drawn across. Dad gave a porter some money to keep an eye on us. We made it to Chicago without Hiram beating me up or throwing me off the train. We stayed with our old neighbors, Hugo and Agnes, out on their small farm. Over the two months I kept busy milking their two cows twice a day and feeding chickens. It's too bad that I didn't have a cow back in North Bend to milk, it would have added at least 25 yards to my drives once I started playing golf.

We also spent a few days with Dad's old friend, Nick Raft. He arranged for us to go to a Cubs game where another old friend of Dad's, who was a sportswriter, took us into the dugout before the game to meet players. From Chicago we were put on a train to San Francisco where Mom's sisters lived. After spending a week with them we were then railroaded up to Seattle. We did have a private cabin at least for both the Chicago to San Fran and San Fran to Seattle legs of the journey. Somehow, I can't picture parents sending kids on a similar venture today. I'm glad we did it, no doubt it helped both of us grow up.

I think it was the winter of my fifth grade year when Mom and Dad went to Panama for two weeks. Hiram and I were left at home alone. However, every two or three days Minnie Stevens (Mom's house cleaner) would come by to make sure we were OK. She would check to see that we had food, clean clothes, had made it to school and that Hiram hadn't injured or killed me.

There was only one bad thing about the trip. We had home delivery by a milkman. Before the trip an offer came out that was for cottage cheese in fancy looking containers (bowls). This called for weekly delivery for one month. Unfortunately, Mom liked the bowls. "Boys, just eat the cottage cheese with canned peaches. I don't want it to spoil, and we have lots of cans of peaches."

Well, true to form Hiram refused to eat any, so Johnny did his best to please Mom. To this day I still can't eat cottage cheese with fruit and that was over 60 years ago. As far as their trip went, they had a good time. The one thing I remember about it was that they went to a bullfight. The best part of that was that they paid almost double in order to be seated on the shady side of the arena, and the bullfight was at night!!

During my fifth and sixth grade years living out on the North Fork Road my best friend was Roger Baker. He lived about a quarter mile towards North Bend from our house. He had three brothers and one sister and a mom and dad. His dad worked for Weyerhaeuser, as did most of the dads in the Snoqualmie Valley at that time. They lived in a big old house located on a 90-degree corner called "Bakers Corner"— go figure.

Roger was two years older than me, was athletic and unlike me was of normal height. We played catch together with baseballs or footballs and shot hoops together. I spent as much time around his house as I could. Mrs. Baker in spite of being up to her ears in kids and house-work, was always kind and understanding to me. She also made what she called Indian bread—deep fried dough that would be kind of like "elephant ears" that you get now at county fairs.

Anyways being around Roger made me better athletically and stronger physically. He was the pitcher, and I was the catcher on a King County parks baseball team for two summers. He and I peeled cascara bark and sold it. We picked strawberries at Bybee's farm together for $0.25 a flat.

So, one day Hiram and his friend Paul wanted to find Jack's Mine. Roger and I agreed to go along. All we knew was that Jack's Mine was located about half the way up on the front side of Mount Si. It was not near the trail up the mountain. After a couple hours of climbing and going through lots of trees and shrubs and downed logs we did find it. It was a vertical mine that was about 6 feet in diameter. There was a partially rotten wooden ladder going down it. There was also a rusty old cable lying beside it. Of course, Hiram wanted to go down into the mine. I begged him not to but I guess he just had to show off. He held onto the cable and started to climb down the ladder while we held the cable as well. He only went a few feet before he realized it wasn't a good idea and quit.

We started back down the mountain and somehow got separated. Roger and I were together, Hiram and Paul were together. I was with a guy who could do things, could handle himself, and had spent time in the woods hunting with his dad. It took quite a while, but Roger and

I made it down the mountain. When I got home Mom and Dad were in a panic. They had called Paul's mom and found out that we had headed up Mount Si in search of Jack's Mine. After several hours they had called mountain rescue and the search was on. I don't remember whether Hiram and Paul got down on their own, but it was a long few days around the Groshell house after that.

Life with Hiram could be tough. He had a paper route for the *Seattle Times*. It took a couple hours a day. I learned the route so I could sub for him once in a while. One day he and Paul were hiding along the route and threw rocks at me as I went by. Thankfully neither one could throw worth a darn or I might have been hurt. If Roger and I had been throwing at him he would have been injured. That was the last time I did his route for him.

One day Hiram and I went inner tubing down the Middle Fork. The river close to the mountain is swift and rough in many places. Of course, as kids it was no big deal, or so we thought. At one point Hiram fell off his tube and it went floating down the river. I didn't jump in and go after it. Hiram became outraged that I didn't and knocked me down on the riverbank and kicked me in the ribs. I was fearful he was going to hit me with a boulder, but he backed off. That was my last rafting the river with him.

I'd say it's quite evident why I liked to hang out at the Baker's house. It wasn't like Hiram and I never got along. We had different interests and different friends. When I was in the eighth grade Hiram was a page in the Washington State Senate. I don't really remember missing him, but it turns out I did. I rode a bus to Olympia, the state capital, to spend a weekend with him. We got along fine and when I climbed on the bus to go home, he gave me a present. It was a small rocket that was propelled by baking soda and vinegar. When I sat on the bus and looked out and waved goodbye I started crying. I really did love him and was really going to miss him.

By the way, that rocket really would take off, especially when loaded with twice the recommended amount of baking soda.

CHAPTER 4

Poaching Trout – Early Sports

Once I became a 7th grader Roger had moved on to high school. He got new friends and new activities. However, before that happened there is a little story about one of our fishing holes. Actually, it was a large pond or a small lake depending on one's point of view. The property upon which it was located was owned by a guy named Paul. He lived in a cabin on that property with no electricity. The cabin was stuffed full of newspapers. Paul (known as "Oddball" by kids in North Bend) spent most of his time panhandling in Seattle. He would hitchhike to and from Seattle, a distance of about 30 miles each way. More than once I was with Dad when he would pick him up and give him a ride part way. What he could make panhandling he bought food for "his trout" in the pond. The food included hamburger. He had the pond dammed up so the fish couldn't go on down the stream that came out of it. Water went through but virtually no fish. My worldly buddy Roger knew about this. There is a rumor that Paul shot trespassers with rock salt.

Anyways, on several occasions Roger and I fished in the river or another small pond until we caught a few. These were always smaller than the big trout he fed with hamburger. We would then go to his cabin to see if he was home. He never was, but if he had, we were going to offer him the little fish we had caught. Being fairly sure he was gone we would get out our hamburger and start fishing. One of us would fish, the other one would be in lookout for a big guy carrying a shotgun. The hungry fish fought over the hamburger covered hooks. We would only catch two or three each before we hightailed it out of there. We didn't want to be greedy, but we really really didn't want to be caught.

When Dad would see my catch for the day it would include more small fish than big ones. A limit of entirely big ones would have been hard to explain. Within a few years Paul's property became a part of the water supply for North Bend. I don't know if Paul had owned, rented, or simply squatted on that property.

After Roger found new friends and activities, I started hanging out mainly with Jerry Mitchell, whose father drove a logging truck, and Louis Roberts who lived about a half-mile from me. Louis was my first golf buddy, starting in the 8th grade.

Hiram and I used to go to Grandpa Paul's and Grandma Truda's house for the weekend two or three times a year. They lived in "The Highlands" in North Seattle. He was a lawyer and had been a Superior Court judge. He was Mom's dad, she was Mom's stepmother. They were the only grandparents I ever really knew. Mom's real mom visited us a couple of times but that was about it. She was an artist—I do have a few of her paintings including one of Hiram and me.

I remember visiting my dad's parents one time. They lived in San Bernardino. I was about 10 years old at that time period. They were nice but the only thing I can remember is him liking to watch wrestling on TV and her remarking about me that "He is for Hollywood"—so what was I, a "drama prince"?

What I was leading up to is that Grandpa Paul is the person that got me started with golf. He would take Hiram and me to Puetz driving range to hit balls when I was in the 7th grade. I guess Hiram didn't care for it because Grandpa Paul didn't get him any clubs. He bought me one club at a time out of a bargain barrel—two or three bucks a club. First was a Wilson 5 iron for juniors, next a ladies' Wright and Ditson 3 wood, then a men's Spalding 7 iron, and a men's Kroydon 9 iron, and finally a ladies' Wilson putter. This is a set that I used until I went to high school.

Besides getting interested in golf thanks to Grandpa Paul, my other sports endeavors through 8th grade were as follows, and remember that I was about 4 foot 8 inches tall when I finished the 8th grade. At that time there was no Little League in the Snoqualmie Valley. We had church league for both basketball and baseball. The drawback to church league was you had to attend Sunday school every week to be eligible to play. I played both, but baseball was my true love. As a 4th grader I was the starting 2nd baseman on the team made up predominantly of 7th and 8th graders. I had to play 2nd base because my childhood hero, Nellie Fox of the Chicago White Sox, played 2nd base.

Nellie was short, scrappy, never hardly struck out and made the All-Star team every year. Nellie always had enough chew in his mouth to look like he had a tennis ball in there. I tried my best to play like Nellie but thankfully I never took up chewing tobacco.

By the time I was in the 7th grade I played catcher mainly, I just loved the action behind the plate. Earlier I mentioned the County Parks team where I caught, and Roger Baker pitched. The grade schools had softball teams for 7th and 8th graders, not baseball. I played second base my 7th grade year and shortstop my 8th. I didn't catch in softball because that was a nothing position, as far as I was concerned.

Hiram specialized in two areas. First, he loved to get our father mad. As often as not that would result in our mother stepping in to protect him thus resulting in a fight (not physical) between Mom and Dad. That usually ended up with Mom crying and me hiding in my bedroom. His second talent was in making teachers look stupid. Of course, in doing so they became quite irritated. They all remembered clearly their year of anguish with Hiram Groshell. Usually, their summer off wasn't enough to heal those wounds. Come September into their classrooms with the new class came another Groshell, little Johnny.

It usually took close to half a year for the teacher to figure out that little Johnny meant no harm. Johnny just didn't care about learning and only cared about sports. At least at that point I was no longer an enemy or a threat to their image or a constant disruption to their efforts to teach.

As mentioned above, if it didn't involve a ball to balance, throw, kick or shoot then Johnny didn't care about it. When it came to sports, I also had a challenge not only due to lack of height but also to age and physical maturity. My birthday is September 24th—six days before the cutoff of October 1st. Had I started school one year later it would have helped my chances of playing on various teams. When I started high school, I was 4-foot-8-inches and 95 pounds. My father thought I should try out for freshman football. Instead, I tried out for high school golf. My dad dreamed of watching his athletic son (me) play Saturday afternoons in Husky Stadium for the University of Washington Huskies. He had season tickets (press passes) for years—I attended many games with him but he wanted to watch me play Husky football one day. I did play four years of golf for WSU. I was the captain two years and finished second in the conference one year. That meant nothing to him, it just wasn't the same thing.

By the time I was a senior in high school my growth crawls (not spurts) had me shooting up to 5-foot-3. I would only top out at around 5-foot-5½ by the time I graduated from WSU. The point of the date of birth and ability to play sports is for any kid, boy or girl, who wants to excel in sports, does not want to be born in July through August or September. So, parents please practice birth control methods of your choice in October, November, December and January.

Four summers in a row Hiram and I were sent to Camp Orkila, a YMCA camp on Orcas Island. The fifth summer only I went. Each session lasted a week give or take a day or two. These were the summers ranging from about my 5th grade year through my freshman year. Campers were assigned to cabins by age groups. Each cabin had around eight kids and one counselor. Counselors were usually college students. Looking back, it just struck me that the kids were all boys. Then after a few minutes of thought before I got a headache from thinking, it struck me that it was a YMCA camp—not YWCA. See, I am sharp!

During the week we swam a lot, in a pool. There was archery, basketball, hiking, beachcombing and some paddling around in row boats. Some nights we had campfires and sang songs.

Most of the years my brother and I were in separate cabins.

The counselor in my cabin one summer had us go out in row boats and get the clear little jellyfish out of the water. We would bring them in and he would eat a couple at dinner. After a night or two of this he asked if any of us would like to have one. While the rest of the guys yelled, "No way," I said, "Sure."

I wasn't going to let him think I was afraid. I managed to chew it up and swallow it in about three bites and keep it down. I even said that it wasn't all that bad. It wasn't totally disgusting, but I have never eaten another one. It had the consistency of soft rubber that you could bite through, and it wasn't really slimy. The taste of it was just very salty, nothing else.

One of the summers I learned a new dive off the diving board. After springing off the board, at the top height of the dive I would rotate sideways so that upon entering the water my back would be facing the diving board. Later that summer when our family took a vacation trip our first night, we stayed in a hotel that had a pool. I tried to show Mom and Dad my new dive, but I was trying too hard and just couldn't do it. I kept splashing down in all different manners until I finally gave up.

My final year at Camp Orkila I was in the oldest group. We loaded up in what would have been a lifeboat for some huge vessel, or so I thought. Whatever it was, it was metal, and motor driven. There were about 25 campers and two or three adults. We stayed out all week only coming back to camp the night before session ended. We camped out on various islands, sleeping in sleeping bags and cooking over campfires.

During one of the days at sea in the San Juan islands, we got caught up in heavy winds. I don't remember it raining so it must not have. Our boat had no cabin or cover over it of any sort. The wind was so strong and the waves so big we couldn't make headway. Some of the kids were scared, some petrified, and the adults were very concerned. I thought it was exciting as I watched the metal hull bend in and out with each bang against a wave. I fully believed that I could swim to shore if need be. After several hours a Coast Guard Cutter came to our rescue. I don't know whether we had a radio or not, we sure as hell didn't have cell phones. Anyways, we were all loaded into the Coast Guard Cutter and taken to Victoria. They dragged our fine craft behind. The Coast Guard guys were nice to the kids but not so much to our leaders, the adults. As I remember we must have been allowed to return to Orkila in our boat the next day when it was calm, but maybe another boat was sent to get us.

Each year at the end of camp one camper was chosen to get the "Order of the Oar." This was given to the camper who showed the best leadership qualities. It also helped if he didn't shoot any other campers with an arrow and didn't burn down more than one cabin. I still have my little carved oar somewhere.

CHAPTER 5

Cruel Girls – My Home Court

In transition from grade school to high school my father gave me the best advice that he ever gave me. "You are now going to a new school where the teachers don't know you. Many of them have not had your brother as a student. You have a chance to make them think you are a good student who cares about learning. If you would just try for one year you will win them over. They will think you care and in the next three years you can screw off and you will be given breaks."

It made sense—I got a 3.8 average my freshman year then coasted. The next three years I did get good breaks—my average dropped some each year, but I coasted in with just under 3.0 overall—good enough to get into WSU.

My high school years as far as classes and learning I just summed up. The parts I cared about involved sports. The other parts of high school would involve socializing. Mount Si High School was where the elementary students from North Bend, Snoqualmie, Snoqualmie Falls, and Fall City first came together. K through 8 were done separately and 7th and 8th grade athletic teams played against each other.

As a freshman at Mount Si, you knew about 25% of the freshman class. Being 4-foot-8 and 95 pounds made me stand out in the hallways, if they could have seen me. I had no trouble socializing with the guys. Even at my height I could play sports. I was sociable enough and made friends easily. However, girls had much more interest in males over 5-foot-6 or so.

There was a group of about eight girls who were mainly seniors who took great delight in humiliating me. In the busy hallways they would get me surrounded and not let me out. One would then step forward and ask me to go out with them on a date. They would all laugh at me and point at me and call me names like midget or freak. Other students would of course be watching this too, some with great delight, some may be feeling bad for me. This activity went on for at least a week at the beginning of the year. Never did a teacher break it up or discipline the girls for their behavior. Needless to say, any self-esteem I had was destroyed. I never dated until I was a senior. A similar thing happened my junior year. I was playing 3rd base for the Mount Si High School team at Bellevue High School. For about three innings in a row when we were in the field playing defense, five or six of Bellevue's girls lined up along the 3rd baseline within 10 feet of where I was positioned and sang, *"5 foot 2 – Eyes of blue – Coochy coochy coochy coo"* to me over and over again. Once again, no coaches, faculty or adults from Bellevue High School broke this up.

As I mentioned I did have a few dates as a senior. When I went to college my freshman year, I had one date with a college girl. When I returned to work at Mount Si Golf Course after my freshman year, I met a girl who actually treated me like I was alright, and not a circus freak. I ended up marrying her and 6/30/22 has been 55 years of marriage.

But I'm getting ahead of myself again. Let's go back to my freshman year in high school. So, I basically covered academics and socializing, the biggest thing, sports remain. Also along the way were several incidents and activities that I was involved in.

Fall is the season for football and golf for Mount Si High. We competed in the Kingco Conference where we had the fewest students of any school. Mount Si had about 400 students for four years. Bellevue had about 2,500 for three years. Most of the schools had over 1,500, the closest to our size was Issaquah and they had about twice as many as us.

As mentioned earlier, in spite of my dad wanting me to play football, I turned out for golf. I really had only played a couple rounds at that point but had gone to the driving range with my grandfather maybe 10 times.

To make the golf team one needed to have a heartbeat and lungs for breathing. So Johnny turned out with his mishmash of clubs and made the team. I finished every round I played in and as a team we had no fatalities, nor did we lose any players in the woods or swamp around the course. Between my freshman season and sophomore season I may have played a handful of times. Basketball, baseball and working at the print shop took up my time, along with trout fishing with Teddy. I also mowed our lawn most of the time. It took about 3 hours with our push mower, no riding for me. I mowed it when I thought it looked like it "almost" needed mowing. With Dad if he had to ask me to mow it, I was already in trouble. Most dads expected their kids to mow when asked to—my dad figured I should not have to be asked.

Sometime during the last summer, I came across an old basketball rim. It was just a rim with no net. Our driveway and parking area were gravel, no cement. There was a grass covered area beyond the gravel that was outside the fenced area that our basset hounds roamed. That area was therefore free from dog droppings. I found a piece of plywood that was 3/4" thick and almost rectangular, good enough for me. I took an axe—no chainsaw for me—and cut down a tree that was about 6 inches in diameter at the bottom. I then cut all the limbs up to about 15 feet. Next, I dug a hole about 3 feet deep and got a friend of mine to help me lift the pole (tree) up and put it in the hole. We filled in around it with rocks and gravel and tamped it down as well as we could to stabilize it. No cement for us! We nailed the plywood to the pole then screwed the rim to the plywood. I'm fairly sure it ended up somewhere between 9'10" to 10'2" high and it was almost level. The right side was just a little higher than the left. Within a couple months most of my court was dirt or mud when it rained. I would shoot baskets hour after hour, the grass never had a chance. As I remember, I never did get a net for my hoop.

Along came basketball season with coach Jim North. Mr. North would later be one of my main golf buddies and also instrumental in my landing the teaching job at Mount Si. He was a real character who I could tell many stories about. However, back to hoops. The team had 12 players that suited up for games. The remaining eight players were put on what the coach called "the gas house gang." I played on the gas house gang. We were sent to the grade schools to play their 8th grade teams. Once you were on the gas house team that is where you stayed! I may have been the only gas house guy to ever be promoted to be on the "big" squad by coach North. Of course, I had sprouted up to about 4'9" by basketball season. I could dribble, pass and shoot. Rebounding was not my specialty. I usually shot a 2-handed set shot in order to get it to the basket, but I could shoot. I even made the starting 5 for a few games. When I would have the ball within 20 feet from the basket, Coach would bellow, "Put it up, Runt. You're not in there to hold it."

Sometimes when a player would goof up, he would yell, "You are embarrassing my good coaching."

Coach North had lettered four years at Central Washington College in football, basketball and track—12 total letters. He had also played with Sammy Baugh for the Washington Redskins.

The next thing of importance to me my freshman year was baseball season. Mount Si didn't have a freshman baseball team, varsity was the only team. The head coach and only coach was Rod Garretson. Here is where brother Hiram comes in again.

Back in those days coaches were also teachers, or administrators. Coaches were never outside people hired just to coach. Rod Garretson taught Biology, a subject all sophomores had to take and pass in order to graduate from high school. Hiram, being one year ahead of me, was a sophomore. Remember back when I stated that Hiram had two goals: one was to piss off our father, the other was to make teachers look stupid. He also didn't mind that they would also get ticked off. I don't know the particulars, but Hiram succeeded to a level he had never accomplished before. After various levels of discipline, sending Hiram to the office or hours of detention, and meeting with parents, Hiram was finally banned from Biology with Mr. Garretson. This wasn't for a day or week—it was permanently according to Mr. Garretson. Our parents finally went to the school board to get him back into this required class.

So along comes baseball season and Hiram decides to turn out, even though he didn't turn out his freshman year. One of his finest moments came during the first week of practice. Coach Garretson was hitting flies to outfielders, and they were throwing balls back to him. Hiram managed to get a hold of several balls even though he himself wasn't fielding any. When an outfielder threw one back to the coach after catching it, Hiram would throw one at the coach at the same time. After three times of ducking away from two missiles at the same time, Coach yelled, "One ball at a time."

To this Hiram yelled, "I only threw one."

That ended Hiram's baseball career at Mount Si and hindered the possibility of Johnny making the team. In spite of this I became the backup catcher and backup 2nd baseman. Coach said that he didn't play me much because at 4'10" and 100 pounds he was afraid I would get hurt. Several seniors on the team wanted him to play me more for my defensive play but he didn't.

However, he would put me into catch when our starting catcher pitched. I think that was because nobody else wanted to catch him. He was about 6 feet tall and weighed over 200 pounds and threw BBs. So, Coach wasn't aware that an undersized freshman faced true danger to life and limb under these circumstances. The first time I went into catch, the second or third pitch just ticked the top of my glove and hit me in the throat. That was before catcher's masks had that hanging guard in the front. The pitch knocked me to the ground, and it took close to a minute for me to get up, get my bearings and get ready to keep playing. I did finish the inning at which point another pitcher came in and Bob went back to catching.

The summer between my freshman and sophomore years was uneventful. When I wasn't working in the print job or mowing the yard I was fishing or picking strawberries for $0.25 a flat at Bybee's farm. I even played golf a few times at Cascade Golf Course. Cascade was a 9-hole course a couple of miles east out of North Bend. Louis Roberts and I rode our bikes, while carrying our clubs, about three miles to get there. We were not very good but had fun. We even painted our golf balls multiple colors for fun. Of course, the paint tended to come off onto our clubs.

CHAPTER 6

Biggest Scare – Biggest Accomplishment

Since I don't know where else to put this, I'll insert it here. Mom and Dad bought a vacation cabin in Ocean Park WA about my 5th grade year. Sometimes all four of us would ride down together. It was at least a 5-hour drive from North Bend. Occasionally we took two vehicles if one of them was going to come back sooner. When we took two cars, Dad and I would always go together in the Nash Metropolitan. For goodly portions of the trip Dad would operate the pedals while I steered. This was from age 13 on.

We had that cabin for a couple of years at which point Mom and Dad bought an ocean lot between Long Beach and Ocean Park. The man they hired to build the house, Herman Eberhart, was our neighbor in Ocean Park. Herman and his wife Berta had come from Germany. Herman, even at the age of 50, could climb a mountain. He had climbed many while growing up. So, this one summer, after my freshman year he was going to take a boy scout troop from the coast on a climb to the top of Mount St. Helens. At that time in 1961 Mount St. Helens was 9,677 feet tall. After it blew its top on May 18th, 1980, it was reduced to 8,363 feet.

Herman asked Dad if I would like to go along. I think Dad told him yes without asking me. When he told me about it, I didn't have the heart to tell him I was afraid to because I didn't like heights. I had climbed Mount Si before but other than the haystack at the top it was nothing more than an uphill trail.

The group which had maybe a dozen scouts and Herman along with two other adults went to a base camp at the mountain. The next morning, we hiked up to the first glacier taking with us picks, crampons and ropes—we were going to practice digging hand and foot holds in the ice and repelling down a glacier. The plan was to come back down the mountain in that manner.

We went across the glacier tied together with ropes, digging holes

Me on top of Mt. St. Helens before it blew up. I begged, "Please send a heli-copter up for me, I'm NOT climbing down!"

for hands and feet. We practiced traveling across using crampons on our boots. They could be compared to roller skates you fastened to regular shoes, but with spikes.

Then it was time to learn how to repel down. So off came the cram-pons and we would get into a catcher squat and start sliding down. We were instructed to just lean back and press the handle end of the pick against the ice to slow down. If that didn't do the trick, we were to flop over onto our bellies and dig the pick into the ice. I got going faster than I liked and was pushing down on the handle end, but that didn't help. Finally, in a panic I flopped over and was swinging the pick try-ing to get it to dig in, but the butt end would hit and bounce. The end of the ice was approaching fast, and I forced myself out of a panic. I grabbed the head of the pick with one hand, the handle with the other, and dug the pick end into the ice. I slowed down and stopped when I was less than 20 feet from rocks. I dreaded having to come down the mountain this way the next day.

We got up before daybreak and readied ourselves for the climb. As soon as we had enough daylight to see, we started up. For at least an hour or so we were walking on pumice rock. You would step two feet and slide back one. We progressed on up to glaciers and snow, using ropes and crampons where necessary. Crevices scared the stuffing out of me. I didn't like getting close to them and looking into them, you couldn't even see the bottom. I dreaded coming back down the mountain sliding out of control and falling into one. They were hard to see and obviously I wasn't skilled in repelling.

About 3/4 of the way up the mountain a rock came tumbling down towards us. Several of us dodged it, then it hit Herman in the foot. After 10 minutes he declared himself good enough to continue on. We made it to the top.

Standing on the top and looking out, it was beautiful. It was bright and sunny and as I remember we could see Mount Rainier, Mount Baker and Mount Adams. Looking out was fabulous, looking down was terrifying. From the top the slope looked much steeper than looking up at it. At the top was a stand that had a notebook in it for successful climbers to sign. There was also a jar of peanut butter there if someone needed a snack. I was so scared of climbing down, I wanted to tell them I was staying, and they could send up a helicopter for me. By the time we were ready to head down Herman couldn't even put weight on his bad foot. The adults rigged up something resembling a stretcher. The idea of repelling down went out the window. We were to go down little by little with ropes, hand and foot holes while sliding Herman along. I was the most relieved guy in the world. We made it back to rocks before dusk and back to camp by pitch dark. It turned out Herman had a broken foot.

Once we moved into the house that Herman built, we were on the ocean. To dig razor clams all we needed was a shovel, a low tide and a bucket. We could walk on out and with the limit at 24 clams a person we could get 96. Dad needed more, so sometimes all four of us would drive a couple miles to another location and get 96 more. Then Dad and I would hit another spot for another 48. Of course, that meant Dad and I got to clean 240 razor clams, an all-day project.

Obviously, our method of digging wasn't good enough for Dad. Professional diggers were "surf diggers." They would dig right by the water. They could take one swipe with a shovel and grab the clam before the next wave hit them. Dad met a guy, who called himself Toad, in the Seaview Hotel bar. Toad told Dad he would teach him how to surf dig. The next day we stopped by the apartment Toad lived in to pick him up. Toad was waiting, but not ready. He was laying in the rose garden sleeping where he had passed out the night before. Instead of leaving him we scraped him up and headed to the beach. Toad kept trying to sing some song about "Rose" then he started crying and saying that was his mother's name. When we parked on the beach Toad got out, took three steps, then fell and his head thudded off the rear bumper. Some 45 minutes later after we got our limits, without Toad's help, we loaded him up and took him back to his rose garden by the Seaview Hotel.

Speaking of the Seaview Hotel. The proprietor was named Louie and he also was the cook at the hotel. Dad liked to go there for their steaks, plus he liked to drink with Louie. When we would go there, Dad would usually bring a fifth of McNaughton's with him. The steaks were good, and Louie and Dad would get loaded, until Dad crossed the line. Next door to the Seaview Hotel was a mortuary. One night after we had eaten and Dad and Louie had finished off the jug, Dad asked Louie if he got his steaks from the mortuary. No blood was shed but that was our last dinner at the Seaview Hotel.

CHAPTER 7

Page in Olympia – Ruins Sports

When school started my sophomore year, so did golf season. I had graduated from my mish mash of clubs to an old set that belonged to Dad. They were definitely old but they were at least matched. They were Byron Nelson autographed and were men's length and weight. The woods were solid wood—no insert like modern clubs of that era had. That year of golf was marked by mediocrity and little success. Between too heavy clubs and lack of practice I certainly showed little promise of success in golf. My love of sports suffered a major let down the remainder of the year.

Hiram had been a page in the Washington State Senate when the legislators met two years before. Hiram paid attention to politics and was involved in campaigning so that he could be appointed to be a page. Mom and Dad got me to get involved too, so I door-belled and put up posters for a guy named Dick Poff who was running for state representative. Hiram and I even attended the state Democratic convention held in Spokane in 1960. It was at that convention that I got JFK's autograph and met Lyndon Johnson.

With this involvement, and Dick Poff winning his race, I was appointed to be a page in the State House for that session of 1961. At that time pages would serve through the entire term. Now I believe they only do a couple weeks each so that their school years aren't messed up. I wish that had been the case then. Hiram got a job in the "bill room" in the Senate so we were together in Olympia for the 1961 legislative session. This started in January and the regular session was to be 60 days long.

To start with I was put in a family's house to stay. I was also supposed to attend Olympia High School every morning for half of a day. Being the very short kid who looked like about a 6th grader and was very shy around kids I didn't know, this was an absolute nightmare. I didn't make it through three weeks of attending Olympia High before

I quit going. I also moved out of the family's home and in with my brother in the cheap place he was staying. I don't remember how this was worked out, or how it could have been legal, but it is what we did.

There were around 30 pages in the House. When the regular 60-day session ended and the extra session started, the number of pages was cut back to two. I actually worked hard during the regular session and was thus kept on. Halfway through the special session I was even moved up to working in the "bill room".

Things I remember from being a page in Olympia, besides my school and housing:

- in the "representatives only" cafeteria they had slices of damn good pie that I would sneak a piece of on occasion if there was no one around.
- there was a "very private and off limits" room upstairs that was referred to as "the barbershop"—later I figured out it served as a "watering hole" for legislators.
- man could have the first name Shirley and apparently be proud enough of it to not have it changed. A state Rep from Eastern Washington was named Shirley Marsh.
- that most of the representatives were nice guys who were nice to me, but I couldn't see that they really worked too hard. I can't remember if there was a single female in the House but I don't think so.

Once I returned to Mount Si High I was in trouble. They failed to see the humor in my attending fewer than 15 half days at Olympia High. Consequently, I had to make up every assignment and every test that I had missed during my three months absence. A couple teachers were nice and didn't make me make up everything. Instead, they had me do some, talked to me about some of it, asked some questions and once they figured I had a grasp of what I missed they called it good. A couple others had me make up most everything, but that was fair to me. Only one teacher made it as awful as he could. That was Rod Garretson, you remember, the Biology teacher who tried to ban Hiram a year before. Not only did he have me make up every assignment and test, but he added a measure of difficulty to some of the tests. He had a fellow student make up some of the questions on some of the tests.

The student was a rather unpopular jerk who took pride in screwing me over.

But back to sports—I missed the entire basketball season which pretty much made my chances of playing varsity basketball the next two years virtually impossible. If I were tall or even if I were average height with skills, I would have had a chance. As a 5-foot-2 guy who could shoot, pass and dribble, it meant game over for the rest of high school.

Due to making up assignments and tests I wasn't able to turn out for baseball. So, I missed out on my sophomore year of baseball but at least I was talented enough to be able to play my junior and senior years. Overall, I wish that I hadn't been a page in Olympia.

CHAPTER 8

Lessons From Dad

I always got along alright with Dad. While Hiram was into antago- nizing him, I was into pleasing him. Dad wasn't around home much because he was busy keeping a business running. I probably saw more of him at the print shop/newspaper than I did at home. The following experiences and activities with Dad took place between my 6th grade year and through my sophomore year.

For two of my birthdays during that span, Dad took me on a "birthday weekend." The first one we went on a fishing trip to Twisp, Washington. Don Buck, Dad's foreman at the shop, went with us. I don't have many memories of the trip. I did get to open their beers in the motel room—they were Olympia beer stubby bottles. On the back of the label on each beer there were anywhere from one to four dots. Supposedly the four dot labels were worth a free beer. Johnny peeled off many labels that weekend.

The other memory was defending the fish we caught. We mainly caught whitefish that were in the 10" to 15" range. We were fishing in a river and threw the fish up on the bank as we caught them. At one point a martin, which looks like a big weasel, decided the fish were his. It took a lot of yelling and rock throwing to back this critter down so we could gather our fish.

Don Buck was a nice guy to me in a man's way. I remember a cou- ple stories about him. One Monday he came to work with a cast on his right hand. The story went that that weekend at the Union Tavern in Issaquah he had gotten into an altercation with another patron. Apparently, Don's left-hand jab was stronger than he thought and when he was coming through with the right to finish him off, the fel- low had already dropped and Don's right hand smashed into the huge oak bar.

On another Monday Don reported to work with a black eye. No, this was not the result of a bar fight. When Don's wife bent over to pick up the Sunday paper on their porch Don had shot her on the backside with a BB gun. She then gave him her version of a right cross. Looking back on it, maybe Don should have worked seven days a week.

The other birthday weekend Dad took me to Seattle where we stayed at the Washington Athletic Club Hotel. On Saturday we went to the Washington Husky football game. The weekend involved bumming around Seattle together, eating good meals, and attending the football game. It must have been Saturday night, after the game, that looking out the window I saw an ambulance or aid car one block over. It was in front of the Gold Coast Restaurant. Medics were attending to someone who was laying on the sidewalk. Dad had me look up the phone number for the Gold Coast and phone them. He had me ask them what their special was that evening. I don't remember what it was, but then I was to ask if that was what the guy on the sidewalk had eaten. The lady on the phone said, "You are sick!" She was right about the guy who had me call. Back then I had never heard the phrase "Don't shoot the messenger," but that would have been my only defense.

I think Dad was training me to have the courage to say and do things without fear. He also was training me to be able to keep a straight face no matter what was going on. Remember, I was a shy kid. Hiram was the outgoing one who could talk to anyone.

When the four of us—Mom, Dad, Hiram and I—went Christmas shopping in Seattle we always split up.

Mom and Hiram together, Dad and I. Dad and I would stand on the sidewalk outside Frederick and Nelson's and look in on the cafe that was at street level. Tables were along the windows with the top of the tables at about our ankles. We would stand and stare, watching people taking one bite after another. As their forks or spoons neared their mouths, we would draw open our jaws like baby robins getting fed. As food went into their mouths, we would close ours as if we were taking the bites. This was done with straight faces, although I was allowed to try to look hungry and pathetic. Generally speaking, the diners would become somewhat uneasy. To my credit, I have never had my sons do anything like this with me.

There was a bank that had a walk-up window along the sidewalk. Dad noticed the teller for that window had a desk at the far end of the bank. He gave me a quarter and had me ring the bell to get help. Dad stayed back so it would look like I was alone. I requested two dimes and a nickel for the quarter. I was following instructions. She gave me those and I went back to Dad, she went back to her desk. Dad then sent me back to get 25 pennies. After her long walk and her look of disgust (rightfully so) she complied. As she walked back to her desk I reported back to Dad. I was then sent back to trade the pennies back in for my quarter. The nice lady actually gave me a quarter and as pleasantly as she could told me to get lost. She must have realized I was being put up to it. I felt embarrassed doing it.

A drug store was selling a combination sponge and bag of bath salts in matching colors. The choices were pink, yellow, green or blue. My mission here was to get the sales lady to mix up colors. The sponges were attached to the bags. I don't remember what colors I ended up buying, but I got her to take apart and re-fasten three different combinations. Each time I was trying to "figure out" what Mom would like best and what color she would like best. I did keep a straight face throughout, and she managed to keep from kicking my ass out. I did buy a combination and Mom did say she liked the present.

As we walked the aisles of stores if I heard Dad say, "Think fast," that meant an object was flying towards me, whatever it was it was always breakable, and he had thrown it. He also did this in our home. The only thing that I ever failed to catch was a piggy bank that Mom had gotten in Mexico. I spent hours trying to glue the many pieces together again, but I could never get it back to original condition. Once again, I felt awful about that.

The toughest assignment came in either Fredericks or "The Bon." Dad did the usual tap on the shoulder and come on gesture to follow him for an event. There was a sales lady, probably a college girl working Christmas vacation, at a makeshift table/booth in the middle of an aisle. She had little wooden figures that were about four inches tall. She was demonstrating how you could push down on the head and a sign would pop out at the top then go back down when the head was allowed to return to the original position. One of the figures was blue, and the sign came up and it said, "I am feeling blue." These were stocking stuffers or the something for someone who truly needs nothing. So, Dad and I stood by the table along with several other people while the young lady demonstrated how they worked. Being short, my head wasn't more than a foot above the tabletop level. So, Dad and I were watching, and I glanced up and he had a look like he couldn't understand how they work. After watching a few seconds, he picked one up and said, "Is this how it works?" as he twisted it and broke it into pieces.

That got the girl's undivided attention, and I kept a straight face. In fact, I looked like I couldn't understand how they worked either. She quickly started demonstrating to Dad how they worked. She was somewhere between panic and "What should I do now?"

"No, Sir, this is how—look—see it's easy, just push down on the top," she was saying as Dad picked up another one.

"Oh, I see, like this," he proceeded to twist that one into splinters as well. At that point she went into full panic and was grabbing the figures off the table as fast as she could. She wasn't mad at him, in fact I think she felt bad for him. Regardless she didn't want him to destroy any more of them. The onlookers were all backed away from the action with various looks of dismay.

Somewhere somehow Dad got ahold of one more figure to which she yelled, "NO!" and grabbed at it. Dad fended her off with one arm and operated the third figure properly on the table. Before or since have I never seen such a total look of relief as I saw on this girl's face. Dad tried to pay for the two broken ones, but she wouldn't let him. I guess one could say that she just figured he wasn't "quite right." Thinking back on it she would have been correct. But most of all I kept a straight face.

CHAPTER 9

Golf YES!

The summer after my sophomore year was uneventful. There were no summer baseball leagues for my age kids in the Snoqualmie Valley. I worked some at the print shop but at that point Dad realized that neither Hiram or I cared to follow in his footsteps.

I did play more golf that summer. My friend Louie and I would ride our bikes to Cascade Golf to play when we couldn't bum a ride from our parents. Towards the end of that summer Dad took me to Warshalls Sporting Goods in Seattle to buy me my first full set of clubs. In those days pro shops at golf courses with a PGA professional sold "pro-line" clubs. Sporting goods stores were limited to "store line" clubs. Pro shop sold "Wilson Staff" clubs, sports stores had Wilson K-28 or Sam Snead BlueRidge or Cary Middlecoff signature. Spalding offered Spalding Top Flite in pro shops and Spalding Kro Flite in stores. In actuality, the store-bought lines were just as playable and about half the price. Golf balls were the same program. Pro shops had Wilson Staff balls, stores had Wilson K-28 balls, Spalding Dot balls were in pro shops, Spalding Air Flights in stores. So, my set was Wilson Cary Middlecoff signature, and I loved them. Being a match set I didn't have to swing them differently because of junior, ladies, or men's weights and lengths. Their technology also was superior to Dad's 20-year-old Byron Nelson autographs.

Towards the end of the summer Mom and Dad realized that I really did like golf. They bought me a series of six lessons from Harry Umbinetti. Harry leased Mount Si Golf Course, the well-established 18-hole golf course in the Snoqualmie Valley. Harry was also a PGA member and one of the best players amongst club pros in the Northwest.

I remember that Harry stressed the importance of keeping the left arm straight throughout the backswing, downswing and through contact with the ball. That was a bit hard to do, but if Harry had told me to stand on my head and grip the club in my toes I would have. Other kids actually made fun of my swing saying I looked like a robot but I didn't care. Since I have never been tall, lean and pliable, my backswing has always been shorter than anybody else's. At two different PGA schools I attended, since I became a PGA pro, instructors tried to get me to lengthen my backswing. Both times it took me over a month to get back to my normal swing that has worked for years. One pro who watched me tee off in a Washington Open later came to me and said, "John, I think I found the guy who stole half of your backswing."

Anyways, back to my lessons. I had taken three or four of the series of six and golf season for Mount Si High had started. This was my junior year. I was teeing off the first tee there at Mount Si Golf Course and my teacher, Harry, came out of the pro shop to watch me tee off. That made me twice as nervous as I was already. I took a mighty swing and actually whiffed it, didn't touch it. In my 76 years of life I have never been as embarrassed as I was then. My second swing I hit what might have been my best drive for the rest of the season, but I was still humiliated. My game improved that season to where I shot in the 80s most of the time. Once the fall season ended, the clubs were seldom taken out for a round. I'd graduated from 9-hole Cascade golf to 18-hole Mount Si Golf where my teacher Harry was pro.

I turned 16 on September 24th, 1961, and with that came a driver's license after two tries. Dad had realized I was not meant to be a newspaperman. There was nothing in the printing business that involved hitting, throwing, catching or shooting a ball. Even though I know it had to sadden Dad, he helped me get a job at the North Bend IGA. One of his best friends was a co-owner there and he hired me. Dad had also gotten an old car as payment for advertising in the paper. It was a Goliath. The Goliath was like a cracker box sized station wagon/SUV from the '50s but it usually worked. So, Johnny was growing up, driving to school, working at the IGA, and baseball practice in the spring. My junior year went along smoothly with brother Hiram going back to be a page in the US Senate from Christmas through the rest of the year.

Changes in the family were beginning to take place. During my junior year Dad sold the newspaper and took a job with King County for the flood control division. Close to the end of my junior year, Mom was appointed to the Washington State parole board by Governor Albert D. Rossellini. Shortly into my senior year Mom moved to Olympia, the capital.

CHAPTER 10

Page in the US Senate

Somehow, between Hiram, Mom and Dad, it was arranged that I would take over Hiram's page position once summer came around. Hiram had been in DC since Christmas and had been sponsored to be a page by Senator Warren G. Magnuson. Hiram and I had both been pages in Olympia, had campaigned for several Democrats, and had attended the state's Democratic convention in 1960. Senator Magnuson and female companion "Jermaine" even came to our house for dinner in 1961. They did get married in 1964.

After my junior year of school, I was put on a plane to Baltimore. Upon landing in Baltimore, I was to catch a shuttle to Washington, DC. Hiram was going to be at the location where these airport shuttles took people. I had one suitcase, one pair of shoes, and a piece of paper with Hiram's address on it. Don't forget about the one pair of shoes!! Also, no phone number to call or name of anybody to turn my dead body over to if things went wrong. But what could happen to a 16-year-old kid from the country who is maybe 5 foot 2 and looked like he was 12?

So, arrive I did, and I found the proper shuttle, or at least I hoped so. But an hour later, sweating profusely due to 100-degree heat in 99-degree percent humidity, I arrived somewhere in DC where Hiram was to meet me. To this day, you could knock me over with a feather, there was no Hiram to be found. After waiting around for a while, I got a taxi. Thankfully I had his address. The taxi ride seemed like it was at least for 30 minutes, and I wasn't so sure that I had enough money to cover it. I got dropped off at the address I gave him, a four-storey apartment building located two blocks from the Capitol. Fortunately cabs in DC charged by districts covered, not by a meter. My ride wasn't even a dollar. Of course, there still is no Hiram. Calling this place an apartment building is a stretch. It had four floors plus a basement. Each floor had 10 rooms and one bathroom. Not one bathroom for each room—one bathroom for the entire floor. Each room had two

Lady Bird's husband meets John Groshell.

small beds and one dresser. There was a basement and that had the kitchen to service the entire building. I was about the only person to frequent the basement regularly. I used it because it was the coolest place in the building, and it had a fan.

So, I'm sitting on the steps outside this luxury apartment house when a guy walks up and asks if I am Hiram's brother. Not having a better answer, I said yes. The guy's name was Ralph Group. He offered to show me around the area, so I said OK. I don't remember what I did with my suitcase but off we went to check stuff out. When we returned in an hour or so, Hiram was there and furious I had seen things without him being the one to show me.

Life in Washington, DC in the summer is hot and humid. Having grown up in Western Washington cool and damp is fine with me. If people in Western Washington want heat in the summer and cold in the winter, they can drive two hours to Eastern Washington and have it.

Pages in the US Senate are separated by party. The Democrat pages have their room and the Republican pages have their own. Your sponsor's party determines what you are. Unlike pages in Washington's state legislature, US pages actually have to work. One or two from each party will sit out on the floor when it is in session. The remainder stay in their room and are sent out to do errands. When sent out, the page punches out on the time clock, and punches in again upon completion.

Within a week or so I was assigned to be the "record" page. Each day I would put a copy of the previous day's congressional record on each of the Democratic senators' desks. I would then haul additional records to the various committees that requested them. Committees that had bills come up the previous day wanted more—some committees didn't want any.

Most days I tried to sit out on the floor the rest of the day. Usually, I could because other pages thought that was boring. I liked to hear what was going on. Most of the time there were only a few senators in the chambers. They spent most of their time in their office in the Senate office building. In Olympia the legislators didn't really have offices so most of them were in the chambers most of the time. In DC the pages really scrambled to get their senators from their offices when the other party was trying to get a quick vote on something.

Remember my one pair of shoes. The Democrat pages were required to wear black shoes. My one pair was brown. The boss of the Democrat pages was named Dickey Darling. Dickey was kind of grumpy—actually you can drop the "kind of." Most every night I would sit in the cooler basement, under 90 degrees anyway, and polish my shoes with black polish. About the only thing that I did at night besides polish my shoes was I would walk eight blocks to the Washington Senators stadium to watch baseball. I did this seven or eight times until I got scared off by groups of black kids threatening to beat me up or even cut me up.

The crowds at games were small, I would get in for $1 and sit anywhere I wanted. You could hear every hot dog, beer or peanut vendor in the stadium. The original Senators had moved to Minnesota in 1960. Washington was given an expansion team in 1961 and when I was there in 1962 there was just no fan base. That Senator team relocated to Texas in 1972.

Back to my job, the first thing I did every morning was take, borrow or how about relocate one *New York Times* and one *Wall Street Journal* from the Senate library to the desk of Senator Henry Scoop Jackson in his office. He was a nice guy and was always friendly to me. My sponsor, Senator Magnuson, was much too important to even recognize my existence.

Most of our errands involved going over to the Senate office building. There was a tunnel between the Capitol and the office buildings. The tunnel on the Senate side had two sets of trolley cars, each with three cars. Each of these cars held around eight people. I was running an errand to the office building one afternoon when I approached the trolley. Senator Hubert Humphrey was seated in the third car, there was nobody else down there but me. I climbed into the first car so that I wouldn't bother him. A second or two later I heard him calling, "Hey, you!"

I turned around and looked and said, "Me?"

"Yes," he replied and then added, "come on back here."

I stepped out of car one and walked back to car three. He asked me my name and I told him. He asked if I knew who he was and I said, "Of course I do, you're Senator Humphrey."

He reached out and we shook hands. He then asked what state I was from and who my sponsor was. I said, "Washington State and Senator Magnuson."

He replied with "Oh" in a tone that showed that he knew my sponsor would be of no help to me. He then inquired as to where I was living, and how I was doing.

I said I was just fine, I didn't describe the dump I was in. I also didn't mention only having one pair of shoes and having to polish them daily. I didn't say anything about not going to baseball games anymore because of being threatened. I just said, "I am fine."

He made me promise to come to him if I had any problems. At least half the times I would see him after that he would call me by

This guy looks like the guy in the sign I'm holding.

name and ask how I was doing. He cared a lot about a 16-year-old kid who looked like he was 12 and was 3,500 miles from home. There was nothing I could ever do for him, he just cared about me. Actually about 25 years later I named a kitten "Humphrey" after him and I loved and looked after him.

Hiram and I did have fun that summer. When not working, Hiram had hooked on with a representative from Illinois to help him in his office, and we did tourist stuff. Hanging out in our small oven with small beds wasn't an option. We went to the Smithsonian several times and other tourist attractions. We even raced up the Washington Monument at least once. There are stairs all the way to the top. As I remember there are plaques for each state joining the union displayed on the walls of the stairway.

While we were in DC, Dad ordered a new Studebaker Lark to be picked up in Detroit by Hiram. He sent Hiram money so he could take a bus to Detroit. Hiram pocketed the cash and hitchhiked instead. His venture went well and a few days later he was back with a nice-looking white Lark with clean blue interior. Little did I or Dad or Mom or even Hiram know that this was not going to be the car that was going to arrive in North Bend six weeks later.

One weekend Hiram and I decided to visit New York City. So, an 18-year-old and a 16-year-old headed north in a spanking new Studebaker to visit the "Big Apple." At that time, I didn't know it was called that. I was driving when we came into the city. I don't re-member if we came in through the Lincoln Tunnel or over the George Washington Bridge. I do know it wasn't the Millard Fillmore Highway. It was a hot day and whatever the route, it took us by the Polo Grounds where a Met game had just ended. The narrow streets were lined with tall apartment buildings. To a country kid from North Bend, they were tall, and the small windows were close together. My recollection was that there were at least two people leaning out each one and they were all eating oranges. I don't know if it was Harlem, which I had heard of, or something similar—whatever the case after being threatened more than once in DC by black kids I was petrified. The narrow roads were packed, and each intersection was full of cars crisscrossed forwards and sideways. The traffic lights were on posts that couldn't have been more than 8 feet high and had only red and green, no yellow. I guess it didn't matter because no one paid attention to them. We did get through it but I was a nervous wreck.

About the only other thing I remember about the weekend was going up the Empire State Building. I don't remember if we stayed overnight and if we did, I don't know where. Whatever the case I was happy to get back to DC and our beautiful apartment.

The rest of the summer was uneventful. Seeing Lyndon Johnson preside over the Senate became old hat, Senator Humphrey was always friendly, and Senator Henry Scoop Jackson always at least acknowl-edged my presence. When the summer was coming to an end, Senator

Jackson's office actually held a little going away party for their little paper-stealing page from Washington.

Loading up my stuff for the trip home was relatively easy. I still had just one suitcase and only one pair of shoes. Hiram had at least twice as many clothes, but he had been there for nine months, and not 2½. Hiram did have box after box after box of envelopes that had franks on them. I guess they were envelopes that were printed with stamps for official federal business purposes. I don't know why he had them, how he got them, or what he was going to do with them. I know that they pretty much filled up the trunk of the Lark and weighed enough that the back end was noticeably lower than the front. The Lark looked more like a little boat with a too big engine going through the water.

So off we go to drive back across the country. We stopped in Cleveland and spent the first night on the road with a friend of Mom's. The next night we stayed with a friend of Dad's in Chicago. Come morning we took off to go nonstop to Billings, Montana where we were to meet up with two of Mom's friends who were from France. Hiram started and got us past St Paul, MN. He didn't want to drive at night, so I took over shortly after the Twin Cities. After five or six hours of driving I was getting sleepy. I had a bottle of Coca Cola to sip on and once it was empty, I was hitting myself on the head with it to stay awake. Somewhere in the Dakotas at four or five in the morning and traveling about 70 mph I awoke to see a sharp turn directly ahead with a cornfield straight ahead. I was smart enough to not try to make the turn. The car couldn't be stopped in time so out into the corn we went. I was able to back out of the field and continue on. While quite dirty there was no real damage to the car. And Hiram hardly woke up. I had no trouble staying awake after that. Once it was daylight Hiram took over driving and we made it to Billings.

We met up with Mom's friends. Actually, one of them was Mom's friend, the other her daughter. She was about Hiram's age.

We went to Yellowstone Park with them and about the only thing I remember about our day involved Hiram and the bears. Many years later when my wife Liz and I took our two boys, Jeff and Willie, to Yellowstone we never saw a bear in three or four days. This visit with Hiram and the French girls there were many bears. You won't see as many squirrels in a peanut covered state park. Hiram was on a mission to get closer and closer to the bears to take their picture. While he was trying to impress the girls with his brave antics, I was scared to death over his safety. Several of them actually lunged at him but nothing ever happened. My only other memory of Yellowstone was of Hiram backing into another vehicle and breaking a taillight out of the Lark.

Leaving the girls after a day or two, we were off to home. When we got within about 30 miles of home, I told Hiram that I would like to stop somewhere and at least wash Dad's "new" Lark.

Basically, Hiram said, "Screw him, it's good enough."

We rolled on into the driveway and into the parking area behind the house. Dad had seen us coming up the long driveway and came out of the house to greet us and see his nice new car. What Dad got to see was a dirt-covered car with a broken taillight and a rear end that was much lower than the front. On top of that when Hiram turned it off, it kept on running, going *ka chunk – ka chunk*. It was a great homecoming.

CHAPTER 11

Senior Year

I was thrilled to be back at home. Dad accepted his "new car" with better humor than we deserved. Our two basset hounds, Jo and Lee, groaned and rolled with glee. Teddy's life had run out a couple years earlier, nothing tragic, just old age. Mom had even written an article about Jo and Lee which was published in 1958 in *The Saturday Evening Post*. The title was "I love my ugly dog."

I'm sure that earlier I mentioned that Mom had nine books published. She also had many magazine articles published. She wrote under her maiden name, Charlotte Paul. While I'm attempting to write a book about my life, many volumes would have to be written to cover hers. Two of her books were autobiographies about our family. The first was *Minding Our Own Business and second was And Four To Grow*. Not only was Mom talented, she was kind and understanding. When speaking of down and out people, Mom would tell me, "There but for the grace of God goes me or you." She also taught me "the Golden Rule." I haven't quite been 100% successful following it but I have tried.

While I have somewhat strayed off the path of my life, I haven't entirely. As I mentioned, shortly after our return Mom was appointed to the Washington State parole board by Governor Albert Rosellini for a four-year term. That was the end of her writing career for the next 10 years. She had to work out of Olympia, so she rented an apartment there. Through my senior year she stayed in Olympia weekdays and in North Bend about every other weekend. After four years on the state board, she was appointed to the federal board by Lyndon Johnson. That was a six-year term. Five of her books were published before parole board assignments, four of them after.

So, my senior year Mom was gone except some weekends and so was Dad. He had sold the paper and taken a job with King County flood control. He rented an apartment in Seattle but came home most weekends. I also never knew when he would show up during the week so I couldn't be a total screw off full time. Hiram was attending Seattle University and living on campus.

I enjoyed my freedom, even though Jo and Lee kept their blood-shot eyes on me. I could trust Lee, the big dumb male, but I wasn't sure if the much smarter Jo wasn't a tattletale. After getting back from DC I played more golf and hung out at Mount Si Golf as much as I could. I would do odd jobs like filling pop machines and picking up range balls in exchange for golf. Gradually I was given more responsibility and paid. My job at the IGA had ended when I went off to be a page in DC. I managed to get around with my Goliath. It had four gears forward and reverse. About every other month a gear shift cable leading into the transmission would break. That would leave me with 3rd and 4th gears forward, no first second or reverse. The only way to go backwards was by pushing. There was a local mechanic who would braze it back together but I would usually go with my limited gears for about a week.

Once the school year got going, I was happier than I had ever been before at school. I had been elected to be the boys club president and served on the student council. My best friend, Dick Sparks, was elected student body president. Girls weren't fighting over me but I hadn't been an object of their scorn for over a year. I even had several dates, usually with freshman girls. There are more of them who weren't taller than me—I was almost up to 5 foot 3 inches by then.

Once again, the golf team played in the fall. Even though I hadn't played for at least four months, due to being a page, I started right up hitting it longer and better than I had before. I was the number one player on the team. I would have been #2 but Gary Barter decided he wanted to play football instead. Gary had played since he was six years old and his mother was one of the best lady amateur players in the Puget Sound area. Gary had already worked at Mount Si Golf for a few years. Gary was a great athlete lettering in basketball and baseball at Mount Si High. He lettered in both at Wenatchee Junior College and lettered in baseball at the University of Washington. Gary and I worked together at Mount Si Golf and were ushers in each other's weddings. Enough about Gary, this is my damn book!

So, I'm playing better but still have not broken 80. For you non golfers, that means shooting a score of 79 or lower. Our first match of the year was at Redmond Golf Course against Lake Washington High School. I may have been the first person to have their first round under 80 be a 70. If one more putt had dropped, I could have skipped the 70s and gone straight from the 80s to the 60s. I'm pretty sure that there was no way another putt could have dropped, I had already made many more than I deserved. The rest of our season I was the medalist (low score) in almost every match. Each morning the office would make a broadcast about upcoming events and about any other newsworthy happenings. If it was a day after a match, they would announce the results including who had the lowest score. Usually, I would catch a bit of flak about it. In the early '60s, playing golf wasn't viewed as a real sport.

After the season ended, I got a tryout with the golf coach at Seattle University. We played Inglewood Country Club. I had never played it before. Inglewood is long and hilly, just plain tough. At that point I had never played a junior tournament and only played a couple of country clubs. I also had never played year-round nor been a member at a club as neither Mom nor Dad played golf. I really was new at the game.

I failed to impress him and therefore was not offered any help. He and I didn't know that three years later in my sophomore and junior years in Washington State U, Seattle University would play against WSU in the Banana Belt tournament at Clarkston. In that tournament six teams competed. Both of those years I finished second overall. One player beat me, I beat 34. His players, all on scholarship, were among that 34.

Early on in my senior year the school bought a soft ice cream machine. I don't remember why or how I was selected to operate it. We had three lunch periods so in order to run it I had to miss half of two of my classes every day. I didn't mind doing that plus I got paid $0.90 an hour to do it. I became known as the "Dairy Queen" which was an upgrade from being called "Frump."

In the fall, Sheri Sparks, younger sister of my best friend Dick, was on the back end of a three-wheel motorcycle. The driver crashed it coming down a gravel logging road from Lake Hancock. Sheri suffered brain trauma and was in a coma for over a month. Once she recovered enough to come back to school, she could only handle half a day. Being a freshman and having missed three months of school, it was difficult for her both emotionally and physically. Sheri and I were in the same study hall daily, the period that her mother would pick her up. I saw her mother pull up in front of the school on Sheri's first day back. Without asking the teacher's permission I got up, carried Sheri's books and escorted her to the car. I did it to physically help, but more importantly help her mentally. At that point I was one of the more popular students at Mount Si and I wanted to show the others that she could use support not any ridicule. Later that year her family gave me more support than I gave Sheri.

While not doing well in classes, at least I wasn't failing any. I was using Dad's system to a tee. Knock them dead as a freshman and coast the rest of the way. I got a D- in second year French. I explained to the elderly lady teacher that I deserved an F but since I was going to college, I needed a C. She then changed it to a C, that was a big break.

Some weekends I was alone, sometimes both Mom and Dad showed up, others just one of them. I had friends over for poker or just goofing off. We never got caught playing ping pong on the living room oak table. I played YMCA basketball at the Snoqualmie Falls YMCA making the All-Star team. The All-Stars then played a game against the Mount Si High junior varsity, which we won. I performed in a school play in which we put on three performances. That was my first taste of drama and I enjoyed it.

When spring rolled around, I started working at Mount Si Golf. I was a starter on weekends and helped with mowing sometimes.

Baseball season started and our new coach was named Marlin Jensen. He had played college baseball then semi pro ball before joining the teaching staff at Mount Si High. Mr. Jensen taught current world problems, a class all seniors had to take and pass in order to graduate. I was somewhat of a class clown and enjoyed getting a laugh. Unlike my brother, I didn't do it to make the teacher look stupid or disrupt the class. Mr. Jensen more than once told me that if my IQ were two points higher, I would be a rock. He also said I was goofier than Joe's dog, and he swam the river to get a drink of water. Knowing that I played baseball, many times he would say, "Groshell, just wait until baseball season."

Starting with our first practice he made me run more than anyone else. In batting practice, I had a lot more inside pitches thrown at me. He would just chuckle and say, "I told you so."

Our first game of the year was at Bellevue High. I started in left field and made several good catches and got two hits. We lost by one run and on the bus trip home, some of the guys were goofing around and laughing. For once in my life I was not joining in. The next day at practice, coach Jensen explained that he didn't like celebrating after a loss. We ran wind sprints over and over until we could hardly stand up. Then he said, "I'm going to race against Groshell. If I beat him, you will all run more."

Coach Jensen beat me easily. He would have beaten all of us. We had to run another few then he made the same announcement. The second time he let me beat him. But I showed him, I continued being a goofball in his class. Little did he and I know that nine years later I would teach with him at Mount Si High and he would assist me with the golf team.

Another member of the team was Chris Dowd. Chris was a freshman and our backup catcher. On a couple of occasions on bus trips Chris would take the part of a preacher and tell the guys to settle down and repent. We named him Deacon Dowd. After one road trip when we returned to Mount Si High, one of the older players took Chris's hat and placed it on the top of a goal post. Chris was afraid to climb up the 20 feet to get it. I hate heights but I still climbed up and got it down. It's funny how things work out but eleven years later he would become a partner of mine at the Snoqualmie Falls Golf Course.

So high school graduation was upon us, the class of 1963. Mom, Dad, Grandpa Paul and Grandma Truda were all in attendance. Graduation ceremonies included speeches by four of the graduates. First was a valedictorian, my buddy Dick Sparks. His grade point was about 3.7. Nowadays 1/3 of the class has a 3.9 plus with several 4.0's. I guess back then we just weren't so bright, or maybe good grades were harder to come by. I cruised in with a 2.9, 13th best in the class of 84 students.

The second speaker was our salutatorian. Faculty selected the third speaker. The 4th was selected by the graduating class—that's called the class speaker. I may not have had much class, but I was selected by a landslide. I don't remember the topic of my speech but I'm sure I spoke with enthusiasm.

When summer started, Gary and I worked full time on maintenance at Mount Si Golf. Mom still lived in Olympia most of the time and Dad in Seattle most of the time. Brother Hiram was traveling overseas after his freshman year at Seattle University. When not working Gary and I were playing golf.

CHAPTER 12

Kaboom

On Father's Day, Mom, Dad and I were all in North Bend. We had Father's Day dinner and I gave him a fancy pipe as a present. All seemed fine with all of us, and I headed to Mount Si Golf to water greens. I knew Mom was headed back to Olympia before I was to return.

Upon my return at about midnight, I drove in our long driveway around the house to our parking area. As I turned towards the parking area the headlights came upon Dad laying in the gravel. I jumped out and as I headed toward him, I saw the shotgun on the ground. I then saw that a good portion of his face was blown away.

He was alive though and groaning and moving a little bit.

I grabbed the shotgun and ran about 30 feet to our fenced backyard where the basset hounds were. I threw the gun out into the yard as I was screaming, "What in the goddamn hell have you done now?" I should have said, "What the f**k have you done now?"—that would have been easier. I was born in 1945, Dad died in 1998 and I don't remember he and I ever using the F word around each other.

Anyways, I then ran into the house and dialed 0—in 1963 in the Snoqualmie Valley there was no aid car. I guess it was an ambulance. I described to them how to find our house and said I would be at the end of our driveway with my lights on. I drove out there and waited for what seemed like a long time, I'm sure it was close to an hour.

When they arrived, I directed them up the driveway and then followed them about five minutes later. I didn't want to see Dad again and truthfully was hoping he had died.

When I pulled back in, they were all in the house. Somehow Dad had gotten up and made it into the main bathroom and they couldn't get him to come out. They asked me to get him to come out and I told them to do whatever they had to do including break the door down, but I wasn't going to help. Eventually they got him out and hauled him away without me seeing him again, I was in my bedroom. I had no idea where they were taking him or what his chances of survival were.

I did know that I could not handle staying there. When I left, the back door remained open and many lights were left on. I drove up to Dick Spark's house, about seven or eight miles away. I'm sure no one was up because it had to be past midnight. Within minutes Earl and Colleen Sparks, along with son Dick and daughter Sheri, were with me gathered round their dining room table. We stayed up talking for at least two hours even though Earl had to work the next day. All four of them were there to do whatever it took to help me feel better.

I never slept that night, but I went to work at 6:00 AM because I didn't know what else to do. After working a couple hours, I started feeling sick so I left to go back to the Sparks' house. I never did call Mom, I guess I just figured someone would, and I wasn't going to return to that house.

Shortly after getting back to the Sparks' house, a County Sheriff car arrived with two sheriffs in it. They took me out and put me in the backseat and started asking me questions. I had to tell them everything I knew, what I had done, and if anyone else had been around. They were not mean, but at the same time they weren't concerned about my feelings. Looking back, maybe the fact that I had gone to work didn't look good for me. At no time since I found him have I ever received any counseling or grief therapy. However, I learned something more important than anything I ever learned before. I learned that there was only one person who would always look after me and take care of me. That person was me.

So Dad survived. He blew away his lower right jaw and with it skin, teeth, gums and part of his tongue. Over the next two years he had numerous surgeries. They cut bone off of his pelvis to graft a new lower right jawbone. The first attempt failed but the second worked.

The hardest part of the whole thing, other than finding him that night, was that I was then expected to live with him. Hiram was overseas playing, Mom was working in Olympia, and good old John was expected to come home every night not knowing what the hell he would find. That's one sorry deal for a 17-year-old kid. I told Mom that I could not handle it. Dad got out of hospital in about a month, the major surgeries were to start months later. Mom came back to

My other mother and brother—Colleen and Dick Sparks. Along with father Earl and sister Sheri, they took me in when I was in need.

North Bend most nights and every weekend. After Dad had been out of the hospital a couple of weeks, I got stuck alone with him a couple nights a week. By mid-August he was well enough to join Hiram wherever he was overseas, I think it was Turkey.

Later I learned that Father's Day night, Mom announced she was leaving him. That was the end of the Groshell family.

CHAPTER 13

Who Ever Bets?

Toward the end of summer Gary and I entered the Pacific Northwest juniors championship which was being held at Tualatin Country Club just out of Portland, Oregon. In 1963 this was far and away the biggest juniors tournament in the Pacific Northwest. This was also to be my first and only juniors tournament. The qualifying round I shot 78 and qualified for the championship flight, but just barely. My first match I played the #2 seed, who grew up playing Overlake Country Club in Bellevue, Washington since he was six years old. I beat him 3 and 2 and saw him shed a few tears as he walked off. The next day I three-putted the 18th green to let it go into extra holes. I then lost the match on the 19th hole. It was the first extra hole, not a drink off the 19th hole bar. Had it been at the bar I probably would have won.

To finish off the summer Mom picked me up in Portland and she and I went down to San Francisco where her two sisters lived. Gary drove himself back to the Snoqualmie Valley. Dad had gotten where he was healthy enough to travel to wherever Hiram was.

Mom and I got to spend about 10 days of "us" time which I greatly appreciated. I remember going to a play with her. We also went to San Francisco Giants game. Willie Mays was, and still is, my second favorite player ever. We were seated down the first base side about 10 rows up. Willie hit a pop foul that could have been the highest one I had ever seen, and it was coming down right at me. I didn't have a glove, but I had my hands cupped together and I was going to catch it. Just as it would have hit my hands, they separated involuntarily. I didn't want them to, they did it on their own. The ball hit the cement between my feet and bounced back up about 50 feet. At that point people were all over us and when the dust settled someone else got the ball.

Aunt Jackie taught Mom and me how to drink tequila properly.

A shot, squeeze of lime in the mouth, and lick salt off the back of the hand. The trip with Mom helped get me emotionally ready for college at Washington State University. The summer had been fun in many ways.

Many hot afternoons students frequented the "Blue Hole". This is a swimming hole on the Snoqualmie River right at the base of Mount Si. The hole had 8 to 10 feet of water in it. We would climb up the rocks to 10 to 12 feet and dive in. The hole was on the mountain side of the river and we had to swim across the river 80 feet or more to get to it. Swimmers would get swept downriver while crossing then walk up the bank over rocks about 50 feet to get to it. Some would enter the river upstream 100 feet or so and then swim across and drift into the hole.

One day I sized up the situation and bet some kids I could enter straight across and swim to it without drifting downriver. I entered the water and went underwater. I picked up a boulder a bit bigger than a bowling ball then scrambled crawling with one arm and two legs on the bottom and came up at the Blue Hole. Nobody figured out how I did it. At our 50th reunion in 2013 several classmates were talking about somebody going across underwater our senior year. They didn't remember that it was me. Since I was the MC for the night, I let them know and had several others at the reunion who verified it.

But I was more into golf than swimming. I played more golf than I ever had before and played better. I joined the Mount Si Golf Club early in the summer and by fall I was down to a 4 handicap. I had played my first tournament and had done well. Working full time in maintenance at Mount Si was enjoyable and I learned a lot. The other plus of the summer was traveling for 10 days with Mom and enjoying her company.

I had grown up abruptly in one night. I wouldn't want any kid to have to go through a similar experience. In spite of the emotional pain and anguish I suffered, it no doubt made me a stronger person. I became determined to never give up. As you will see in later years, especially in college, I did a lot of foolish things. Maybe it was because I just didn't care and didn't think about consequences. I certainly didn't worry about what my father would think. The one thing that I would never get over is my father doing what he did when he knew I was the one who was going to find him dead. I wasn't the wife who was leaving him. I wasn't the son who tormented him. I was the son who loved him and wanted to please him. Dad passed away 32 years later and not once did we ever talk about that night.

If you didn't notice, when I went underwater from one bank to the other without drifting downriver it was a bet. I had tried the boulder under one arm and crawl method when no one was around. Thanks to Dad's training I was no stranger to betting. There used to be Wednesday night and Friday night fights on TV. Dad and I watched them whenever we could, which was most of the time. Back then one fighter always wore white trunks, the other fighter wore black. There were no red, blue, green or any designs or tassels—just white or black. We bet $1.00 per bout, and I always got white trunks and Dad got black. This gave me a slight advantage if it was a championship fight. In championship fights the defending champion always wore white, the challenger black. Without a doubt this is the only bet Dad ever gave me the advantage in. We really had fun watching these together.

We had a dice game that instead of having dots on each side had cards. The six sides of each had 9, 10, Jack, Queen, King, Ace. There are five die with the standard leather cup to roll them out of. The object was to come up with the best poker hand. After a few rolls trading wins, Dad started winning one after another. When he got up aways we started going double or nothing on each roll. He kept on winning, over and over. It got up to where I owed him over 60,000 dollars. I just figured it out and starting at $1 and going double or nothing it would take 17 losses in a row. At the time I was around 10 years old and trusting and gullible. He had to be cheating in some manner.

Once I owed him the 60 grand, he refused to let me go double or nothing again. He said he shouldn't have let me go this far and that was it. I begged and pleaded to roll just one more time and he refused. I kept telling him I couldn't pay, and he said I could pay little by little. Day after day when he got home, I would beg for one more chance. It really was driving me nuts.

Finally, after about two weeks he said, "OK, we'll roll but only for $5."

"What good will that do?" I cried.

He said, "Forget it, we won't roll then."

After a couple more days of sweating it out, he finally let me roll double or nothing. I won and that was probably the biggest relief in my life.

Our whole family would go to Longacres horse racing track once a year, sometimes twice. Mom and Dad would let Hiram and me bet. Each one of us could pick one horse a race and they would match the dollar each of us would put up to make it a $2 wager. Between two consecutive trips to the track, I had lost twelve straight bets. I wouldn't take favorites or longshots. I liked horses between 3 to 1 and 10 to 1. Horses with interesting names and jockeys wearing colors I liked also attracted my attention. So after not cashing a ticket in 12 races over two visits to the track, a horse named "Mr. Miracle" was in the next race. Obviously, I needed a miracle. I think it was Mom who matched my dollar to place a $2 win on Mr. Miracle. I don't remember what color the jockey was wearing but he won.

One night while having dinner as a family, Dad told us about how they had what they called a "ghoul pool" at the *Chicago Times*. I was about an eighth grader at the time. If we were interested, we had to come up with a list of at least 40 elderly people who were famous. They could be actors, entertainers, singers, politicians or royalty. They also had to be in the news. We would then randomly draw the names out of that hat so we would each have 1/4 of them. Each of us would put $5 in the pool to start with. If no person on our list died in the week, we would each ante up $0.10 to the pot. If someone on the list died, the person who had him would collect the pot and everyone would put in $5 to start up again. So, we set about the task of making the list. We used newspapers to help come up with names. Mom and Dad were both highly educated and worked in the news world for years. They could come up with lots of names. The list was growing, Hiram coming up with some names while I only knew names of baseball players and they were in their 20s and 30s. Things were going fine until Hiram suggested that Dad be put on the list. Dad was a bit put off by this one while Mom was appalled. Both stated that that wasn't nice, and it was not going to happen.

Hiram stuck to his guns that,"It's supposed to be a list of those who could die at any time, so Dad certainly belonged on it."

Once the smoke cleared the ghoul pool died before anyone on it had a chance. Hiram once again succeeded in creating mayhem. Gambling was certainly not foreign to me. I don't think Dad was trying to make a gambler out of me. If anything, I think he wanted me to have a bit of experience with it but at the same time be wary of it.

CHAPTER 14

Two Cross State Trips

There were 84 graduates in the class of '63 from Mount Si high. Nine of us went to WSU and one to UW. Being small town kids, we preferred a smaller school. WSU had just over 9,000 students. The mighty UW had 25,000 plus or minus 2. Pullman, the home of WSU, was 250 miles and over five hours driving time away. The UW was 30 miles in 40 minutes. The mantra for Mount Si students was to "get out of the Valley." More than half of our fathers were employed by Weyerhaeuser and virtually every graduate was determined to escape that trap.

I was set to be Dick Spark's roommate at McAlister Hall, and on the 4th and top floor. I had spent many nights that summer staying at his house. Another member of our class going to WSU was Pam Austin. Pam and I had been in every class in K through 8 at North Bend Elementary and had many high school classes together. I never dated Pam, who we called Ozz, because she was taller than me and always one of the cutest girls in school. What is the saying? Oh yes, I got it: "out of my league." But Pam was always nice to me and never gave me a bad time. It was the upper-class girls my freshman and sophomore years in high school that tormented me.

Anyway, the first love of my life was Pam's mother. It was at Ozz's birthday party our second grade year that I fell in love. I followed her mother around like I was a little puppy, trying to be cute to win her over. My best trick was acting like I couldn't operate the straw in my bottle of pop. She would smile, unbend the straw and put it back in the bottle. I quit trying that move about my junior year in high school, it just didn't work. I had no car. I got settled in at McAllister Hall with pretty much all of my possessions. That consisted of one suitcase of clothes and my golf clubs.

A couple of weeks before semester break my dad had another surgery to graft bone off of his pelvis to rebuild his jaw. The first attempt had failed. I wanted to see him but had no car. Pullman to North Bend was about a six-hour drive.

A friend of mine in the dorm, Paul Taylor, wanted to go home to Kirkland to visit his new girlfriend. Little did we know that would lead him to becoming the owner of Cadman Gravel years later. That made him a very well-to-do individual, but at that time Paul didn't have a car either.

Paul suggested that we hitchhike. I had never hitchhiked in my life. When we decided to embark on this venture it was afternoon and at the end of January. Eastern Washington is cold in the winter, but we weren't hindered by something like practical thinking.

Our first ride took us under one mile into downtown Pullman. Our next ride ended in Colfax, WA only 16 miles away. By then it was after 1:00 PM.

After 15 minutes we got our third ride. This person was only going as far as Dusty which amounted to 18 miles. Dusty was famous for their grain elevator. The population couldn't have been over 25.

As it got colder and threatened to snow, we stood with thumbs out. Finally, someone stopped, picked us up and took us to their destination. That was the next town 22 miles down the road which was named LaCrosse. A year later I was going to meet their sheriff.

At this point it was hard to get a ride because nobody was driving anywhere. It wasn't because we looked shady, it was because it was winter in eastern Washington and snowing.

Finally, a car came along and picked us up. His destination was one town away in Washtucna. Every ride had been for a one-town jump. This time it amounted to 23 miles. We had gotten five rides for a total of 80 miles. This left us with more than 175 miles to go and it was snowing, and dark out as it approached 6:00 PM.

One car came by after 15 minutes but went on by. Paul threw a couple rocks towards the car as it was going out of sight but as a pitcher for WSU he couldn't throw a strike so he missed.

Finally, we walked about a hundred yards back to a small café/gas station in Washtucna. They were just closing but there was a couple leaving who offered to take us to Connell. That was not on the path to North Bend, but they did have motels and restaurants. We took the ride. Fortunately, we had enough money to get a room.

The next morning, we hitched a ride that took us about 10 miles back to the road going the direction we needed. We stood there for over an hour and decided it was time to hitchhike back to Connell and buy bus tickets to North Bend.

We entered a café there that also was the bus depot. A guy at the counter heard us talking about getting tickets while we were counting our limited funds. He said, "Hey guys, I'm going to Kirkland. I can drop you in North Bend and go on to Kirkland." Wow—life was good after all.

Once in North Bend I was able to borrow my roommate's '55 Chevy that he had left at home in Snoqualmie. I also stayed the next two nights with the Sparks family and drove Dick's car in to see my dad in the hospital.

I vividly remember my trip over by thumb, but I can't remember how I got back to Pullman a few days later.

The tale of two trips continued one year later also on semester break.

The summer after my freshman year I was able, with financial help from Mom, to buy a car. It was a 1959 Chevy Impala convertible. I wish I still had it but upon graduation I traded it in for $500 to buy a Plymouth Barracuda. Unfortunately, that wasn't the only mistake I ever made.

But back to the trip from Pullman to Snoqualmie a year later. My '59 needed to have the engine rebuilt and Dick Spark's dad was a mechanic. He insisted on doing it for me at his own expense. The Sparks family had taken me in when I had nowhere to go, and now he was fixing my car as well.

Anyways, I had a friend riding with me and was being followed by an old high school pal, Herb Johnson, in his '58 Impala. It was a clear sunny day in January but close to freezing. Since my convertible top was always down when the sun was up that's how it had to be that day. With the heater on full bore, it was actually comfortable if you were in the front seat.

As we came into LaCrosse, I saw that Herb took a right onto a gravel road that hooked back up with the main road in about a half mile. It bypassed the downtown area. The downtown area had two or three small stores and a few chickens in the street.

Seeing Herb in the rearview mirror pull this stunt I knew he was trying to beat me to where the roads joined back up. At that point I stomped on the gas in an effort to win the race.

At the same time my passenger was going through my glove compartment. There was garbage and old napkins and papers and who knows what all in there. I was just barely beating Herb to the junction so as I came to it I turned slightly and went onto the shoulder where I sprayed gravel towards him.

We were laughing and yelling, and my pal asked, "Do you want these papers and junk?"

I said, "Hell no!"

With that he threw the armful up in the air thinking it would hit Herb's car.

In the meantime, another car had slid in behind us and had a red light flashing. I spotted it as the papers bounced off his windshield.

I pulled over and this old station wagon with a flashing red light pulled in behind me. Out of it climbed a tall and big individual who was wearing coveralls and a beat-to-crap baseball cap.

With the top down I still had to roll down my window. It stayed warmer with the windows up. He sauntered up and in a slow drawl started in on my buddy. "I could have you clean up ten miles of road if I wanted. You college punks think you can come through my town any way you want. I could throw your asses in jail and make you sit for days. Etc. etc. etc."

Thankfully I had been raised to keep a straight face. I didn't think it was funny but when scared sometimes it makes you kind of laugh in fear. Plus, here is this giant in coveralls yelling at us sounding like he belonged on the *Andy Griffith Show*.

Then he turned on me. "And you punk gunning your fancy car through my town thinking you're some big shot! Driving with the top down in freezing weather. You're nothing but a spoiled rotten punk."

At this point I'm sure we are headed for jail. Finally, he said, "Okay—get out of here. If I ever see you coming through town like that again I will give you a handsome fine. Now git outa here!!"

I drove away slowly and felt lucky to have gotten off with no jail time or fine. At least when I hitchhiked the year before I didn't have a run-in with the law.

CHAPTER 15

Can't Read? Box Instead

The house in North Bend was on the block plus most anything else that I owned and would never see again, including what would now be thousands of dollars' worth of baseball cards.

My set of golf clubs now were Haig Ultras made by the Walter Hagen division of Wilson sporting goods.

Soon after I started working full shifts at Mount Si Golf and playing to a single digit handicap, Harry Umbinetti picked these out for me. He sold them to me at less than his cost and I was allowed to work them off gradually. I now had "pro shop" clubs.

But back to starting college. The first thing was to sign up and register for classes. First step was to go to your advisor and have them establish a list of the classes you were to sign up for. When I reported at my assigned time at his office I had barely sat down before he said, "You are going to flunk out."

This wasn't comforting to a 17-year-old who had no family or home to go back to. Of course, I asked him why he said that. He replied that it was because I couldn't read. I probably said something convincing like, "Can so." He said the Stanford achievement tests indicated that I couldn't and that was that.

Apparently, he didn't want to be proven wrong so he required me to sign up for 18½ hours of courses for credit plus a 3-hour remedial reading class for which I would get no credit. Included was a four-hour Chemistry class with lab time. WSU was on a semester system so most classes are three-hour credits. Class is either Monday, Wednesday, and Friday for one hour each day or Tuesday and Thursday for an hour and a half each day. In a quarter system, students usually have three classes of five hours each with three finals to take. The standard semester system means five classes of three hours each with five finals to take. So, my advisor, or maybe executioner, signed me up for seven classes because I couldn't read.

I decided to make a strategic and economic move and not buy books. Why waste money buying something you can't use, or waste time trying. I did buy a lab manual for Chemistry since we wrote in them in the lab. Dick Sparks was also in the same Chemistry class with me so I could, if needed, refer to his textbook. I religiously went to every class, took notes, and rewrote or organized them later.

Someone had told me—I couldn't have read it—that you could get a C by reading the books or by going to every class. To get an A or a B you had to do both.

Without books to read I had more time and money than I would have ever if I bought them. I played a lot of ping-pong at the student union building, it was free. I played basketball and even did a bit of weightlifting. I also got into boxing.

The ½ hour of my 21½ was a PE class. I took a class called "Bag Punching." The class was taught by Ike Dieter. Ike was about 60 years old and had coached and trained boxers for years. There had been AAU boxing for years, but it was dying out. Ike trained Golden Gloves boxers and was always looking for sparring partners for them. I spent a lot of time at the gym working out punching speed bags, heavy bags and skipping rope.

After about a month working out and hanging around the gym with Ike, he asked me if I would like to spar with his Golden Gloves guys. I thought it was a good idea to learn how to get beat up without crying. I looked like a world beater jumping rope and punching speed and heavy bags. The key factor was that they didn't hit back. In the ring facing a real person who threw punches my feet moved like I was wearing cement shoes. The worst thing I could do was actually land a punch and tick them off. Even then, Ike would tell them to back off and take it easy. Ike called me Tiger. Tiger never became a good boxer, but he did learn to not be afraid. The guys in my dormitory started calling me Cassius Clay (who later changed his name to Mohamed Ali).

With time to spare, somehow I started reading John Steinbeck books. Yes, I did say it, reading. While Dick Sparks studied at night, I read *Cannery Row, Of Mice and Men, Grapes of Wrath* and every book of his that I could get my hands on. The final Steinbeck book I read was *Travels with Charley*. That was several years later and probably my favorite largely because of my love for dogs.

I ended up the first semester with a 2.65 GPA. When I checked in with my advisor, he was shocked that I did as well as I did. I thanked him for helping me save money and have time to have fun. I explained that because he told me I couldn't read I had skipped buying books. I bragged that my ping pong game had improved, and that I was in much better shape and that I had learned how to get hit and not cry. I also mentioned that I had saved money and then in spite of not being able to read I had read a number of Steinbeck books.

He was perhaps a bit shocked but I'm not sure he believed me. He advised me to buy books the next semester, after all he was an advisor. He proceeded to sign me up for the standard 15½ hours the next semester and allowed me to drop the remedial reading class. The half-hour class was for PE which I got credit for being on the golf team the spring semester.

My first blemish, as far as behavior goes, happened this spring semester. There was another Mount Si graduate I knew who lived on the 1st floor of McAllister. He was roommates with one of the pitchers on the WSU varsity. The dormitory was holding a dance one night. Four of us were drinking in my friend's room on the 1st floor. I hadn't organized this or gotten the beer or vodka for it—I was just there. My fellow Mount Si friend got the drunkest the fastest and decided to throw all the empty bottles out his window into the parking lot. We got caught and while no punishment took place apparently it went on my record.

CHAPTER 16

Meets Liz – Gets Social Probation

So, golf season rolled around which for the freshman meant very little. I was a walk-on since no golf scholarships were given at WSU at that time. There was a freshman team; freshmen were not allowed to play varsity then. We played a few matches against junior college teams but there weren't many. We didn't hardly have a coach but the guy who drove us to several matches was the freshman basketball coach. I had watched every WSU home basketball game, both freshman and varsity. I had plenty of time, no books to read. The freshman coach was very demanding and tough on his players, and they responded by winning virtually every game. With us he was friendly and funny. Anyways, his name was Jud Heathcoat. He went on to be the head basketball coach at the University of Montana and lead them to one NCAA tournament. From there he became the head coach at Michigan State University where he led them to 10 NCAA tournaments. He and his Spartans won the NCAA championship in 1979.

So back to me. On the freshman golf team I played number one. From what I gathered I would have been number one on the varsity. We practiced on the 9-hole goat ranch on campus while the varsity played and practiced at Clarkston Country Club, about 35 miles away. That season was pretty much a waste, but I did get a cardigan with a 67 on it. No, that wasn't my IQ, that was the year I was supposed to graduate. The next year WSU was going to give a few golf scholarships, but they never even told me that much less offered me one.

The second semester was relatively uneventful. My grade point that semester was a 2.45. During that semester my parents were able to sell the house. The Sparks family welcomed me into their home for the summer. Back to the 1959 Chevrolet Impala convertible that was my first car. I bought it at a used car dealership in Seattle for 1,500 dollars. When I was a mile from the golf course the steering got a bit ragged, so I slowed down considerably. At about 30 mph the back left wheel fell off and I skidded to a stop. The hub actually landed on the wheel and tire as I slid to a stop. All the lugs were gone so I took one off each of the other three wheels. I then jacked the car up and replaced the wheel with them. I was able to continue on to the course and get replacement lugs the next day. I did check the rest of the lugs to make sure they were tight. Other than that one episode the car ran well all through summer and into the next year in school.

I worked at Mount Si Golf mainly outside in maintenance and in the pro shop a bit on weekends. Harry Umbinetti hired a guy named Hugh Peterson to be his assistant pro. He had been in the service, and he became the first ever assistant pro for Harry.

Hughie was tall, blond and handsome. He was also very outgoing. Working in the pro shop with Hughie taught me to be more outgoing. I wasn't exactly a wallflower before but watching him in action made me realize that people enjoyed being kidded with and even being made fun of to a certain degree. I also learned when to back off and how to soothe things if things went too far.

There was a girl named Eileen Wilson who I had met the previous summer at Mount Si Golf. On occasion she played golf with her parents, Bill and Ann Wilson. One day when working with Hughie I said, "I think I'll ask Eileen Wilson out on a date."

He said, "No, you won't."

I said, "Why not?"

He said, "Because I am dating her."

Obviously, I couldn't compete with a handsome 25-year-old who is 6 feet tall and outgoing. That would have been the end of my story. I was 18 years old and 5-foot-5 tall and had one date my whole freshman year. Then he said she does have a younger sister.

Hughie arranged through Eileen to have kid sister Liz come out to Mount Si with her parents so we could meet. About three years later we got married. As I'm writing this right now, we had our 55th anniversary a few months ago on June 30.

On our first date we went to the Cinerama theater in Seattle to watch *It's a Mad Mad Mad Mad World*. Most nights the rest of the summer we spent visiting in the front room of the Wilson home in Kirkland. Generally, I was encouraged by her mother to leave by 11:00 PM. I reported to work most mornings by 6:00 AM.

One night I took Liz to a restaurant called Canlis. I don't think I was trying to impress her but since it was one of the most expensive restaurants in Seattle, I guess I was. At Canlis you pull in and they park your car for you. That was a first for me. We ordered the Chateaubriand for two with whatever all came with it. Since I was only 18 and she was 17 we saved money. Coca Cola was much less than wine and/or mixed drinks. When I got the bill I was able to cover it with about a dollar to spare for a tip. I was a big spender!! Upon stepping out the door our car was waiting for us. That is another feature of Canlis, one's car is waiting when you're ready to go. Unfortunately, I didn't have a cent to give the valet parking guy. I was embarrassed but that's just how it was. He looked at me with a sympathetic smile, he understood. It's just a good thing I had enough gas to get home.

Gary Barter and I played a lot of golf in the afternoons after work and before I would head into Kirkland to see Liz. Gary talked me into entering the Northwest Open with him. It was being held at Everett Golf and CC. The only other tournament I had ever played in was the PNW juniors the year before. For their first adult golf event doesn't everybody pick the biggest non-tour professional event in their region of the country? Needless to say, I was in over my head. The club pros that I was paired with were kind and understanding. While I failed to make the 36-hole cut, I didn't totally embarrass myself or hurt anybody.

Summer came to close, so it was time to kiss Liz goodbye and head back to WSU for my sophomore year while Liz completed her high school years at Lake Washington High. Yes, Liz and I did kiss and even held hands.

The Sparks waved goodbye to their son and their sorta son as we headed back in my Impala convertible. We were headed for a new 12-storey dormitory named Orton Hall. McAllister had been changed to a women's dorm. The occupants of 4th floor McAllister were transferred to 9th floor Orton. Just for variety Dick and I decided to change roommates for our sophomore year. We still got along just fine but thought a change would be fun. Our rooms were beside each other and we did things together socially. Of course, I did more socializing, and he did more studying.

I decided to buy books my sophomore year. My major was Business Administration because that is what most guys signed up for who didn't know what they actually wanted to do. My freshman year I took about half college requirement classes and half business classes. My advisor signed me up for 15½ hours of classes. I continued working out occasionally as a sparring partner, playing a bit of basketball, and even studying a little.

There was a loudspeaker situated on the wall directly across from my room. Most announcements were made between 8:00 and 9:00 in the morning. One Saturday morning I awoke to some loud message at about 8. I came out of my room and was looking at the speaker which happened to be higher on the wall than I could reach. A buddy of mine came out of his room just down the hall from mine. We agreed that the speaker would be appreciated more if it were torn down. Being taller than I, he decided to handle the operation. The head resident put up posters asking whoever did it to come forth. Neither of us wanted to come in first or second let alone fourth. When it was announced everyone on the 9th floor was going to be charged $5 to fix it, a stool pigeon flew in and gave us up. Apparently, he had looked out of his door when we removed it.

This was considered my third infraction of rules. I mentioned the first earlier when I got caught drinking in McAllister with three other guys. The second infraction had taken place the year in McAllister as well. The head resident of McAllister was a nice lady of about 50 years of age. She would go to tea or lunch every Friday at noon with friends. She always came out of the building through the same door. Once out the door, which could not be seen from windows on that side of the building, there was an overhang of eight feet. The guys who had the room at that end of the hall planned to throw a bucket worth of water out to land on her. So, one of them went down to the parking lot to signal the guy back in the room when to let it go. The timing was a one in a thousand chance of actually hitting her, maybe more like 1 in 10,000. Anyways they hit the bullseye. She set a time record in climbing four floors worth of ramps. There were several guys who weren't involved but had witnessed it, I was one of them. So, the loudspeaker caper became my third strike. I had done several other stupid things which I didn't get caught doing.

A buddy of mine who also lived on the 9th floor came up with a large heavy duty plastic bag. We took it up to the 12th and top floor where there was a rec room. We put as much water in it as we could handle and threw it out a window. We did it where it would land on a breezeway below and not hurt anyone. At least we were that smart.

We watched it fall 11 floors before impact. When it hit the cover on the breezeway, we could actually feel the impact shake all the way up on the 12th floor. The circle of water spray was huge.

Fortunately, the cover withstood the impact and as far as we know suffered no damage. Best of all we weren't caught.

I never thought of the consequences. Had I been thrown out of school I would have been drafted and sent to Vietnam. Looking back, I'm guessing that the whole deal with finding Dad that night made me not give a damn about anything.

There was a meeting scheduled in the conference room on the 9th floor of Orton. The head resident at Orton, the Dean of University living facilities, and the Dean of Men were to discuss my punishment and future at WSU.

Whatever the case, the conference room was next door from my room. There were two wings to the building and between them were bathrooms, conference rooms, washing machines and elevators. The middle section jutted out so one of the walls of the conference room stuck out to the left of my window. On that wall was a fan to the room.

When I was asked if I tore the speaker down, I replied, "How could I? I have to stand on a chair just to brush my teeth in the morning."

Once again, I was just pissed at the world or really stupid, but I thought it was funny. I was sent to my room while they discussed what to do with me. There was snow on the windowsill. So just to prove that I had a bad attitude, I decided to try to throw a snowball through that fan and into the room. The fan was running and therefore open. There was also snow on our window sill. I fixed up about four snowballs and got my roommate to hold on to my belt as I leaned out the window to throw. I didn't want to make a nine-floor freefall. The fan was about 12 feet away and my third throw hit dead center. I doubt that much snow actually went through, but enough so that they knew what I had done. When they got to my room, which was in less than 10 seconds, I was sitting at my desk with the window shut. I'm sure I looked innocent.

Once they finished telling me how stupid my actions were, they told me what was going to happen. I was being kicked out of the dorm at the end of the semester, about two weeks away. I was to clean the 12th floor recreational room every Sunday night for eight weeks. I was also fined $25 for the speaker repair. I didn't realize how lucky I was to get to stay in school.

I signed up for rush to find a fraternity to live in. The first one to invite me for dinner was a small group. It turned out to be a Catholic fraternity, which for me wasn't a good fit. After going to a couple other frats, I got invited to the Sigma Phi Epsilon house. I knew nothing about any of the fraternities but my visit there was enjoyable. Sigma Phi Epsilon was at that time somewhat the *Animal House* of WSU. Besides being a bit wild, it had 5 football players, 3 baseball players, 1 wrestler, 1 basketball player, and now 1 golfer. All 11 were starters on the varsity teams. I was all set to move in there in two weeks once the semester ended. With the aid of textbooks, I dropped to a 2.3 grade point that semester.

Since I was going to play varsity golf the next semester, my advisor signed me up for only 14½ hours of classes. Playing on the varsity required two different five-day trips plus other matches and practice every afternoon at Clarkston Country Club.

CHAPTER 17

Frat Life

Even though the Sig EP house was on the wild side, there was much more structure living there than there had been in the dorms. Pledges had to be out of the house weekdays by 8. If you didn't have a class, you were supposed to be in the library. Lunch was back at the house between 12 and 1, then back to classes and or library until 5:00 PM. We had a 6:00 PM curfew period. Failure to observe these hours resulted in a swat with our ¾-inch thick leather paddle.

As pledges we had to take a test every week on our pledge manual. Pledges also had to observe certain rules of etiquette at meals. Never talk with food in your mouth. When passing food, reach across your body to receive the platter then transfer to the other hand to then reach across your body again to pass it on. If the plate was coming from your left, you reach for it with your right hand. You then switched it to your left hand and passed it on to your right. If eating soup, you had to spoon it from your bowl thitherwardly. That meant spooning it in a backhanded type of motion away from your body and towards the center of the table. Failing to observe any of these rules put you on the auction block. The member who bid the most got to give you a swat with the leather paddle. Generally bids to swat me were higher than on other pledges. I'm sure it had nothing to do with me being a smart ass.

There were two sleeping dorms in the fraternity. The 2nd floor dorm was a no talking dorm. There were basically no regulations on the third-floor dorm. Usually, it was pretty quiet but a couple of times a semester there would be a rack session. There were bunk beds in both dorms. Due to some sort of fire regulation the windows had to be open in the sleeping areas. Pullman, Washington is cold in the winter, so everyone had an electric blanket.

I started out sleeping in the second-floor dorm, but the quiet well-behaved atmosphere just didn't fit. I was soon switched to the salt mines. That was one room in the basement where they put the two pledges they thought they most had to control. Along with the two pledges were the two members deemed most worthy of controlling these troublemakers. I actually liked it down there. Our study area was bigger than the ones upstairs and our sleeping room with bunks wasn't as cold.

One of the members down there kept a list of demerits he gave to us. They could be from anything he deemed necessary. He had the list taped to the side of his file cabinet. One night he gave me a demerit for something, so I responded by lighting his list on fire. That got me an extra hard swat, but it was worth it. After the semester I got to move to the third-floor dormitory, where there was the occasional rack session.

The rack session happened when anyone in there said, "Rack 'em." That meant every mattress and sheets and electric blankets had to go out of the windows. That meant everybody's! With most of the football players on that floor things could get interesting. It would take two or three guys to hold one down while his stuff was being thrown out. Once everyone had carried their things back up three floors and settled down, someone would say, "Rack 'em again." After two of these everyone would be tired enough to actually go to sleep.

There was also a ritual in the house that if anyone was born out of the state of Washington they would have to be initiated into the "sons of the frozen North." I didn't know what that was, but I also didn't want to find out. I didn't tell anyone that I was born in Chicago, IL. Someone must have found out. During lunch one day after I had been in the frat for a month one of the guys said, "Get him." I was hauled out of the dining room. All my clothes were removed in the front room. I fought it but was outnumbered about 50 to 1. Once stripped totally naked I was hauled out into the front lawn. I was dragged by my ankles all around the front lawn with about 6 inches of snow on the ground. In addition, the Main Street leading up to the classroom buildings ran by our house. Several hundred students, both male and female, got to watch as they walked back to class. I was locked out of the building and had to climb a fire escape to get back in. George, on *Seinfeld*, never knew what shrinkage was really about.

I could rattle on about rough things in the house but there also was a closeness to it. Hell Week had the pledges doing disgusting things but surviving it and becoming members was actually an accomplishment.

My first semester in the frat I got the worst grades of my four years at WSU but it wasn't the fault of the fraternity. I will get into the rest of the semester next, but I thought I would finish frat stories now.

I did stay through the next semester. Towards the end of that next semester several alumni who had positions with the national branch of the Sig EP house came in to clean up the joint. Three of our members were kicked out so 23 of us moved out at the end of the semester to show support. I then moved into an apartment with Dick Sparks and two others. I will pick up about that later but now I will swing back to that second semester of my sophomore year.

CHAPTER 18

Major Change

Among the 14½ hours of classes I had a 2-hour computer class. Computers then were the size of refrigerators now. We punched out cards and fed them into the computer. I just couldn't get the whole thing. I had never had a class before that I flat couldn't understand, although high school calculus came close. Regardless I knew that there was no way I could pass it. If you dropped a class within the first two weeks, it was like you never signed up for it. The last day of the two-week period, I went to my advisor and asked to drop it. He said fine but told me I would have to change majors if I did. Passing the computer class was required to graduate in business administration. I said fine and asked for a course catalog so I could go back to the frat and pick out my next major.

I leafed through the whole thing looking for what would be the easiest thing in which to graduate. When I read about a speech major I thought, "I could do that!" I went back to the counselor. He informed me that with the speech major I should get an English minor. I would also take education classes and become a teacher. He was right about the English minor since most schools offered very few Speech classes.

I'd still have to finish that semester with my remaining classes. Two of those, Botany and Advanced Accounting, had me needing a B or better on their final in order to get even a D in the class.

Botany I just plain didn't like. I just couldn't get into it and my attitude towards it didn't help. One day in the lab the teacher passed around an apple and a banana as examples of something. All I could think of was how stupid it was to pass these around, like none of us knew what an apple or a banana looked like. So being an act-be-fore-thinking fool, I ate about half of each of them. While the professor didn't really see the humor in it, at least he didn't kick me out of the class. Fortunately, the last several weeks of the class were all about heredity. I enjoyed that and found it interesting. The best part is most of the final was about heredity. That is how I got a B on the final.

Upon returning from our PAC 8 conference championship in Palm Desert I came down with a sinus infection. Landing in Spokane I thought my head was going to blow up. It was a Sunday when we returned to campus, and I got one of my frat brothers to take me to the hospital. There were no doctors on duty, so they gave me two aspirin and sent me back to the frat house. There happened to be a party going on at the Snake River. Another frat mate took me there since the two aspirin did little and they had a keg full of pain killer there.

Monday morning, I was in agony and could hardly see out of my right eye. I walked into my Accounting class, and he was giving a big test. I could hardly read, let alone think. I told the professor this and he said, "Tough, just take it."

He didn't care for student athletes, especially one that missed a week of classes to play golf in Palm Desert. I failed the test miserably. That is why I needed a B on the final to get a D in the class. During final week I studied Accounting more than anything else and came through. The other two classes I might have been able to get an A in if I could have studied for them, but I was busy trying to pass Botany and Accounting. I ended up with two B's and two D's plus an A in my half-hour PE class for 2.08. That was OK, next year I would be taking classes that I liked and learning things that I would actually use.

CHAPTER 19

My First Varsity Golf Season

Now to the golf part of my sophomore year at WSU. Basically, there is no golf at WSU until March. Most college teams have some form of golf, be it playing or practicing, year-round. We had no indoor facility and winter in Pullman is winter.

When tryouts started, I qualified as the #1 player on the varsity. There were a couple other sophomores and several upperclassmen. Our schedule involved mainly playing smaller schools in Eastern Washington. These included Whitworth, Whitman, Eastern Washington and Gonzaga.

The first event was the Banana Belt Invitational played at our home course, Clarkston Country Club. The teams involved included those I just mentioned plus ourselves and Seattle University. I placed second in the field, and I beat every Seattle University player. You might remember, I wasn't good enough to get any sort of scholarship from them.

Most of the matches with the smaller schools were played at Clarkson or in Spokane. I had little trouble winning most of them.

The University of Oregon came to play us in Clarkston once. I played against their #1 player. His name was John Hedland. We had a good match which I think we split. One of us each won a side, and we tied the 18. I'm fairly sure our other players lost all of their matches.

Our other big match was against the University of Washington at their home course, Rainier Country Club in Seattle. Their team included seniors Bill Tindall and Bruce Richards. Tindall went on to become a PGA member and one of the best players among club pros in the northwest. Richards later qualified for the British Open, otherwise known as "The Open Championship."

As a team we didn't want to get shut out *aka* skunked. Our players tried to get our coach, Roger Seoul, to play me at #6 so we would have a better chance at winning a point. He refused and had me play #1 against Bill Tindall.

There were three points for each of the six matches: front nine, back nine and total 18. That was the usual for dual matches. On this day a best-ball was added for players one and two—three and four—and five and six. This would add nine more points to the overall score.

So, I played Bill and we were paired with the number two players, Bruce Richards for them and Greg Mulvihill for us. I beat Bill on the back nine and we lost 26-1. We weren't skunked!!

The big event of the year was the Pac 8 championship. This was held at Indian Wells Country Club in Palm Desert, California.

There were highlights and lowlights of this event and it started with the night before we were to travel to Palm Springs. I was to report to Bohler gym by 7:00 in the morning. We were to drive to Spokane to catch a plane to Palm Springs. I was living in the salt mines located in the basement of the Sig EP fraternity. My roommates down there knew I had to get up by 6:00 AM. I went to bed earlier than usual and as difficult as it was, I finally fell asleep. Being in the basement it was dark all the time. All of a sudden, they were shaking me and telling me to hurry because it was after 7:00 AM. In a panic I was throwing on clothes and grabbing my suitcase, my clubs were already in my car. As I came out of the bunk room, I saw a clock on the wall and it was only 1:00 AM. Needless to say, I hardly slept a minute the rest of the night.

The flight to DC to be a page was my first, this was my second. I don't remember what airport we flew to, but we went by car to Indian Wells after landing. We even stayed in the apartments right at the golf course. I had never seen any golf course as beautiful. I was awestruck with the palm trees and lakes. The fairways were mowed as short as the greens I played in the northwest. The tees were all grass, at Mount Si they were rubber mats. So, this kid who had played one junior tournament and in matches against mainly small schools was going to tee it up against the best college players on the coast on the nicest course he had ever seen.

End of May there it was hot. The Pac 8 finals involved playing 36 holes a day two days in a row. Even then I didn't like heat. Using my usual poor judgment, practice round day I played 27 holes and walked it. During the tournament we used power carts. During the last couple of holes during the practice round a windstorm came up. Sand was flying everywhere. When we got back to our room, we found that one of us had left the sliding patio door barely open. The room had about ¼ inch of sand throughout. We had to switch rooms.

The first day I was paired with three other number #1 players. One of them was named Sherman Fingers. He was the number one for USC and had won the PAC 8 title the year before. Thankfully he was a nice guy, not intimidating in any way. The stage was set for the biggest round of my life.

After 16 holes I was even par. It was like an impossible dream. I was playing the best and most beautiful course of my life, in the biggest tournament in my life with the best player I'd ever played with.

My drive on the par-5 17th hole went into a fairway bunker on the right side. For my next shot I could have easily hit a 5 iron up the fairway into position to get on with a wedge for possible birdie or routine par. But I was flying high thinking I could do anything. I decided to hit my 3 wood to get on in 2 or just off the green to make a birdie almost certain. There was a palm tree about 30 feet from me and in my path, but I intended to go left of it and fade the ball back to the target. I hit the ball cleanly, but I also hit the palm tree cleanly. The ball came back towards me as I flopped back so it would miss me. I flopped too slowly, and it hit me in the chest. So now I'm laying in the sand with my ball beside me. Physically I'm fine but I am now laying 4 and hitting #5 thanks to the two-stroke penalty because my own ball hit me. I ended up with an 8 on the hole, a triple bogey. I parred the 18th for a 75 but my bubble had burst. In the afternoon round I shot 80 something. The next day I had two more rounds in the 80s. I couldn't hold it together.

Landing in Spokane my head felt like it was going to explode— here was the sinus infection leading to the failed Accounting test that I wrote about earlier.

CHAPTER 20

My Big Mouth

Several weeks before the end of my sophomore year I called Harry to make sure I had a job that summer at Mount Si. He said that I didn't. They had hired another person to work maintenance year-round, so I wasn't needed. I was still going to be allowed to play golf there for nothing.

Dad at this point was working for King County in the flood control division. He lined up a job for me with Segale Construction. Most days I would report to the maintenance shop and help the head mechanic. I had a pickup with Segale Construction on the side and a walkie talkie radio. I ran for parts, flagged for trucks, signaled cats to dump into a belt loader, dumped trucks and even weeded Mario's garden. A few days I even babysat his kids.

I spent the summer getting up early, going to work, going to see Liz in Kirkland, getting three to five hours of sleep at Spark's house and then going back to work. My only golf was on weekends occasionally.

Towards the end of the summer, I found out from Hughie why I was laid off at Mount Si Golf. One day the previous summer I was working in the pro shop on a Saturday when a small tournament of 20 players had not shown up. We had filled in almost all the spots with walk-ons but he just kept on crying about the no-shows.

Finally, I said, "You can afford it."

That earned me a one-year layoff.

Looking back on things, there may have been a second motivation for my sabbatical leave. One day that summer I had come across an old manual-powered push mower that probably came from Sears in 1940. It cut a swath about 20 inches wide and had probably not been used or sharpened for at least ten years. We pulled a seven-gang set of mowers with a tractor that mowed about an 18-foot wide swath. After all there were about 100 acres to mow.

I may have been the first to worry about emissions and global warming and this push mower was powered by muscle not a gas engine.

So one day after I had finished my regular 8-hour shift working on the course I set out to mow the first fairway with the 'little hand mower'. The first fairway was about 350 yards long and 60 yards wide. I figured that cutting a 20-inch swath each pass would only take me about 16 hours.

The first hole was also right in front of both the pro shop and clubhouse so everyone could watch me work.

I made the first run of 350 yards and the return to in front of the pro shop. I then started my second pass, completed it and started back again. As I was approaching the pro shop there were about a dozen people watching me from the first tee. My buddy Hughie, the assistant pro, came out about 50 feet to meet me.

He said, "What the f—k are you doing?"

I replied with a totally blank, no expression face and in a monotone, "Mowing."

Then he asked, "No really—have you lost your f—king mind?"

I said, "I got to hurry up, I have a lot more to mow!"

He finished with, "Knock it off! Harry [the boss] thinks you've lost it and told me to make you quit—so STOP, you dumb ass!!"

I did stop—but those four swaths I cut of about 72 inches total looked really good.

CHAPTER 21

Liz and Drama Too

A long came September and back to school I was going. Harry and his wife Betty told me that they would like to have me back the next summer. They decided to have a closer in the pro shop to cut back Hughie's long hours and they wanted me to fill that position.

Going back, I had two things going for me. Liz was enrolled to attend WSU and I was going to be taking classes in my new major. I was still going to be living in the fraternity but that was fine with me.

Over my junior and senior years most of my classes were in the Speech and Communication School. I had finished virtually all of my college required classes. Besides the public speaking classes there were classes in discussion and debate. There were Drama classes along with everything involved in putting on a play. I had classes on stage lighting, set building, makeup, and directing. I found most of my English classes to be boring with only English Literature being awful. The English class I enjoyed the most was English Grammar. We had a workbook that made sense. No memorizing terms or diagramming sentences. As far as my teaching English, this course proved to be the most valuable. Education classes were easy. Most of the stuff was just common sense.

Due to changing majors I did have to take many hours of classes in order to graduate in four years. I ended up taking 15 hours of summer school at the University of Washington the summer after my junior year. That fit in fine with my closing job at Mount Si Golf. I also got to live in the back room in the pro shop free. It had a shower, bathroom, and Betty did my laundry.

Enough on classes and education, these last two years I averaged over 3.5 while learning things I liked and that I would actually use. The School of Communication was fairly small and close knit. Being involved in play production was a blast.

I set up and operated the lighting for a play done in the round. That is where the stage is in the middle with seating all around. There were about six performances and Dick Sparks sat up in the rafters with me while I operated the switches. He did this for two of the performances.

My two biggest accomplishments were acting in a production and being the stage manager for *Guys and Dolls*. As an actor I was the British butler, bartender, do everything guy in *Outward Bound*. I was on stage for virtually the entire performance. For the part I had to do extensive makeup as I was supposed to be an older butler. I enjoyed it tremendously and made it through without ever forgetting a line.

Dad and Hiram were going to drive the six hours from Seattle to see it, but Hiram failed to show up for the trip. Dad, who at that point didn't like to drive, drove all the way over and back to watch me.

Being the stage director for *Guys and Doll*s would be right up there with climbing Mount St. Helens for being the toughest thing I've ever done. I actually had control of everything to do with set and scene changes. I used actors to move things around when stagehands couldn't handle it. The faculty director/producer was the only one with more power than I.

CHAPTER 22

The Rat House

As I mentioned, during the first semester of my junior year, I lived in the frat. I made grades and became a member. Those in power of the frat decided to clean it up and remove three members. There were 23 of us that moved out because of that. I moved into an apartment with Dick Sparks and two other guys. One of those, Leo Bustad, had been in the fraternity with me. He went on to become a brain surgeon. We lived in that apartment for the second semester of my junior year.

Finishing off my living situation at WSU, Dick and I lived in a converted garage for my senior year. The rent was $40 a month, kind of like $20 each. It had a dirt floor in the bedroom with two cots to sleep on. Between the bedroom and the bathroom was a door opening but no door. The bathroom had a crapper and a small shower stall. The sink was in the shower stall. Then there was another no-door opening into the kitchen. The kitchen had a sink, a small stove and a small refrigerator. Then came a room that was the end of the building where we had one chair, a small sofa and the heat source for the entire apartment. That was a 55-gallon oil drum that oil dripped into. The first time we dropped a match we discovered that it must have been dripping oil for a while. It groaned, moaned, and turned orange. We were hauling out our belongings as fast as we could, but it settled down. Joined to that room but running down the other side of the building was our study room/closet. The first time Liz saw our beloved apartment, which we called "the rat house", she was irate that I made Dick live in a dump like that.

It had its advantages, mainly low maintenance. During the first month there someone accidentally broke a bottle of wine in the front room. As the floor was far from level it all ran to the wall behind the small sofa. We threw an old towel over that and just left it until the end of the year when we moved out. We did clean up the broken glass.

Liz was also pleased when we found a door to fill the opening between the kitchen and the bathroom. My rent of $20 a month was also nice when I had to go to Moses Lake for 10 weeks to do my student teaching.

CHAPTER 23

Pac 8 All Conference –
Horse Handicapper Too

Now that I've polished off the living facilities and education of my junior and senior years, I will turn to my golf life over that period.

During my sophomore golf season, the coach, Roger Seoul, realized I was better than all the varsity players. He also realized I was better than all of the players on the freshman team even though five of them had been given scholarships. When I started at WSU as a freshman there were no scholarships for golf. Coach Roger lobbied the Athletic Department to give me a scholarship based on how I had performed and based on my beating scholarship players. They must have figured that I wouldn't quit school or the golf team if they gave me nothing. They were right. Over the years I have insinuated that I was WSU's first scholarship winner in golf. I was only the first one who should have been given a scholarship in golf.

After the usual no golf from September to March we started up in the spring. We had a new coach, who was also the alumni director. His name was Pat Patterson. He wasn't a good player nor was he able to coach golf, he just kept track of things and arranged our trips. Roger Seoul also wasn't truly a coach, but I soon wished that he had continued to be our coach.

I qualified as the #1 player. I also was given the name "Jumbo" by my teammates and that stuck through my senior year as well. Our scholarship guys did strengthen the team. The guy who had played #2 in most matches my sophomore year didn't crack the top eight players in my junior year. Our first competition for the year was the Banana Belt Invitational. Once again, I placed 2nd individually in it and finished ahead of all Seattle University players.

This year the Pac 8 added a new 72-hole tournament. I guess it

Groshell swings hot club on Oregon trip

Competition was tough, as expected, last weekend when the WSU Varsity golf team opened Northern Division play against Oregon, Oregon State and Washington in Corvallis.

JOHN GROSHELL

All six Cougars shot in the seventies Friday at the Corvallis Country Club. John Groshell fired a one over par 72 to cop medalist honors for Washington

State in the first round. Earl Jones earned the runner-up position for the Cougars with a 75. Bill Bleakney (76), Ron Pence (77), Craig Lee (78) and John Perkins (79) completed the Cougar scoring.

Oregon State, playing on its home course, led the four team point totals after the first day with a six-man aggregate of 437. Oregon was second with a combined total of 450. Washington edged the Cougars for third place by a stroke, 456 to 457.

Saturday, the same four teams moved over to the tough Eugene Country Club where the Cougars were hindered by the unfamiliar course. Despite the handicap, Groshell again had a fine round with a one over par 73 to win medalist honors for WSU.

Perkins dropped to 79 strokes, while Bleakney and Jones found the going tough on one hole which boosted their totals to 82. Pence and Lee rounded out the Cougar scoring with 83 and 84 strokes.

At the end of 36 holes Oregon State leads with a team total of 895 strokes. Washington is second with 907. The University of Oregon occupies third place with 911 and Washington State follows with 940 strokes.

These were the two rounds after our trip to Portland Meadows. They helped get the coach to forgive my taking the car to the track.

actually added two since there was a Northern Division championship in which the Oregon schools and Washington schools competed. The Southern Division championship was for the California schools.

My sophomore year when traveling to matches, the coach drove one car and another faculty member drove another. My junior and senior years I guess they knew I would make the team, so I was named Captain and given a special license to drive the second state vehicle needed. I guess they thought that made up for not giving me scholarship money. Before we left campus, the coach gave each of us $40 for

Bleakney, Groshell pace WSU golfers

Oregon State captured the 72 hole AAWU Northern Division golf title with a team total of 1,770 strokes. Oregon took runner-up with 1,778 strokes. The Ducks were followed by Washington State with scores of 1,302 and 1,838.

Despite the fourth place finish, two WSU golfers, Bill Bleakney and John Groshell, played well throughout the tournament and brought distinction to the Cougar linksmen.

Bleakney fired a four under par 67 at the Clarkston Country Club to take medalist honors for the Cougars. His 67 score was one off the 66 shot by Oregon State's Lloyd West who won medalist honors for the tourney.

Groshell recorded the second low score of 288 for the 72 holes to take claim the runner-up spot

BILL BLEAKNEY

behind West's 281 strokes. The consistent little golfer, a junior from North Bend, was named to the All-Northern Division link team for finishing in the top five. Other All-Stars included Jim Gannon of Washington (294), Mike Davis, Oregon (290) and R' Niles, OSU (294).

I finished second individually in the conference and was named to the all-conference team.

food on the trip. This amounted to 8 dollars a day and it was a five-day trip. We drove to Portland the first day and I had my two buddies, Earl Jones and Ron Pence, ride with me. The other three drove with Coach Patterson. Once checked into the hotel we were allowed to do whatever we wanted, within reason, for dinner and entertainment. We were to be ready to leave the next morning to go to Corvalis for a practice round at Corvalis CC.

Portland Meadows is the horse racetrack in Portland and at that time they raced at night. The three renegades decided that a trip to the track was in order, and I had the keys to one of the cars. No, we didn't ask permission or say where we were going. So, Earl, who is from Calgary, Ron, who we called Sus (short for Sus-pence) and I went to win a fortune.

The track had what they called a big Q. It was like a daily double where you try to pick the winner in two consecutive races, but the big Q was on the last two races instead of first two. They had a nine race per day format. After 7 races and going into number 8, I had $7 left out of my $40 meal money. Earl had $10 left and Sus still had most of his, since he had only placed a couple of bets.

Looking in the race program at the eighth race I spotted a horse named Johnny G. That was me, Johnny Groshell. It was projected to be a 20 to 1 odds. I immediately placed a $2 bet on Johnny G to win before I could smarten up and save the $2. I now had $5 left to feed myself for the next four days. I figured I could survive with one milkshake a day and they were about $1 then.

Earl looked ahead to the ninth race in his program. Amongst the horses was one named Dunbrokus. He was projected to be a 35 to 1 shot. Taking him could certainly done broke us. So Earl decided he would get a win ticket on him in the 9th which would leave him with $8. We put our great minds together and decided to each put in a dollar and get a $2 big Q ticket pairing Johnny G in the 8th with Dunbrokus in the ninth. That would leave me with $4 and Earl with $7. We were in line to place the bet and the guy in front of us was placing all kinds of combination bets. He gave us time to think about whether we should really place this stupid bet. If he had placed his bet more quickly, we would have made our bet but too much thought made us step aside and not place it.

Of course Johnny G did win, and I collected $45. Earl did place a bet on Dunbrokus but I didn't. I don't know why I didn't, but sure as hell Dunbrokus won and paid $84 on Earl's $2 bet. The big Q on Johnny G *and* Dunbrokus paid *$1,600!*

We were pissed off!! I don't think the coach ever knew that we went to the track. I didn't get into trouble over it anyway.

The next day we played a practice round at Corvalis Country Club. Earl, Sus and I played together, and we had a small bet with the foursome made up of the coach and the other three team members. I shot a 72 and the rest were in the high 70s or low 80s. The coach insinuated that we must have cheated to win.

The next day was round one of the tournament. I shot another 72. As I walked off #18 green, Coach came up to me to see how I did. I handed him my card which had been kept by another player in the group. I then said, "Are you going to accuse me of cheating today too?"

The rest of the team all broke 80 with the scores of 75 – 76 – 77 – 78 and 79. I'm fairly sure that was the only round all season that the scholarship players all broke 80.

Next day we played at Eugene Country Club. It was a much tougher golf course. If our coach had used his brain, or better yet someone else's, we would have used our practice round day to play there. In spite of never playing there before, I shot a 73. The rest of the team came in with a 79, two 82's, an 83 and an 84. The last two rounds were played the next week at our home course, Clarkston Country Club. I shot 72 the first day and 71 the second to finish with a total of 288 for 72 holes. I finished in second place individually. The winner was Lloyd West who played for Oregon State. I was named to the "All Northern Division" team. None of our scholarship players finished within 15 strokes of me.

Our last event was the Pac 8 Finals which were held at the Stanford University Golf Club. No excuses, but the course beat me. I was mediocre at best with all four rounds in the upper 70s or lower 80s.

My senior year of golf was one of mediocrity as well. I just couldn't get over the fact that Coach Patterson screwed me out of my dream to play in the collegiate finals the year before.

I had done my student teaching at Moses Lake High School from January through most of March. WSU had paid Moses Lake CC to allow me to play and practice there during this time. Since I was going to miss qualifying, Coach had assured me that I was still going to be the Captain and #1 player. I was even going to be the guy to drive the second car again. He must not have ever known about our night at Portland Meadows.

Any good feelings towards Coach Patterson went out the window after talking to him upon my return from Moses Lake. He said that the NCAA had contacted him about inviting me to play in the Nationals.

He had told them that based on my performance at Stanford I didn't deserve to go. They felt I should, based on my second-place finish in the northern division. They dropped it after that. There are very few individual invitations to the Nationals. A number of players I had beaten during the year went as players on teams that qualified.

Anyway, I played the first two thirds of my senior year as the #1 player. The last part I was dropped to number #2 by a sophomore named Pat Welch. Pat had grown up playing golf and, at the time, Pat's dad was the PGA head professional at Indian Canyon Golf Course in Spokane. Pat was a fine player and had the #1 position. I was very discouraged when I didn't do well in the Pac 8 Finals which were held at Corvalis Country Club. The finals were 36 holes a day. It didn't help that I got heat prostration the second 18 the second day. I did finish all 36 while being dizzy and weak. I even threw up a couple of times. I had always played well there and had thought that I would again. I wasn't awful, but I didn't excel. Now it was time to graduate, get married, and start teaching school.

CHAPTER 24

By "The Babbling Brook"

I went to my graduation because I thought I had to. We were told that if we skipped it we would not get our diplomas for a year. Mom was living in Alexandria, Virginia, at that point and there was no sense in her traveling that far to see me be handed a piece of paper. Same deal for Dad to drive from Seattle. Liz attended so that I at least had a future relative in attendance—we were to be married in just two weeks on June 30th. About the only thing I remember is that it was too damn hot and took too much time. Around 2,000 graduates were handed a form to mail in to get a diploma. They should have put the paper in a crackerjacks box so we would at least have gotten something to eat.

The night before graduation Liz and I had shared a bed in a motel in Lewiston, Idaho. We not only shared it, we used it. This was only the second time that we did more than make out. The first time we closed the deal it was a few miles out of Moscow, Idaho. On a blanket by a stream in the woods. The location was very private and romantic. The surroundings were pleasant and calming with only the sound of water in a brook and two chipmunks laughing.

We rented an apartment in North Bend where we were to live upon returning from our honeymoon. One afternoon we were checking it out, before any furniture had been brought in. A kiss led to another which led to our third moment of bliss on the floor of the unfurnished bedroom.

Before our vows we succumbed to lust on three occasions. Liz gave me permission to write about these since her parents have been gone for a long time.

My father had said that he would not attend the wedding. This was four years since the split with Mom and I think he just didn't want to see her. I was somewhere in the church close to the back door when I heard his voice say, *"John—over here."*

He was peeking in the back door and wanted me to step outside

Liz and Me: "I Do!"

I'm thinking, "We can make it to the motel in 20 minutes."

Liz is thinking, "Did I really say I do?"

Mom and me at my wedding. Mom is thinking, "I never thought anyone would marry my baby boy!"

with him. I did and he pulled a pint of McNaughton's out of a bag. We took a couple pulls out of it apiece. He congratulated me on getting hitched and said he would watch from the back row. He snuck in without being noticed except by me. Immediately after the ceremony he exited before Liz and I walked up the aisle.

The marriage ceremony went just fine with only one flaw. My wedding party included Hiram as best man with Dick Sparks, Gary Barter and Hugh "Hughie" Peterson as ushers. Gary, Hughie and I had worked together at Mount Si Golf for three summers. One of the sick sources of humor was jokes about people with speech impediments. Apparently when I said, "With this ring I shall wed" it came out "With this *wing* I shall wed." Hughie busted out laughing and Bart did as well.

Following the reception Liz and I headed out for a honeymoon in Calgary. We were going to attend the famous Calgary Stampede and I was going to be an usher in Earl Jones's wedding. If you forgot, he was on the golf team with me.

Even though it was an afternoon wedding, we only made it as far as Everett before we pulled into a motel. The drive from the church to the motel was 25 miles at the most. I don't remember if the room had a TV or air conditioning, but it did have a bed. At some point I was trying to explain to Liz that I needed to get some sleep. It wasn't that I was tired or bored with our activities, but I had to do all the driving since she had no driver's license.

The next day we made it to Harrison Hot Springs. From there we drove to Banff where we stayed in the old hotel. I remember the high ceiling in the room that matched the high price to stay there. To soothe the sting of the price I borrowed a silver cream pitcher and small silver casserole dish. They were outside a room down the hall where they had gotten room service. A full 55 years later we still have them. I may have set a *Guinness Book* record for longest borrow ever.

We also played the golf course at Banff. I was surprised that after three nights of the honeymoon I still had the strength to walk that long and hilly course. The course is fabulous with more sand traps than any course I had ever played before it. They actually had guys that walked around the course and raked traps all day as their only duty.

The next day we made it to Calgary. The Calgary Stampede was fun with the chuck wagon races being the highlight. Earl's wedding went off without a hitch. Before we knew it we were back in North Bend in our once used apartment, but now with a bed.

We had to be back because I was to be an usher at Gary Barter's wedding. On July 14th the day before the wedding, Hughie had taken Gary to Bellevue to pick up the tuxedos for the wedding party. I was working the closing shift at Mount Si Golf, so I missed this outing and the wedding rehearsal as well. On their way back from Bellevue he pulled into the El Nido to introduce Bart to happy hour martinis. On their way back to North Bend, he pulled up beside the pro shop. I looked out and saw Hughie in the driver seat but no Bart. After maybe 30 seconds one hand appeared on the dashboard, then one more. Bart was bombed. While he had made it to the rehearsal and the dinner, he didn't remember either one the next day.

July 15th for the afternoon wedding it was somewhere around 130-degrees in the shade. After pictures with an hour before the actual ceremony, Hughie got the ushers to go uptown for a drink. We only had one but when we got back there were over 100 people waiting outside in the sun waiting to be seated. Bart's mother, Mildred, was furious. Rightfully she blamed Hughie. A SWAT team would run from Mildred, but she decided to spare Hughie for the time being. Once all were seated the wedding went fine. Gary had gotten a refresher course on what he was expected to do, and I received a crash course on my duties as well.

That summer Gary and I worked full time in maintenance at Mount Si Golf. In addition, we each worked one weekend day in the pro shop with Huey. Gary and I played a couple days a week after work, but we didn't play in any big tournaments. I was soon to become a full-time teacher.

CHAPTER 25

Cupcake Teaches School

Every year there was an event where school districts from Washington and Oregon sent school administrators to Spokane to meet with prospective teachers. It was called Inland Empire Days. I think a few school districts from Idaho and Montana went there too.

I went to it with a friend who was also looking for a teaching job. I had already been offered a job by the Snoqualmie school district and one from Moses Lake where I had done my student teaching. Apparently, they had forgotten about the fist fight two of my students had had in my classroom.

After interviewing with five or six schools I was offered two jobs. One was to teach at an Oak Harbor junior high and the other at Burlington High School. Both districts were about an hour north of Seattle. Ultimately, after visiting both of the schools, I decided to take the job at the Snoqualmie middle school. The deciding factor being that I could also work at Mount Si Golf weekends, evenings and summers. Having a second job was necessary in that my starting salary for the entire year was $6,000 gross. My monthly take home was around $375.

This was in 1967 and it was to be the first year ever for Snoqualmie Middle School. Up until then students went K-8 in North Bend, Snoqualmie, and Fall City before coming together to attend Mount Si High School.

There was pride in each town and being thrown together for the first time, 7th and 8th graders added on to other hormones called frustrations. On top of that the school itself was due for demolition. The gym was old with dead spots in the floor causing irregular bounces from basketballs. There were old style radiators for heat that either cooked you or left you cold. There was a lunchroom for students to eat lunch in but no kitchen in which to prepare it. The school was staffed with the principal, 12 teachers and one secretary. Of the 12 teachers, nine of us had never taught school before.

Jim Satterlee was the man chosen to lead this bunch of rookies into the lion's den. Jim had never been a principal before but had taught there in the Valley for over 20 years. Apparently, the district was looking for someone with experience but had been unable to locate one willing to take on this mess.

Without a doubt Jim Satterlee was the best principal I worked under. I also think he was the best principal that my kids would have had when they attended school. He was a disciplinarian over the students, and as a teacher you damn well had to do a good job under him. He was tough but fair. As a teacher I always knew he would back me up. Jim referred to his staff as "the dirty dozen."

The 7th grade and 8th grade were each divided into 6 classes. The classes ranged from 30 to 35 students apiece. Teachers now complain about class sizes between 20 to 25. Each class stayed together all day. Half the day they would go to different teachers each period for Math, Science and PE. The other half day they would be stuck in what was called "block" with one teacher and no breaks. I taught block where I was to teach English, Spelling, Reading, and History. The classes were arranged in ability levels from highest #1 to lowest #6. These ratings were from a combination of Stanford achievement tests and past performance in school. The #6 group was mainly boys who could hardly read and would do anything to not be in school.

The block half of the day was torture for most. Being stuck in one room half of the day taking everything they disliked was so much worse than changing rooms every hour to take classes they could tolerate.

There were three block teachers for each grade each with a morning group and an afternoon group. One teacher got Group 1 in the morning and Group 6 in the afternoon. Another got Group 2 in the morning and Group 5 in the afternoon. The third got Group 3 in the morning and Group 4 in the afternoon, that was me. I lucked out.

The teacher for groups 1 and 6 was Gayle, a nice gal who was a first-year teacher. Group 1 is tough because you have to keep them interested and not bored. When bored they're capable of coming up with creative ways to express their displeasure. Group 6 is difficult because they don't want to be there. Having them spend their dreaded "block" in the afternoon instead of morning didn't show much forethought. In the afternoon they really wanted to escape. Jim Satterlee didn't organize the schedule, he just got thrown in to run it.

Within a month of the start of the year I had to go next door and settle down the mayhem that Group 6 was raising, at least a couple times a week. About a month before the end of the semester I went to Jim and requested that I switch afternoon classes with Gayle. I had asked her if she would like to switch. We finished out the year, she with #4, me with #6.

So going back to the beginning of the year. Swats were allowed as one form of discipline. There were several male teachers who gave a few. The one regulation was that you had to get another teacher to witness it.

After a couple of weeks of school, I came up with my formula for punishment. I made an official game ball out of crumpled up paper with a tape cover. It was about the size of a tennis ball but lighter and it didn't bounce. Then with tape I established the official foul shot line, about 15 feet from the wastebasket in the corner. If anyone did anything that I deemed worthy of punishment, they took a shot. If they made the shot that was it, go back and sit down. However, if missed they had a choice of punishment. One—take a swat. Two—write sentences: "I won't do...." Three—make up time.

Of course, the girls never got in trouble. The boys always opted for the swat, the only manly thing to do. One of the students had even made a paddle for me. On the blackboard I started a list of "makers not takers." The first semester with Groups 3 and 4, I don't think I had more than four take shots. I had taken more swats as an eighth grader than I gave out as a teacher. For example, I got three swats for getting a special education student to give the principal the finger. I was the one who needed help for not thinking it through. The principal simply asked David, "Who told you to do that?" and David said, "Johnny." The main thing I learned was that the third swat hurt more than the second and the second hurt more than the first.

One day one of my students asked if he could shoot without having done anything wrong. I said I guess so, but if you miss you will get a real swat. He missed and took the swat. The next day he wanted to shoot again. I reluctantly let him, and he missed again. The next day he wanted to and I said *no!!* I thought he just wanted to make it into the short list of makers not takers.

A few days later Jim Satterlee came to me because the student's parents had come to him. It turned out the other kids were paying him to shoot, and he wanted the money to buy a new fishing pole. Jim backed me up and got them to back off—I felt awful and that was the end of any shots for fun.

Last quarter of the year my students and I didn't really need more discipline. There were only three times that a student did something I deemed necessary to take a shot. One of them made the shot and two missed. Both times the student and I went out in the hall to carry out the task.

There were stacks of books in the hall that were supposed to be hauled away but hadn't been. So, on both of these occasions I said to my victim, "I am going to hit a pile of books then go back into the room. I am going to look pissed off and throw the paddle in the corner. You wait about five minutes and come in with a sad, hurt look on your face and sit at your desk quietly."

On each occasion the student asked me, "You aren't going to swat me?" and I replied, "No, it's no fun hitting any of you, but if you tell anyone that I didn't, I will later kick the crap out of you!"

These kids kept others in line the rest of the year.

There were to be more swats that year. Starting the last quarter, I told my Group 6 class that whoever got the best grade in each of the four subjects would get to give *me* a swat. These four swats were to be given on the front lawn of the school on the last day of the school year. That quarter students who got D's and F's were mostly getting C's with an occasional B. There were two girls and two boys who had won the right to swat me. The class wanted the girls to be able to relinquish their rights to the two biggest boys in the class. I vetoed that and took the four swats in front of over 100 cheering kids.

As you can see, I may not have been the most orthodox teacher. I tried to treat the kids with respect. I tried not to embarrass them in front of other students. If I needed a kid to run an errand, like taking a note to the office, I would ask the so called "worst student" to do it. This would be the one that had never been given a privilege from any teacher before. Sometimes they would say, "You want *me* to do that?"

I would say, "Why not, you're not capable?"

They would reply, "Yes, I am."

I'd say, "So do it and thank you."

I also believed that learning subject matter was important but gaining confidence and a desire to become successful were equally important. I would start most morning and afternoon groups with discussions about virtually anything they wanted. It could be about school or local activities, or individual problems, or anything of interest to them.

It was amazing how much I could learn from them about what was going on in the school and in the Snoqualmie Valley.

Also, to get their attention I would memorize their names the first day of school. I would make out a seating chart and study it while I had them working on something. Then after about a month I would memorize them backwards. For instance, the first year one boy's name was Jeff Stevens, so he became Ffej Snevets. Another name Vernon Berg became Nonrev Greb. The first class that I started referring to them that way they loved it. We had to go over what all of their names became. Of course, I became Nhoj Llehsorg.

Fairly soon after that I managed to get myself another name by accident. I became my own victim by talking before thinking. On Halloween night I was playing in a men's league basketball game. Liz and I were living in that apartment in North Bend. It never occurred to me that my students knew where I lived. About a dozen of them came to trick or treat and got Liz to allow them to enter the apartment. Being just 20 years old and not used to dealing with kids, she wasn't able to control them. Other than a couple of eggs under our pillows, they didn't do any real damage, but Liz was fairly shook up.

So, the next day I started our BS session talking about their Halloween activity. I was actually getting them to feel a little bit sorry for upsetting my wife. I said, "Do whatever you want to me, but it's not cool to upset her."

Then one of them asked, "What name does she call you?"

It is hard to explain why I say many things I say, but out came "Cupcake." We have never used honey, sweetie, dumpling, or even lamb chop. As Cupcake came flying out, I tried to stop it but couldn't.

While at that time teachers went by Mr., Mrs. or Miss, I would on occasion hear *Cupcake* from a distance. I had to act like I didn't like it but I actually did. Back then we male teachers had to wear ties and sport coats too.

My fun wasn't always confined to my classroom. My planning period was 1st period that year. Teachers, at least then, got one period to plan, correct papers, or whatever. About once a week I would spend my time in the office helping Jan, our secretary. One of her daily jobs was to call the high school kitchen to order the number of lunches to be sent over to the middle school. This one particular day the lunch was Navy beans, hold the meat and flavor. Basically, the meal was beans and day-old bread.

Being the big helper that I was I volunteered to call this in for Jan. Once I got the kitchen on the line I said, "I'm calling to report the number of lunches we need."

She said, "Fine, how many?"

I replied, "We need 147 of your finest navy bean lunches."

At this point Jan was climbing over the desk to get the phone away from me as she knew it was only going to get worse.

I continued, "And please throw in 145 barf bags. I figure two kids will drop their trays before they get a chance to eat."

Jan then wrenched the phone out of my hands and apologized profusely for my transgressions. Believe it or not, that was the last time I ever got to call in a lunch order.

The year finished with a sore butt for me, and with the principal, Jim Satterlee, being let go. The district had taken him out of the classroom and thrown him into a difficult spot as principal in the first ever middle school. He had done a masterful job. The district managed to bring in an experienced principal to take over the next year.

Earlier I mentioned that Jim hadn't organized the class schedules, he was only saddled with it. However, he did reorganize it a bit. Recognizing that I was a Speech major with no History background, he changed classes to where I had all six Speech classes on a rotating schedule and Mr. Moeller took my two classes for History.

Jim was able to land a new job as principal at Tolt High School in Carnation the next year. Bob Drake became our principal the next year. Out went my teaching Speech and in came my teaching U.S. History. I did include Speech into my English, Spelling and Reading classes here and there. I was also given the number #1 and #6 ability groups to teach. I enjoyed the challenges that came with both of them. With Mr. Drake as the principal my teaching Speech went out the window and I had History as one of my block classes. The first day of school I explained to my group #1 that History wasn't my mainstay. I pointed out that instead of searching for what I didn't know about History, why couldn't we all learn it together? They bought it and I learned more about U.S. History than I thought I could. I did have an advantage though—I made up the tests.

Bob Drake gets my credit for virtually ending swats. There were a few but he discouraged it. My last ones were on the front lawn the year before, and I received them.

Both years I was referee for flag football and basketball games. There was a team from Duvall and one from Carnation. We had teams from North Bend, Snoqualmie and Fall City. Even though they were students at the same school, they were opponents in sports. That also made for friction at times, but Satterlee had settled that down in year one.

A student named John Krona played basketball for the Snoqualmie team. He was a 7th grader this second year of middle school. His older brother Rick was in my #1 block class that year as well. Anyways, I knew John fairly well. He was a lot like I had been as a kid. Sometimes he would speak without thinking. Before his first game I warned him that I would give him a technical foul if he mouthed off. He just laughed it off.

His first "T" came in the first quarter. He started to complain, and I just gave him the "you better shut up" look. He did and he got to finish the game. John is now my accountant and has been for over 30 years. He is also a good friend.

During that year my classes wanted to paint "our" room. I don't remember if I got permission from Principal Drake, but my students and I spent two weekends painting. The room went from ugly tan or cream to blue with orange trim. It really became "our" room.

Before the end of the year Jim Satterlee came to me to invite me to teach at Tolt High School. I agreed to do it not knowing that I was going to love it as much as I did.

Speaking of getting invited (how is that for a segway?), a few months ago I received a call from one of my 8th grade students from

my first year teaching. On behalf of their 50th year high school reunion committee she invited me to attend their reunion. Even though
I wasn't their high school teachers for most of them, they wanted me
to be there.

Cupcake replied, "HELL, YES!"

CHAPTER 26

Lucky Me

So, before I go into my two Tolt High School years I need to go over some of the non-teaching stuff from the two middle school years.

When I started teaching school in 1967, teachers were required to take what was called "a fifth year" of classes. They could be summer school classes or evening classes. At that time there weren't internet options.

One summer I took a series of coaching classes at the UW for a total of 12 hours. They included football, basketball, baseball, wrestling, track, and taping ankles, wrists, and medical problems. Each class was two weeks long, five days a week and for two hours.

Tex Winter, the Huskies head coach, taught the basketball class. He was fabulous. He went on to coach in the NBA. I still remember a saying of his about taking criticism:

"They say this and they say that—.
it makes me wonder where they're at.
You identify who are they
and I will have more respect for what they say."

The head football coach, Jim Owens, didn't teach the football class. I felt like that was a disservice to himself. He chose to pass on an opportunity to impress over 50 football coaches. I felt that he passed up on a great recruiting opportunity.

Baseball, track and wrestling were all taught by the respective head coaches.

For the taping and conditioning class, I got paired up with a double amputee. He had no ankles to tape. He and I would each do one of the ankles of another classmate.

Hugh Peterson, the assistant pro at Mount Si, had a brother Jack, who taught at Central Washington. I had played a lot of golf with Jack and he and I were usually partners in matches with betting. Usually, Jack and I would win money.

Jack knew that I needed credits for my fifth year. One quarter he was teaching a five-hour extension class and asked me if I would like to take it. When he further explained that beyond paying the modest tuition fee, I wouldn't have to attend class, do assignments, or take any tests. For about $100 I would get five hours of credit and receive an A. Like they say, it's not what you know it's who you know.

The next quarter I signed up for a 3-hour class with him that required the same effort and gave the same grade. I became a 4.0 student at Central Washington university with eight credits.

I actually earned a few more credits taking a class here and there. My final class was a night class at the UW in Communications. It was one night a week on campus for three hours a night. Basically, we had to read the *Seattle Times or Post-Intelligencer* every day and be ready to take a test on their content.

The first several weeks I did little reading, and while I wasn't failing the class, I was not far from it. The last couple of weeks I called in sick and stayed home to read papers all day long the day of the class. Thanks to that I was able to do well enough to at least get a C.

The last night of class when I learned I passed the course I was greatly relieved. I went by my brother's house in Seattle to celebrate. He and I had several beers and then I took a couple "for the ditch" with me. I wasn't wasted but I shouldn't have been driving. Fortunately, I didn't open either of the beers I took with me.

I was rolling along just fine feeling happy and relieved. At this point it was close to midnight so there was no traffic. As I was taking a curve by Preston, WA I heard my tires squeal. I looked at the speedometer and I was doing 90 mph. At this point I was less than 10 miles from North Bend and home. I slowed down and carried on. About another five miles along the tires squealed again as I was making a slight curve by Nelem's hospital. Once again, I was doing close to 90 mph. When I looked back up from the speedometer, I saw a car in front of me. I went on around him and as I was slowing down observed that it was a Washington State Patrolman. His blue lights came on and I pulled over off the road. I thought I did so quickly but realized later it took me two miles to accomplish it.

I decided that with two beers sitting on the passenger seat, it would be good if I got out of the car before he walked up. I opened the door as fast as I could and was surprised when I hit him with it. He was already standing there. I closed it then and rolled down the window.

He asked: "What is the deal here?"

Me: "Just take me away—I screwed up—*just take me to jail!*"

He: "Settle down, relax, what is going on?"

Me: "I just took my last night class to finish my fifth year. I teach here at the Snoqualmie Middle School. I thought I was going to flunk. I celebrated at my brother's in Seattle. I shouldn't have driven—I screwed up—go ahead and arrest me."

He: "Please get out of your car and let me see your license."

I got out of the car and as I took my wallet out of my pocket, I dropped it. I leaned against the car while I picked it up. Being dark out it was hard to read the cards in my wallet. I decided I would hand him the first card I came to with my picture on it.

There were three possibilities. First was my driver's license. Second was my UW Student ID card. Third was my Washington State liquor card. I knew it wouldn't come off as being funny if I handed that one to him. Fortunately, I did hand him my driver's license.

At that point I felt totally sober, maybe adrenaline does that to you. He asked how far I had to go to get home and I replied it was about two miles. He asked if I felt alright, and I said yes. He then told me to drive straight home, and he would follow me to make sure I was safe.

I lucked out again. He never even commented about me passing him at 90 mph. Nowadays the patrolman would have granted my wish to be arrested.

CHAPTER 27

Bud in The Mud

Not long after Halloween with kids upsetting Liz, we moved into a new house about 1/2 mile out of North Bend. We bought it through Jim North, my old PE teacher and freshman basketball coach. He was also one of my best friends and golfing partners. His name will be brought up again as he was quite a character.

Anyways, the three-bedroom house with one-car attached garage cost all of $14,500. It was located one block from my buddy Hugh Peterson's house. Hugh, who I worked with at Mount Si Golf, had married a stewardess named Kaye. Over the next four years we had dinner with them three or four nights a week, sometimes at their house sometimes ours, or more often out.

My best buddies amongst the teaching staff were the two Science teachers. They taught classes together and had a really great program that had students involved with experiments and hands-on activities. Kids enjoyed their classes. One of them was named Dick Kirby but every non-student called him "Kirb." Another was Doug Curry but he went by "Bud." Doug, oops I meant Bud, called everybody Bud. I don't care whether it was a man, woman, child, or dog—the name was Bud. He was a lot smarter than I, one name fits all. I was learning every individual name forwards and backwards.

Both Kirb and Bud coached a basketball team in the middle school league. I refereed all of the games played there in Snoqualmie. Games were held afternoons after school.

After a couple of Friday afternoons Kirb, Bud and I went bowling. The alley was only three blocks from the school. After bowling we would drop into Smokey Joe's Tavern for a couple of cold ones. It was located between the bowling alley and the school. It was about the third Friday when we decided bowling was not necessary and we went straight to Smokey Joe's. That only made sense because it was closer and since I'd refereed one or two games, I needed to hydrate myself.

Two or three beers later we moved a block to the "two by four" room in the "Timber Café" for hard drinks. A couple drinks later we went to my new house so Liz could join in on the good times. An hour or so later Kirb and Bud were going to head home. As Bud slung his coat around to put it on, he managed to break the light fixture over the dining room table. He must have had two pounds of keys in his coat pocket. That should have brought attention to Bud's condition, but Kirb and I didn't notice. Bud climbed into his VW bug and started it up. Instead of driving down the road he took a hard right into our front mud yard. I had not planted grass yet so some days it was dirt and some days it was mud. It has been known to rain in Western Washington.

So, Bud was stuck. Kirb took over behind the steering wheel while Bud pushed from behind and I pulled from in front. We were all still wearing our sport coats. Fortunately, we got the bug back on the road without having it run over me. We decided to have Kirb drive Bud home in the VW and I would follow in my car.

It was about two miles to Bud's trailer house. Kirb and I had never met Lois, Bud's wife. By the time we got there, we had to help Bud into his house. While their three-year-old son, David, was jumping up and down on the sofa laughing, Bud was trying to get Lois to say "Hi" to us. For some reason she was not going to greet two mud-soaked drunks who obviously got her husband drunk.

After that Lois showed up every Friday to take Bud home after the basketball games. It only took a couple of Fridays before she would talk to us. Within a year he bought a house one block away from ours. Bud and I remained friends even though I moved to Yakima for a year. His son David even took golf lessons from me at Snoqualmie Falls golf course 30 years later.

Christmas vacation my first year of teaching I worked on a railroad line crew. Gary Barter, who was still attending the University of Washington, and I signed up along with about four other students for a two-week gig. We were to reset anchors along the tracks from Carnation to Duvall. Anchors keep the rails from sliding forwards or backward. A sledgehammer is used to wedge them tight to the ties. We had done this for a couple of days then a heavy snowfall came. That ended the anchor setting but Bart and I along with one other guy stayed on. At that point we had four of us counting our foreman. Our job was to chip ice out of switches from Duvall to Snoqualmie Summit. The work itself was easy but riding in that little car all day was awful. It was like the little hand cars you see in movies but was engine driven. It had side curtains, but your lower legs and feet were exposed. Most of the time was spent riding and freezing.

After several days of this I started filling my thermos with hot buttered rum instead of coffee. Bart and I still froze but we did so with better attitudes. While we signed on to make money, we hardly cleared any. We had to pay railroad union dues. Since schools didn't reopen when scheduled due to snow, we stayed on further into January. We ended up having to pay dues for both 1967 and 1968. In addition, what we had leftover was mainly spent at the Riverside Tavern in Fall City on the way home.

When Liz and I got married we decided to wait at least five years before having kids. The thought was that we would travel. The first trip we decided to go to Hawaii for Christmas my second year of teaching. Teachers, at least back then, got a three-month check for the three summer months. With my first such check we bought furniture. My second one went to our Hawaii trip.

We flew to Honolulu where we had a room reserved at the Reef Hotel. We had no idea that Christmas was the busiest time of the year in Hawaii, and Honolulu was the most crowded spot. We had no idea that it was necessary to reserve a car. I was able to get a car two of the days by waiting at the car rental agency to snag one if the party that reserved it didn't show up.

Most of the days we hung out by the pool or on the beach sunbathing. We met a lot of military men who were on R&R from Vietnam spending Christmas with their wives. We spent a lot of time at night in the bar at the Reef where there was a window into the swimming pool below the water level. Most people swimming didn't know it was there which made for some interesting viewing.

One of the car days we drove out to Makaha and played golf. The other car day we drove all around Oahu. We were able to play a round of golf at Waialae Country Club. At that time Mom was on the federal parole board and through that knew someone who was a member there. The course was fabulous, and Liz had the best shot of her life.

Off one of the tees, she hit it way off to the right. There were condos lining the fairway and her shot was heading right for a sliding door in one of them. Fortunately, the door was open about 3 inches. Liz's shot went right through the opening. Who knows what or who it might have hit inside, but we didn't hang around to find out. All in all, the trip was fun, never since have I seen so many Hawaiian Santa Clauses.

Other than that, we only took one more trip before son #1 was born in 1972. We drove to Las Vegas to visit Liz's sister, Eileen.

CHAPTER 28

Bees in The Pants

I worked both summers, after my two middle school years, at Mount Si Golf doing maintenance. I also worked in the pro shop on weekends.

As I recall, Mount Si Golf was the second golf course in Washington to get a triplex riding greens mower. Up until then we mowed greens with walk-behind mowers. I had the distinction of being the first person to catch his hand in one of the reels of a triplex mower. Fortunately, I was wearing leather gloves otherwise I would have lost at least three fingers.

The night before I was working in the pro shop, Hughie had hit range balls from beside the putting green on over to the driving range. In the process he had a few divots that he left on the green. When I came to mow it, I removed the divots and put them back where they came from. While I was doing that Harry came out and accused me of taking the divots the night before when I was working. I told him I didn't, but I didn't tell him who did. I was really ticked off for being blamed. As I mowed all I could think about was what an ass Harry had been to me. Seeing the baskets were overloaded with grass I pulled off the green.

The first thing I did was reach into the basket to push grass back because being over full I couldn't see the reel spinning. My fingers were caught momentarily, and my glove was ripped off. I was afraid to look at my hand as I ran into the pro shop to get help. Harry took one look at me and almost fainted when he saw my bloody hand. All he could say was, "Why did you come in here?"

I then headed for the maintenance shed and, on the way, looked to see how many fingers I had lost. Pete, the superintendent, looked at me and he too almost fainted. Bill Easter, who also worked outside, was calm and got me to relax. He got a bucket full of ice and water and had me hold my hand in it. That really, *really* hurt but I left my hand in it for at least an hour.

Since I not only didn't lose any fingers, and could still bend them all, I didn't want to skip the golf game that afternoon. Three fingers were cut up on the upper side and one fingernail was ripped off but none were broken. I saw no reason to go to a doctor, so Liz cleaned and bandaged it up. I took about half of a fifth of Canadian Club as a painkiller and went off with Bart and Hughie to play Oakbrook Country Club. I shot 39 on the front nine but had 50 on the back nine when the painkiller wore off. One week later I was the low amateur in a pro-am at Overlake Country Club with an even par 72. I could hardly hold on to the club with my right hand so the left dominated. Golf is a game of opposites. If you play right-handed the left has to dominate and control.

As for the mower, now riding mowers have kill switches that turn off blades or reels when the operator climbs out of the seat.

During those two summers I played in the two Lilac Opens in Spokane with my buddy Mike Calabrese. Mike, along with his wife, Helene, would join Liz and I for this four-round event. I was always in the 0-4 handicap group and Mike was in the 13-16 group, so we were always in opposite shifts for starting times. Whoever played in the morning the other would caddy for him. The same applied in the afternoon. I would walk and Mike would ride. Mike had to ride as he was in his upper 50s and Helene was a great cook. We both won some money most years and had fun. I had a tendency to try to hit my sand wedge from farther than I should. Mike would often refuse to let me and would only hand me my pitching wedge. We actually played this tournament four years in a row.

The summer after my first year of teaching, Bart, Jim North and I played in the Washington Amateur. It was held at Oak Brook Country Club in Tacoma. Going into the final round Bart was a couple strokes ahead of me and I was four or five ahead of Jim. We traveled together each day to and from the course. Anyways, Jim's tee time the last day was almost an hour before mine and I was about 15 minutes before Bart.

That last day I shot a 72 which was the low score for the day. When I went into the bar to find Jim, I spotted him at a table in the back. As I approached him, I could tell he was drunk. He went on to tell me what happened to him. He went like this, "Hey, Runt, you'll never guess what happened to me. On the 12th hole I got a bee in my pants, and it stung me about 10 times. Guess what, now I have a stinger on me about this long. Ha ha ha ha!!"

He had already told all the waitresses along with several golfers he knew.

I decided I had to get him out of there as fast as I could. Being the final round of the tourney there were a lot of couples there to watch the awards ceremony. I looked out at the 18th hole and could see Bart headed up to the green. So, I got Jim up and got him started for the door. He spotted another old buddy named George Skarich who was the president of the Pacific Northwest Golf Association. Jim stopped and was telling him his story. When he got to the part about having a stinger on him this long, he dropped his pants. Fortunately, he didn't drop his fruit of the looms too.

So here is a 6-foot 2-inch, 300-pound ex-lineman for the Washington Redskins. He is barely standing up with his pants down to his ankles in the middle of a couple filled bar in a country club. I just kept walking and left him standing there.

I sent Bart in to get him about 10 minutes later.

CHAPTER 29

Fun Teaching at Tolt

My third and fourth years of teaching were at Tolt High School in Carnation. As mentioned before, Jim Satterlee recruited me to teach there after my two years at the Snoqualmie Middle School. Jim had already been the principal there for one year.

The high school opened in 1914. Sadly in 1990 it was replaced by Cedarcrest High School that was built in Duvall, Washington. My two years at Tolt High School were the two most fulfilling and enjoyable of my five years of teaching. When I started there, I thought I had left my nickname at the Snoqualmie Middle School. Tolt was in a different school district. About one month into my first year at Tolt as I was walking down a hallway I could plainly hear, *"Cupcake – Cupcake,"* and I loved it.

Tolt was a small high school with about 70 students in each graduating class; as such, teachers had to wear several hats and run at least two extracurricular activities. The school was actually Tolt Middle and Senior High school. My first year there we split shifted. The high school ran from 7:00 AM to noon, with five minutes between each class. The middle school ran from noon until 5:00 PM.

During this school year a new building was being constructed so that the next year both the middle school and high school would attend during the same hours.

As a high school teacher my classes were in the morning. Once or twice a month I would be asked to sub in the afternoon and for that I would receive $25.

My class schedule for the six periods was two senior Speech classes, two junior English classes, one Journalism class and one study hall. For extracurricular activities I was the public address announcer for varsity football games, the assistant/JV basketball coach, the only baseball coach, the advisor for the school newspaper, and the director/stage manager for all school plays. I almost had enough to do. Many of my students I had for more than one class and for at least two activities.

Principal Satterlee was a believer in public speaking classes. He brought me to Tolt because he liked how I handled students and teaching Speech was my specialty. Consequently, the senior Speech classes were created for the first time at Tolt. In addition, he made them a required subject in order to graduate. Overall, the senior class was irate over this new requirement. While my two Speech classes didn't revolt or even hold marches on the school, they did not like it. I was 23 years old when the year started but looked like I was 19, at the most. The seniors were mainly 17 or 18. I was at the peak of my height at 5 foot 5-1/2 inches. There may have been one boy shorter than me.

By Halloween of that year the classes resigned themselves to the fact that they had to take and pass senior Speech class. I had several instances where male students displayed their displeasure. I would simply take them out in the hall and explain that they needed the class, and the class didn't need them. Quite often I would include the F-word in some form to help them understand.

My classes were never truly difficult as long as students would put forth a little bit of effort. I understood that standing up in front of a crowd or class to speak is terrifying to many. The first round of speeches I would allow them to stay seated at their desks if they preferred. Usually several of the girls would do so. That first assignment required only a minute of talking about anything they wanted.

The next speech assignment was to give a demonstration speech. They had to explain how to do something while demonstrating how at the same time. In doing so their minds were taken off the fear of standing alone to speak as they had to perform the activity at the same time.

I required them to inform me of their topics. I didn't want irate parents over their children seeing something bad. I never did veto any subject matter. Being a farm community, both years someone wanted to demonstrate chopping the head off a chicken and plucking it. In both cases I had all the students get permission slips signed by their parents so they could watch it.

Another assignment I had them do pantomimes and the class would guess what they were doing. A student named Roy got the biggest applause for his rendition of a garbage collector.

Through the year we had various speeches, debates, discussions and drama. Actually, by mid-year I had two classrooms full of hams. I wasn't fighting them, and they weren't fighting me. One of my classes wanted me to do a pantomime after they had done theirs. I did a performance like I was a stripper. Amazing as it may be, these country farm kids knew what I was doing. More amazing, I didn't get in trouble for it.

The junior English classes went fine. The first year one of my classes had 41 in it and the other had 38. For the 79 students I had 25 books. I didn't even bother passing these books out. Instead, I printed material on our antiquated ditto machine. The students knew that I was putting out an effort for them and they responded by putting out an effort for me and themselves as well. Tolt High School was part of the Lower Snoqualmie Valley School District. The district lacked funds to provide the finest educational activities since their special levies usually failed. Students understood this and appreciated anything teachers did to help them.

The journalism class was really quite easy. Most of the students were young ladies and while we did some study of news writing, most of the time was spent putting out the weekly school newspaper. This class was held the last period of the day and was really a great way for me to relax and wind down. Most every student that I had in that class had been in either senior Speech or junior English earlier in the day.

Among this wonderful class I had three girls who hung out together all of the time. Somewhere around mid-year I had named them "the three stooges". By actual names they were Mary, Mariane and Deb. To me, they were the Three Stooges.

Toward the end of the school year, they came to me and asked if I wanted them to buy me a new tie. They were going shopping in Seattle that afternoon. Classes were over by noon so they had lots of time. I gave them $5 which at that time was like about $25 now.

The next morning, they presented me with a purple tie with yellow dots on it. It may not have been the ugliest tie in the world, but it was in the top 5. I put it on and thanked them for getting it for me.

I wore it all day while getting glances and snickering from students both in the hallways and in the classroom. When Journalism class convened sixth period, the Three Stooges came to my desk and presented me with a nice-looking tie. The tie that I had worn all day they had bought at Goodwill for 10 cents. The real tie that had stripes of pink, purple and white had cost about $5. I put on the nice one right away, but the real show was yet to come.

Close to the end of class Jim Satterlee came into the room with the guy who represented the Washington State Department of Education. He was at Tolt to get a firsthand look at how the school was doing in spite of a lack of funding. To be friendly I started telling him the story of the two ties. The Three Stooges were standing close by and trying to get my attention as I was telling it. I ignored their efforts and continued on.

At the point where I held up the ugly tie and said, "I actually wore this ugly thing all day," I noticed that it looked exactly like the tie he was wearing.

He and principal Jim exited quickly. Regardless of my big mouth, Tolt High School was allowed to stay open. I also never heard the end of it from the Stooges.

As a study hall teacher, all you do is take roll and keep it quiet. My study hall was 2nd period. I didn't even allow eating in my classes. While they didn't get a lunch period, their classes ran from 7:00 AM until noon. They could snack between classes. I also didn't like cleaning up the wrappers and packages they left behind. One morning I spotted a student, Mike Sunnich, smuggling in a Hostess cherry pie. After I took the roll, I left the room and went to the office for about five minutes to give Mike a chance to eat it.

When I returned to the room I casually sat at my desk for a while pretending like I was working on something. Acting like I just remembered something I looked up and said, "Hey, Mike, how about you bring me that pie you brought in? I know you wouldn't eat it in my classroom, so I'll just hold it for you, so you won't be tempted."

Mike started to reply, "I don't have—" but I cut him off saying, "Mike, I know you would never lie to me so just bring it up here and I'll give it back at the end of the period."

Mike: "Well, I ate it."

Me: "Are you kidding! You know not to eat in here! I am really surprised that you would actually do such a thing!"

I left it at that and didn't say anything until the class period was almost over.

Then just conversationally I asked, "Hey, Mike, what types of cookies *don't* you like?"

Not realizing what a mean bastard I was he replied, "Fig newtons and ginger snaps."

"Oh," I replied, "just curious."

The next morning the Three Stooges were in my first period class, so I sent them to the closest store to buy fig newtons and ginger snaps. At the end of first period my class helped me arrange the desks into a big circle with one desk remaining in the center. I put the wastebasket by that desk. I ran out to the gym and got the two-handed paddle that was in the coaches' office. It was never used to my knowledge but was a bit intimidating.

As my second period study hall group filed in, I had them take any desk that they wanted except the middle one that was for Mike. Once all were seated, including Mike, I announced that since Mike insisted on eating in my room, he was now going to have the opportunity to eat and eat and eat. Also, when he stopped eating, I was going to start swinging "the paddle." Mike was another one of those kids who was kind of like me. He liked to get a laugh and was quick with making funny remarks. I knew this wasn't going to scare him and, ultimately, he would enjoy the attention.

Anyway, somewhere around 50 cookies—yes, we were counting—in came the nurse for the school district. She was rarely around our school but there she was, and somehow heard what was going on in my room. She was a bit worked up and told me that having him eat all of these cookies could hurt him and mess up his blood sugar.

I explained that the only thing that was going to hurt him was me with the paddle when he quit eating. She ran to Principal Satterlee but the cookie eating continued, and I never got in trouble. I'm sure Jim explained that I probably would do what I said and that was OK with him.

Between 50 and 70 cookies, Mike was going from pale to gray to running to the bathroom to throw up. I let him do that instead of into the garbage can in front of his classmates. After that nobody ate in my classes and Mike gained notoriety as Tolt's biggest cookie eater.

Before I get into the coaching and non-classroom activities, I will finish off the teaching assignments. The second year with the new building ended the split shifting. All grades from 6 through high school attended at the same time. I had one of the rooms in the new building.

I had all of the same classes to teach except instead of a study hall to babysit I had a Mathematics class. This class was designed for anyone who needed a Math credit to graduate. I believe it only took one year of Math to graduate so this class was for anyone who didn't pass Algebra or Geometry or anything else with numbers.

The class, as I remember, was made up entirely with boys. It wasn't huge, probably around 25. After about three weeks I divided them up into three groups. One group could almost add but hardly subtract. The next could add and subtract but multiplication was questionable and division unlikely. The final group was good through multiplication and division was a 50-50 chance. These groups weren't formed to embarrass anyone but to make working with them easier. The kids weren't insulted, they were fine with the program.

Physically I separated them in the classroom without ranking them or pointing out what each group could do or not accomplish. Once in their seats with their groups, this one kid named Max who was seated with the add-but-not-subtract group raised his hand.

I said, "Yes, Max, what's up?"

Max said, "Mr. Groshell, you know what you just did?"

I said, "No, Max, what did I do?"

He replied, "You just created an atomic bomb."

I then looked over his bunch and I had to agree. Max was no dummy. He just wasn't much for Math or school.

That class and I had fun. They all learned a bit of Math. They also learned how to write checks and keep track of them. They learned how to make change if working in any type of store. They learned about pints and pounds and measuring things. We even made a map for the school district marking where trees, fences and brush were located on a 2-acre plot by the school. That class beat the stuffing out of babysitting a study hall.

CHAPTER 30

More Fun Coaching

Starting my first year at Tolt, my first outside activity was as the public address announcer at home football games. I had never done anything like that before in my life. The entire atmosphere at the Friday night games was so totally alive. In fact, everything at that small high school in Carnation was alive and enthusiastic.

I was a one man show. I tried my best to call the names of players who made the catches, throws, runs and tackles. The games were important to the students, parents, and even teachers. We were a community as well as a school. I don't think big schools enjoy the closeness and feeling of belonging that small schools do.

I had the pleasure of handling this job for the two years I was there. My highlight film would have been quite short, or maybe nonexistent if not for the game against the Granite Falls Tigers. The opening kickoff was being delayed while one of the Tigers was changing his shoes in the middle of the field. Rain was coming down sideways and the crowd was more than ready to get things going.

So, I announced, "There is a time out on the field while a Tiger changes his paws!!"

Sorry, I guess you had to be there.

Next came my first ever George Plimpton imitation. You know, *Paper Lion* or even the *Great Impostor*. I had played freshman basketball in high school. I played two years of YMCA run and gun basketball. For me to step in as a high school basketball coach was a stretch. Head coach Karl Albrecht was a for real damn good coach. Under the circumstances he was willing to take me on as his assistant. I was to coach the junior varsity team and assist him with the varsity. When it came to helping with the varsity the best thing I could do was stay out of his way.

Since we were double shifting at the school, the gym wasn't available for practice until 5:00 PM each day. Karl needed the entire floor for his coaching purposes. He featured full court presses and run and gun offense. The Tolt Demons would wear out the other guys, then conquer.

I was allowed to use half of the gym between 2:30 and 4:00. All through basketball season I started classes at 7:00 AM and finished varsity practice at 7:00 PM. We had games usually on Tuesday and Friday nights. Home game night I would get home around 10. Away game nights would get me home around midnight. My pay for assistant basketball was $330 for the year. I think it came to $0.25 an hour. The varsity team played well, winning more than half their games. Coach Albrecht got them to district but not to state. That would hold true the next year.

My junior varsity squad had an uphill battle all the way. Nine of my players were freshmen, the other three were sophomores. Most JV teams had sophomores and juniors. My tallest player was about 5 foot 10 inches. On top of everything else, the JV team the year before was good. They had run up scores on a number of other JV teams. Consequently, a number of coaches from the other schools were ready to return the favor. The problem was, I wasn't the coach who had done that and not one of my players had been on that team. We didn't deserve to have teams run up the score on us.

One night we were playing at Stanwood High. Apparently, they were one of the victims of the previous year drubbings. Their players were all bigger, older, stronger and more talented than my little scrappy bunch. The first half they played only six players and full court pressed the entire time. The score at halftime was 44–8.

The gym was old with dead spots in the floor. Our dressing room was in a dingy, cold, damp basement. My kids were getting beaten both physically and mentally. They were sitting on benches with two or three of them crying. All I could do was tell them they were doing as well as they could hope to do under the circumstances. We went over how we wanted to beat their full court press, which looked good on the chalkboard but with our lack of size and skill meant nothing.

The second half went just the same, same six kids played, same full court press, same score of 44–8. Then their coach came over to shake hands after that 88–16 drubbing, I refused. With all the class I could muster I said, "Go f**k yourself."

In the locker room I told my kids I was proud of them and that we would improve.

When Stanwood came to Carnation to play about a month later, I tried something new. I told my guys no shooting unless it's an uncontested layup. They played only the same six players and full court pressed the entire game. With my stall in effect, the score after one quarter was 5–1.

After one quarter I took the stall off and we played the best we could the rest of the way. The final score was 56–31 even though his full court press was used the entire game. This time when he came over to shake hands, I did, but I told him he was still an asshole.

I didn't know he was also their baseball coach, and I would be seeing him come springtime. If I had known I still would have said the same thing.

My kids did improve as the year progressed. After about 13 losses to start the year, we actually won 38–37 against Darrington's JVs. My kids went nuts like they just won a state championship. That night made the whole season feel worth it. We went on to win a total of four games. The next year I had pretty much the same squad but with a couple of new freshmen. That team won about 9 or 10 games.

I had two highlights those two years. Both had to do with making a statement to officials. One was at Kings Garden when I attempted my version of Bobby Knight. Instead of throwing a chair into the court I kicked one. I caught the edge of the steel folding chair on my ankle as I did it. I didn't break anything, but my ankle did swell up considerably.

The other happened at LaConner where the officials were letting their bigger and stronger players physically beat on my guys. One of my players had to leave the game with a gash on his head from a flagrant elbow. Three others had to come out for a while with other inflicted injuries. After another assault where no foul was called, I lost it and ran on the court where I put a bear hug on one of the officials. I screamed in his ear that he was letting my players get killed.

Nothing happened to me. I should have been hauled off to jail, or at least thrown out. Instead, the rest of the game they cleaned things up and no more kids got hurt.

It's funny because when it came to helping with varsity games my role was good coach and Karl's was bad coach. When talking to officials, Karl believed that it was better to intimidate officials than to be nice to them. Other than my couple of meltdowns I thought nice was better than mean.

Karl would send me out to raise hell during a stop in action. I would go up to them waving my arms and look like I was raising hell but saying, "Hi guys, you're doing great. Karl just sent me out to yell at you. Now I'll go back and sit down."

Over the two years the highlight for both varsity and JV was the weekend trip we took to play Onalaska one night and Mossyrock the next. From Tolt High to those schools was about a two-and-a-half-hour drive. The trip included two nights in a motel. On the trip were both teams and all the cheerleaders. Karl and his wife Sherry along with Liz and I were the chaperones. Most of the players' parents along with many students drove in their own vehicles.

Saturday for sightseeing and for entertainment we went to Yard Birds, a big variety store in southwestern Washington. Looking back, it was so refreshing to see what was fun for all of us at that time. For music at that time the hands down favorite for the group was *Knock Three Times on the Ceiling If You Want Me*. Those two nights had more than a little bit of knocking on the ceiling by players who had cheerleaders in the rooms above them.

Those two years would be the sum total of my basketball coaching career. I did learn a great deal from Karl about the game.

CHAPTER 31

"Wheels" Taught Me

With spring came baseball season. I was comfortable coaching baseball since I had played it through high school. I didn't feel like an impostor as a baseball coach. There were still many hurdles to leap as a baseball coach. These weren't the high and low hurdles used in track. However, getting kids to play baseball at Tolt rather than turn out for track was a big hurdle. For whatever reason springtime at Tolt meant track, not baseball for most of the boys. Consequently, I only had 13 turn out of which 9 were freshmen. Most of my players were kids I had coached in JV basketball, and most had played very little baseball.

Another problem was we had no field to play games on and worse yet no field to practice on. I was able to get the grade school in Fall City to let us use one of their softball fields. Looking back, I'm surprised they let us because they were in a different school district. We had to put temporary bases on the outfield grass to make the diamond big enough. The pitcher's mound, without the mound, was moved from 45 feet to 60 feet from home plate. The field was rough as it was never dragged. I would drive there for practices and players carpooled to make it.

As far as actual games, with no home field we had to play all of them away. Normally home teams provided the umpire so everyone we played picked from their staff of coaches and teachers. If you ever heard of getting homered, this was it.

There was one more bonus. Being a small school, we had to travel quite a way to play other league schools. Because the travel was so far, all of our games were double headers. With only 13 players of which only one was really a pitcher, it was virtually impossible to handle double headers.

This was my first ever experience to be the head coach of a team, let alone a high school team. I had come up with a couple of rules and a basic philosophy of what I expected. These were largely developed from coaching JV basketball under Karl's guidance. At the first practice I sat all the players down and made them listen to the following:

Number one: players were there to be a part of a team. They were there because they wanted to play as part of that team. They were not there to help me or because I wanted them to be on the team. If any one of them thought they were doing me or the team a favor, then they should leave.

Number two: when I gathered them together to talk to them, I expected them to keep eye contact with me and listen. They should not look away, play grab ass with another player, toss a ball in the air, or in any way not pay attention.

Number three: the only person on the team who could criticize a player about their play was me. No question about it!!

After a couple of practices, I came to the conclusion that only three of my players had a prayer of hitting a pitched ball. Consequently, while we practiced a lot of hitting, we also worked a great deal on bunting and running bases.

The first three double headers I only allowed those three to swing away. The rest were bunting only. If they actually got the bunt down, they were to keep running until they were called out or had reached second. Once on second if the hitter got the bunt down the runner was to keep going until they scored or were called out. I figured this beat watching every hitter strikeout and sit down. We did get the other teams to throw the ball around a bit chasing our runners and we did score a few runs.

Only a couple of parents grumbled about it but when I explained I would let their kids swing once they had a chance of touching the ball they understood.

On defense I stressed keeping things under control. Always hit your cutoff man who would then run it into the middle of the diamond. We would not throw the ball all over chasing after runners. It was easy for them to understand that since our offense was based on getting the other team to throw the ball all over chasing our runners.

After three double headers I let all of them swing away sometimes but we still did a lot of bunting.

On the team bus returning from our first double header, one of our outfielders, Steve Rush, was giving our catcher a bad time for letting a few pitches get by him. As soon as I heard this going on I shut him up immediately. Our catcher, Mike Guisti, already felt bad and as a freshman he had played pretty damn well.

For practice the next day I found an old chest protector, old shin guards, old catcher's mask, and an old catcher's mitt in storage. I dressed Steve up in this gear before practice and had taped the shin guards on because the snaps were broken. The glove was for the left hand but since Steve threw left-handed, he had to wear it on his right. I made him get behind the plate and I started throwing pitches to him. I threw half of them in the dirt in front of him. After about 15 minutes of beating him up, I asked him and all the rest of the team if they had any more complaints about other players' performances. It was unanimous that I would be the only one to make any comments in the future. From that point on I called Steve "Yogi," in reference to famed catcher Yogi Berra.

When I rolled up to our field in Fall City one day I was greeted by my squad to a chant of "Wheels got pissed on, Wheels got pissed on, Wheels got pissed on."

Wheels, *aka* Ted Morris, had fallen asleep under a tree by the practice field. While dozing away a dog had come up and peed on him.

I had given Ted the name of Wheels because he was the slowest runner on the team. Wheels was tall and skinny. When he ran, he looked like he was going to break apart at almost any given joint. While he wasn't fast, he could catch a ball and throw it. To start the year, he was our backup first baseman. Early in the season he woke me up and taught me a valuable lesson.

So many coaches have their best lineups and best players determined early on. Quite often they know who they are going to play at whatever position before the first practice even takes place. That wasn't me since this was my first year but by the first game Ted was destined to be a substitute or backup in my mind.

I think it was in our third double header I had to make a switch at first base. Ted had not gotten in a game yet. I would shuffle other starters around to fit my best sub into a spot he could play. As I was moving this guy here and that guy there, I called on the third baseman to move to first base and as I said it I spotted Ted looking at me. Tears welled up in his eyes when I called for someone else to move to 1st. In an instant I thought *Ted has been at every practice, Ted has tried to do anything and everything I've asked, Ted deserves a chance.*

Quickly I said, "Forget that—Wheels get on First!"

Wheels finished the game well and the rest of the season he was my starting first baseman. Thanks, Wheels, for waking me up!

We won a few games that year but most importantly the kids had fun. They had enough fun that word got out to others that baseball was an alright alternative to track. The next year I had 22 turn out. We were much more competitive, winning close to half our games in spite of still having no field for games or for practice. We also got "homered" by the umpires more often than not.

The first practice I tried to hold on the lawn in front of the school. I didn't want to go to Fall City anymore. I switched locations to the practice football field after one of my players threw a ball through one of Mary Balenti's windows. Mary was an English teacher who had very little love for sports.

CHAPTER 32

Plays With Ladies

M y summers between all my teaching years involved working at Mount Si Golf and playing golf. I mentioned Lilac Opens with Mike Calabrese earlier. I also won two club championships during those years and finished second in the other two. The summer between my second year at Tolt and my year at Mount Si High I had quite a run. I played 90 holes (5 rounds) at Mount Si with no score higher than par on any hole. Included in the rounds were two consecutive scores of 62. The course record was 61 and I wanted that so badly I could taste it. Twice I choked on the taste.

One Saturday night between my two years at Tolt High, Gary Barter called me to invite me to play the following day at Ocean Shores in a two-man best-ball. At that point Gary was the assistant pro at Ocean Shores. I called Mike Calabrese and he and I along with Liz and Helene arrived Sunday morning at 10:25 in Ocean Shores for the 10:30 starting time.

Gary met us with the cart saying, "Hurry—*hurry*—you're on the tee."

Neither Mike nor I had ever played Ocean Shores golf course. The wind was also blowing quite strongly which it does there more often than not.

The competition was a two-man best-ball. However, we were to both finish out every hole because the low individual for the day was going to win a $300 entry fee into the Wendall West Open to be held in September. $300 was close to my take home pay for a month teaching school at that time.

Anyways, I shot a 69 individually. We had a best ball of 69. Mike wasn't able to help on any hole, but he really wasn't expected to, especially in that wind. The next low best-ball score was 76. The second low individual score was 78.

So, I won the entry into the Wendall West Open in 1970 in the amateur division. The Wendall West Open was a golf tournament for the Ladies PGA. Among the participants were Carol Mann, the 1969 Ladies leading money winner. Kathy Whitworth, Joanne Carner, Betsy Rawls and Patty Berg were all included. This was the real thing.

The only problem was that the days of play were on a Wednesday, Thursday and Friday in September when I would be teaching school. I called my principal, Jim Satterlee, and asked him what I should do.

He said, "Play in it, just call in sick but if you get caught it is on you."

This was like the third week of school, so I called in sick ahead. The first day I played with Leslie Holbert who was a pro in the Northwest. I played just OK and shot a 74. The second day I was paired with Carol Mann and Betsy Rawls, two of the best on the Ladies tour. In fact Carol had been the top money winner on the ladies tour the year before. After 11 holes I was four under par, so I switched into my gag-and-three-putt routine. After three straight 3 putts, Carol came over to me and bent over to put her arm over my shoulder. Carol was 6' 3" to my 5' 5-1/2" of height.

She draped her arm over my shoulder and said, "John, knock this shit off, you are better than that!"

I said, "Okay, Miss Mann, I'll try."

I finished with a 72.

For the third and final round I was paired with Patty Berg and Sharon Miller. Once again, I was choking on the back nine, three-putting several holes. I had a 15-foot putt on #18 for birdie when Gary came up to me and asked how I stood with par. I said I was even, and he said if I two-putted for my par, I would win the amateur division by one. Miraculously I did two putt it to shoot 71.

Patty Berg had overheard what Bart had told me. She came over and held up my arm and announced, "Here is the winner! Here is the winner!"

Patty was past her prime, but she was revered as one of the best to play the game. She was to the Ladies' Tour what Arnold Palmer was to the Men's. The tournament was a great experience, and all the girls were very friendly and nice to me.

As far as calling in sick I hadn't thought about newspaper articles. Both the *Seattle PI* and *Seattle Times* listed the golf results every day.

Wendell West Open - 1970

Patty Berg   John Groshell   Sharon Miller

Patty Berg was to the LPGA what Arnold Palmer was to the men's PGA Tour.

As the leading, then winning amateur I was listed every day. In the teachers' lounge that Monday before school, Mary Balenti made some comment that insinuated that she knew something. She was known as a troublemaker. She had been fired several years before and had sued to get her job back.

I waited until she went to her room. I followed her and approached her.

I said, "Mary, I have no idea what you know or don't know, but if you want to cause trouble for me, then do it. But I won't be taking any crap off you. Do what you think you have to do or just shut up!"

She replied, "Don't worry, John, I've got no problem with you."

And that was it.

CHAPTER 33

Sad Leaving Tolt

As the year wound down, word came out that the district was going to let one principal go to save money. Our principal, Jim Satterlee, took care of the secondary schools. Another principal had Carnation Elementary, and the third principal was at Duvall's Cherry Hill Elementary. Neither one of them was qualified to lead a secondary school, let alone a combination middle school /high school. Problem was that Jim was not a yes man. He didn't kiss the superintendent's rear end, so he was the one chosen to go. In protest of that I decided to leave Tolt. As my second and final year teaching at Tolt High wound down, I was saddened knowing it was my last there.

I had tried my best to both teach Speech and English but more importantly, to instill confidence and positive thinking. I wanted my students to become self-reliant and successful individuals. With large classes and limited supplies, I tried to go the extra mile by printing materials almost daily. My baseball team practiced in a field for two years and had no home field for games. All of our games played away. I tried to do my best with what I had to work with.

Being a small school, many students attended one or more of my classes every day. Many of the boys played either JV Basketball or Varsity Baseball with me as their coach. I was a member of the Tolt High School family. At the point I knew I was leaving I didn't tell any students. As I mentioned earlier, I was leaving because "my" principal was being let go because of politics.

In spite of my efforts, everybody knew I was leaving several weeks before the school year ended. The graduating class requested that I be their guest speaker at graduation. Considering that most of them had listened to me more than one hour a day for two years, I took this as a compliment.

On the last day of school with graduation that night several students invited me to a little get together. There were about a dozen students and one teacher (me) that met on the bank of the Snoqualmie River that afternoon. Beer happened to be the beverage of choice, but I was not the one who provided it.

So, there I was at 25 years of age drinking beer with 18-year-old ex-students. They were ex-students by at least two hours. I honestly didn't know there was going to be beer but when I got there I sure as hell didn't leave before joining in. It never occurred to me that if caught I would possibly never be allowed to teach again. I was there to say goodbye and share laughs and stories with kids that were family to me. We all laughed and shed a few tears. I then went home, ate dinner, cleaned up and returned to speak. I didn't talk about drinking beer on the riverbank with students.

While it wasn't smart of me, I'm glad I did it. My connection with the students at Tolt has never died. The 50th anniversary of that graduation in 1971 was last year and I was invited to attend. I did and was thrilled to see my ex-students.

Two years ago my first class at Tolt, the class of 1970, was to have their 50th reunion. Due to Covid 19 the reunion was called off. In reply to the announcement that it was cancelled, I wrote—to all—"I'm sorry I won't get to see you all. I worked very hard to teach you nothing. If there is a reunion next year, I would love to attend it."

Here are several replies I received....

"Thank you for making me laugh this morning. I was looking forward to seeing you to share some of the things in my life I have done because of you. Hopefully we can get together next year."

"You were one of the most positively influential educators in my secondary school years. I do hope to see you someday. I can still see the twinkle in your eye and your quick grin as one or more class of 1970 teenager does something only a superb teacher would understand."

"For many of us getting away from the small-town environment was what we had to do to find ourselves. Your validation of each of us was a gift whether we knew it or not."

Money can't buy what those words did for me.

It was a pleasure teaching at Tolt High for two years. Had it not been for the unfair and ridiculous removal of Jim Satterlee I would have never left. The feeling of belonging and of community with my students and their parents was something I cherished. Perhaps when a new high school was built in Duvall and named Cedarcrest High the feeling of community and belonging might have diminished. At that point there was no more Tolt High School. That campus became Tolt Junior High alone.

At that point I probably would have stayed on, but I will never know. Instead, I ended up in golf full time and ended up owning a golf course. Financially I did much better than I ever would have teaching. However, I have always felt I belonged with the kids helping them work their way through life, even if the path was a bit twisted.

The Terry family was one of those that was a big part of the Tolt High community. Pat and Nina Terry had several children of which I had a daughter as a student and two of their sons as players on both my JV basketball and varsity baseball teams. The Terrys also put on the annual party and dinner for the varsity and junior varsity basketball players and coaches.

Mike and Mark were the Terry boys I coached. They were twins but not identical. Mike was taller and bigger than Mark, but both were athletic and really good kids. All "my" kids at Tolt were good kids!

It was my second year at Tolt when Mike and Mark became freshmen. I already knew them when they were in 8th grade because the campus contained both the high school and junior high. While we split shifted with the high school 7 AM to noon and the junior high noon to 5 PM, a number of activities mingled. I also substitute taught on occasion in the afternoon after already doing my normal high school classes in the morning.

Mark and Mike both turned out for my JV Basketball team. Mike, being taller, played forward. Mark played guard and could handle the ball, shoot and pass quite well.

I wasn't concerned with political correctness since I had never heard of it. I would tell Mike and Mark not to eat too much spaghetti before games so they wouldn't get bogged down. The Terrys were of Italian descent. They would fire back that I should take it easy on the sauerkraut. My father's side was German. Whatever ribbing I handed out I expected ribbing in return. As long as there was no disrespect either way it was all good.

One day when we had basketball games that night Mike and Mark brought me a container of hot dogs and sauerkraut. It was meant as a good-natured jab and at the same time it served as a great lunch.

That late afternoon when I went home for dinner before the games Liz had cooked pork chops with sauerkraut. I also enjoyed that very much.

I returned to the Tolt High gym in plenty of time to coach the JV team. We played our game before the varsity game was to be played.

Until that time I had never known what sauerkraut could and would do to me. Somewhere during the second quarter a grumbling and growling sensation started in my mid-section. Within minutes I knew there was no holding back. The head coach, Karl, was sitting in the stands on the other side of the court. I sent a player over to fetch him as fast as possible. As soon as Karl reached the bench, I moved as fast as I could toward the locker room. I barely made it. From then on there was no sauerkraut on game days for me. The Terrys could eat all of the pasta they wanted. To this day, if I need a laxative, I eat lots of sauerkraut and drink some of the sauerkraut juice as well. It works!

My other Terry brother story involves Mike in a varsity baseball game. Mike played outfield most of the time. Mark was my full-time second basemen. Both were better than average players, but Mark was a bit more focused on the game that was going on.

During one game Mike had doubled and was standing on 2nd base. Actually, he was *nearly* standing on second base. He was stationed about two feet off the bag on the third base side. His mind was not on the game at the time. He was staring off in the air at nothing. Maybe he had lost his virginity the night before and he was searching the sky to find it and get it back. Maybe he was thinking about whether Santa Claus was real or not. He might even have been thinking about a fish that got away. Whatever it was, it wasn't about standing just off the bag while scratching his ass with one hand and picking his nose with the other.

I was watching him and noticed that the pitcher realized he was off the bag. The pitcher waved to the shortstop to cover the bag for a pick-off throw. At this point I was calling, "Terry! Terry! Mike! Mike, watch out! Get on the bag. Wake up! – etc." —And I even kept it politically correct not yelling dumb dago or stupid wop or anything.

The shortstop moved over to the bag, took the throw, and tagged the dreaming base runner out. When he was called out, he woke up and headed for the dugout.

Even though I was always in total control of myself, I ran out and met him by the pitcher's mound. I was calmly explaining his mess up as I took the baseball cap off of his head, threw it on the ground, and jumped up and down on it.

While I wasn't necessarily proud of my actions, I was successful in getting his attention. Another bonus was that back then parents supported teachers and coaches, especially in small towns where we were all in it together. I think his dad, Mel, wondered why I didn't throw Mike on the ground and stomp on him instead of his cap.

CHAPTER 34

Returns to Dedicate Field

After finishing the last school year at Tolt, I applied for an opening at Mount Si High. I was hired even though there were 56 applicants. I did know people in the system and had taught two years of 8th grade there. All those students were attending Mount Si High at that point. Probably 50% of the teachers had had me as a student just nine years before.

As I mentioned already, one of the biggest compliments of my life came at the end of my year at Tolt. Even though everybody knew I was leaving to go to Mount Si, the graduating class asked me to be their main speaker for their graduation. These kids had just spent two years listening to me in classes for one to three hours a day. Then there were those that I coached in one or two sports plus the ones I directed in a play. They actually wanted to listen to me one more time. Wow!!

I was to be asked back to speak on another occasion when I was teaching at Mount Si. Steve "Yogi" Rush had drowned that summer after I left Tolt. During the school year they finally built a baseball field for the Tolt Demons. The field was to be named after Steve. I was invited to do the dedication speech, and I was proud to do it. Now, 50 years later, when I run into one of Yogi's brothers or sisters they say, "Hi, Coach, how are you doing?"

My two years at Tolt were the most rewarding years of my life. Had Jim Satterlee not been let go I would never have left. I would have retired as a schoolteacher many years later.

CHAPTER 35

Prank Call

Jim did sue the district and they were forced to bring him back, which they did as a teacher. A couple of years later he got on as a teacher at the Snoqualmie Middle School. He taught there for a number of years until he came down with Lou Gehrig's Disease. Jim finished the year even though he couldn't lift either of his arms for most of it. He is the toughest and bravest guy I've ever known.

Before I move on to writing about my next year at Mount Si High School, I would like to add a story of a prank call I made. It was a snowy day and various school reports were being made on the radio. Tolt High was in the Lower Valley District where my ex-school, Snoqualmie Middle School, was in the Upper Valley. I had driven to work at Tolt that morning where there was to be a one-hour delay. I had been listening to reports on the radio and the Upper Valley was waffling from one hour late to two hours late to closing for the day. I decided that I should call my old friend Jan who was still the secretary at the middle school. You remember the lady who had me call in the order for navy bean lunches. At this point I hadn't seen or talked to Jan in over a year and a half. Here's how the call went

Jan: "Good morning, Snoqualmie Middle School, Jan speaking."

Me: "I want to know what the hell is going on?"

Jan: "What do you mean, sir?"

Me: "My kid has been out in the snow waiting for the school bus for almost two hours."

Jan: "This is the middle school."

Me: "This is ridiculous, he was in the hospital for pneumonia two weeks ago."

Jan: "You need to call the administration office; I can't help you."

Me: "Don't pass the buck, damn it. I want answers."

Jan: "Sorry but I can't—."

Me: "What is going on here?"

Jan: "Is this you, John?"

Me: Laughter

Jan: "You son of a bitch, are you trying to kill me?"

Me: "Heck no, I just missed you."

About two years later Jan pointed me towards what turned out to be my full-time job from 1973 onward at Snoqualmie Falls Golf Course.

CHAPTER 36

HA HA BANG BANG – And I'm Gone

Teachers and administration reported for a day of orientation the day before school was to open. To kick the day off we went to the music room to listen to our principal give us the lowdown on what was up. He was a tall man of about 6'3" and had big ears. His mother and father had given him a name which probably appeared on his birth certificate. I learned very soon that to the students he was "Bullwinkle."

The vice principal was a short skinny guy who face-to-face with students had a different name than "Squirrel" which is what they called him. When Bullwinkle passed around printed material to start the orientation, I feared that the year was going to be long and painful. After listening to him for five minutes I knew it to be true. At the top of the sheets was printed "Mount Success High School" rather than Mount Si High School. My gag reflex kicked in immediately.

Mind you, in this room were all the teachers. Of the 25 to 30 teachers, probably 50% of them had had me as a student nine years before. Consequently, I most likely couldn't have shocked them much if I made any comments. Nonetheless, when I sat down, I planned on being a good little quiet soldier. I had no intention of making waves or drawing attention to myself. The Mount Success headings did weaken my good intentions subconsciously if not consciously.

Bullwinkle babbled on mindlessly and I remained quiet until he proclaimed, "Every teacher should provide a meaningful educational experience for every child every minute of the day!"

That did it, little Johnny couldn't be mute Johnny any longer. I raised my hand and when called on said, "Really? If I can get most of my students to learn a couple of things in a period I'm doing quite well!"

Oops—wrong start with my boss.

So, then he started going over the class schedules of all of the teachers. If I needed to know what everyone taught, I could look it up.

I sat quietly like a good little trooper. Eventually he got to my schedule of classes. I had all freshmen for Speech classes and a couple of English classes. One of the English classes was named American War and Humor. That is quite a pairing: So 17 guys got shot while their children back home were watching the three stooges and giggling. I mean, come on, *really?*

So little Johnny raised his hand again and Bullwinkle reluctantly called on him.

Bullwinkle: "You have a question, Mr. Groshell?"

Me: "Yes, I do."

Bull: "And what would that be?"

Me: "I was thinking about changing the title of one of my classes."

Bull: "Which one?"

Me: "The one titled *American War and Humor.*"

Bull: "And what do you have in mind?"

Me: "Instead of war and humor could we just call it *Ha Ha Bang Bang*?

That brought the house down, my ex-teachers laughing as they thought, "Little Johnny is back."

Bullwinkle had nothing to say.

I could see education was changing. We were supposed to entertain, not teach. The three Rs were more than halfway out the door. By the time the meeting ended, I realized Bullwinkle cared more about procedure and lesson plans than about teaching and learning. For four years I had worked for realists, now I had to make it through one year with a spineless dreamer.

Soon I learned that the teacher next door could not control her classroom. Fortunately, my room was at the end of the hallway, so I only had one neighbor. Besides noise next door she constantly had students break off pencil leads in her doorknob so the door couldn't be opened. Part of the class period would go by with a classroom worth of students and the teacher waiting in the hall while the janitor got the door open. I tried to go over to her room as little as possible to quiet things down, but I had to on occasion.

My classes actually went along just fine with no complaints from students, parents or other teachers. At the end of the first quarter, I found a note in my school mailbox from Squirrel asking me to please come see him. I went to his office, and this is how it went:

Squirrel: "Hi John, how are things going?"

Me: "Just fine."

Squirrel: "Great but we do seem to have a problem."

Me: "Really, what's that?"

Squirrel: "You haven't written any referrals."

Me: "You're right, I haven't. So why is that a problem?

Referrals are written when a student has caused a problem that the teacher can't handle. Description of the action and/or problem is written on the referral and accompanies a student to the office where a counselor, vice principal or even principal handles it. The key part to me was "problem a teacher couldn't handle." So, to continue....

Squirrel: "So you haven't had any problems with any students?"

Me: "None that I couldn't handle."

Squirrel: "Well, we all need help sometimes."

Me: "Have you had any complaints about me from any students or parents?"

Squirrel: "Well, no."

Me: "Are you aware that not only do I handle my classes but have to settle things down in the room next to mine on occasion?"

Squirrel: "I guess I've heard that."

Me: "So what do you want me to do?"

Squirrel: "Just understand that referrals are the system to be used when needed."

Me: "OK, I won't forget."

After one more quarter with no referrals I was able to climb the ladder. Once again I wrote no referrals. There were improvements next door though. By Thanksgiving the teacher next door had quit after a nervous breakdown and was replaced by a retired teacher who had taught me years earlier. He didn't take any crap from the students.

So, climbing the ladder I got a note to see Bullwinkle. When I reported in, the conversation was identical to the one I had with Squirrel a quarter earlier.

At the end of it I didn't ask, "So what do you want me to do?" Instead, I said, "So, if I understand what you are telling me, I'm supposed to write referrals."

Bullwinkle: "Yes, that is the system."

Me: "So, no matter if I need to or not, you want referrals?"

Bullwinkle: "Yes, I do."

Me: "OK, no problem."

First period the next day I asked, "Would anyone like a referral?"

Four or five kids said, "Sure, I'll take one."

Each of them got assigned one from me with instructions to describe their misbehavior. I repeated this every period all day long. Every class I sent anywhere from two to five kids to the office. The kids thought it was funny. The referral system was a joke to them. They would get out of a class and listen to a bit of crap, and nothing would ever happen.

The next morning my mailbox had a different note. *"You must see me now!!" Signed, Bullwinkle.*

I marched back to his office and walked in. I acted like everything was just great, wonderful and as I entered joyfully said, "It's a beautiful day today, how are you doing?"

Oddly enough, he looked like he could kill me as he muttered, "You know what's wrong!"

I said, "Oh yes, I know, the referrals—didn't I send enough of them?"

He said, "Don't be smart with me."

I replied, "Sorry but as I have said I haven't needed to yet. The first time I have a problem with a student that I can't handle I will march them right in here and put them on your desk!"

Bullwinkle said, "OK."

I realized I'm not being positive about that year at Mount Si. I had been spoiled having a principal who was a positive thinking realist who believed in discipline. Another principal, Bob Drake, had been fine too.

So, onto the next thing that pissed me off. Actually, this took place during that second quarter. In November Liz had a miscarriage. She was over five months along and the baby was a girl who was kept alive a short while. Nowadays she may very well have been saved. We had rushed into the hospital in the night and through it all I didn't call in my upcoming absence from school the next day fast enough.

Bullwinkle was at least consistent. I got lectured over late notice. Never did I get a "Sorry about your daughter. How is your wife?"

After that I knew I couldn't handle more years at Mount Si.

I had good communication with the students. Half of the student body had me as an eighth-grade teacher. There were a couple of times when I learned of drug deals that were going down. I would know who, when and where. Both times I went to Bullwinkle about it and was told to stay quiet. If these things weren't broken up or reported, Mount Si didn't have a drug problem.

My dream had been to teach at Mount Si High and be the head baseball coach. I coached the freshman team that year and the head coach was leaving. The head coaching job was to be mine. Instead of going for that, I decided I had enough of Mount Si High. Starting after the first of the year I decided to look for a job as a golf pro.

My buddy Hughie was going to show me any PGA notices of job openings. The first one was for the assistant pro job at the Yakima Elks Country Club. On the notice it said apply in writing only, no phone calls. The guy who was going to be the new head pro there was still at Helena Country Club in Montana. He was in the process of switching over to the Yakima head pro position. This was actually in March. I found the phone number for the Helena Country Club and phoned. His name was, and still is, Don Williams. He answered the phone and I said I called about the job in Yakima.

He said the application was supposed to be in writing only.

I said I knew that, but I just wanted him to know that I really wanted the job. He had me meet him in Yakima on that coming Friday night. I did, and he hired me. I then worked with him that weekend at The Elks.

For the next 2½ months I taught school Monday through Friday and coached baseball with games on Friday afternoons. I would then drive for 2½ hours to Yakima where I would work Saturday and Sunday. Sunday night I would drive back to North Bend to teach and coach until the next weekend. Over that period, we got rid of most of our furniture and stuff. We sold our Barracuda and our Roadrunner and bought an economical Chevy Vega. We had to cut all unnecessary expenses since my new job only paid $450 per month. The only good part of that was that a one-room apartment in the Yakima Elks building was ours to use.

The last day of school I signed out of Mount Si and went home. We signed papers for the sale of our house. A buddy of mine who owned a moving company brought a moving van to the house. He filled it with a small amount of furniture we had, except our bed. Liz and I slept that night in it. The next morning, we loaded that on the moving truck and drove to Yakima. My buddy and I emptied that into the tiny apartment, and I reported to work by noon. It was less than 24 hours between one job and the next.

I will try to sum up the transition from our position in my fifth year of teaching to our new situation in Yakima. About the only thing that stayed the same was Liz was pregnant again. What I was leaving:

- The teaching position of my dreams that would have paid about $11,000 for the year.
- A side job at Mount Si Golf where I would have earned over $5,000 that next year.
- A nice 3-bedroom home with a recreation room that I put a shuffleboard in.
- A good-sized yard for us and our two basset hounds.
- Two really sweet cars: a Barracuda and a Roadrunner.
- A climate in Western Washington that I liked. I'll take rain over heat any day.
- The Snoqualmie Valley where I had lived since 1949 and where most all my friends lived.

Pregnant Liz and I were moving to:

- A job in Yakima, WA. As an assistant golf pro that would pay $450 per month.
- No side job so my annual gross would come to $5,400.
- The head pro would give all the lessons so there would be no extra bucks for me.
- A small one-room apartment in the clubhouse where golfers could knock on our door 24 hours a day.
- One Chevy Vega for transportation.
- No yard. We had to leave the basset hounds with my mother.
- A climate that was hot in the summer and cold in the winter.

I have never claimed to be smart. My mother, who was very intelligent and a positive thinker, summed it up this way: "John, are you out of your mind?"

CHAPTER 37

Beginning Golf Pro

O K, let's review our situation. Liz and I, along with our two cats, are off to Yakima for my first golf pro job. We get to live in a one-room apartment with no air conditioning. In Eastern Washington air conditioning is a must from April through September. We had to leave our two basset hounds with my Mom on Lopez Island, but at least Liz has the cats, Moosey and Boom Boom, to talk to.

Liz and I have never been to Yakima before. She and I don't know a single person within 75 miles of Yakima. However, Liz has it made. She has a Chevy Vega and a one-room apartment with running water, a full bathroom, almost a kitchen, and a promise that I will get an air conditioner to put in the window. Plus, remember that at the point when I got the job, she was pregnant again.

We discovered that golfers expected service 7 days a week and 24 hours a day since we lived on the premises. Most members kept their clubs in the club storage room. On occasion, when returning from a pro-am at 1:00 or 2:00 AM, we would get a knock on our door to let them in the room. While I wasn't scheduled to open the pro shop before 7:00 AM on weekends and 8:00 AM on weekdays, there was the occasional knock somewhere between 6:00 and 7:00 AM. Liz was basically stuck in that one room 24/7, while I worked six days a week from 7:00 AM to 8:00 PM or later. At the time I didn't really think about it but looking back she was really a trooper. But at least on $450.00 a month gross income, she didn't have any money to spend either.

My job was simply to open the pro shop and work until closing every day except Monday. After three months at the Yakima Elks Golf Club, the PGA allowed me to play in pro-ams. They were on Mondays, so there went one day a week to do something with Liz.

At Mount Si Golf, I had worked in maintenance and in the pro shop. Mount Si Golf was and still is a very busy public golf course located in the crowded Greater Seattle area. The hours at Mount Si were basically when it was daylight. In June/ July/ August, starting times ran from 5:15 AM to 7:00 PM, and those starting at 7:00 PM didn't finish until dark. There were many days that we had 250 players. I was used to that pace of work.

In comparison, the Yakima Elks GC was a private club open only to Elk members. Weekdays almost nobody teed off before 8:00 AM and that was really about the same for weekends. We didn't even bother with starting times. Basically, golfers showed up and teed off. If it got at all busy, there was a little gravity fed metal golf ball chute by the first tee. Golfers would drop their golf balls in it and the next ball at the bottom would indicate who teed up next. Maybe once a month I might have to settle a dispute over who was next.

Basically, my duties amounted to unlocking the door to open and locking it to close. In between, I would take in a greens fee from an out-of-town Elk who wasn't a Yakima Elk member. Also, I would sell a little bit of merchandise, but very little.

I played golf every Wednesday afternoon with Men's Club members. I mixed it up and played with different guys almost every week. After golf I got to go into the bar and socialize with the guys I played with. I liked Wednesday afternoons except for the heat. For me, anything over 65 degrees is too hot. In Eastern Washington, summer days are almost always in the 90's, with days over 100 degrees not unusual.

Yakima people kept telling me that, "It's a dry heat." Dry or wet, heat is heat to me and I hate it. I also played every Friday night in what they called the Friday night fights. This was couples' night and there were usually more girls than guys, so I would pair up with one of them.

Anyways, what I am trying to explain, while my hours were fairly long, I really didn't work very hard.

My boss, Don, would come in most mornings between 9:00 and 10:00. He would then give lessons until noon. At that point, he would have lunch and then tee off with the same guys. His playing partners were the same six to eight guys who liked to bet. As a club pro you are advised to play with different players, not to show favorites. Don must have skipped those classes in PGA school. After his round he would finish off his day socializing.

Don's wife, Linda, did the merchandising. She ordered things and displayed clothing. Linda also took care of the paperwork and all billing.

As you can see, I put in the time but didn't do much. I did create a bunch of work for myself though. One guy brought in his clubs and complained about his grips. They were worn down a bit and sucked. I suggested new grips, and he went for it. I ordered grips, got some two-sided tape and some charcoal lighter fluid and proceeded to re-grip his set of clubs. Apparently, this was a service no one had offered there in years. I ended up doing more than 50 sets that year. Don made about $4 a club for my efforts.

The Elks course itself was, and still is, a fine golf course. It is difficult but not discouraging, and always in good condition.

The first time I played it, members were betting amongst themselves whether I could shoot a 75 or better. I started with a double bogey 6 on the first hole, a par 3 on the second hole, and then a triple bogey 7 on the tough third hole. So, after three holes I was 5 over par. I went on to play the next 15 holes two under par to finish with a 74, three over par. That did gain me an ounce or two of respect.

As a club pro you are expected to play well, but not expected to be great. Most assistant pros back then didn't play much because of working many hours. Today the PGA tries to limit the hours put in by members. One day I shot a 5 under par 31 on the front nine but ballooned to a two over par 37 on the back for a 68. After the round, while socializing in the bar, one of my playing partners was telling other members about my 31 on the front nine, which at that time was the course record. One of the crusty old members commented, "He should, he's a pro, isn't he?"

The first pro-am I played in was in Richland. It wasn't like most pro-ams where a pro plays with three of his own members. It was a 3-day senior statewide amateur tournament where pros were invited to play one day with three amateurs. Don didn't want to play in it so he sent me. I was very nervous with it being my first so called professional outing plus playing with strangers who expected me to do well. I DID NOT play very well!

I think I broke 80, but it didn't matter. Never, before or since, have I had three amateur partners knock in so many long putts. My guys were absolutely putting lights out. We, and I use that word lightly, won by several strokes. My partners never realized how poorly I played because they were having so much fun!

The rest of the year I played moderately well in most of the pro-ams. The first PGA branch pro-am I played in I had a 73 for 3rd place. I finished somewhere in the money in every one of these pro-ams.

As a club pro it is good to play well enough that members want to take lessons from you. However, it is more important to be a nice guy that members want to be around. It also doesn't hurt to be a decent businessman who caters to his members' needs.

Most all golf clubs have some interesting characters, and the Elks was not an exception. One of them was Art Schneider, who was a short, somewhat feisty guy who happened to be a pickle salesman for Seinfeld pickles. Art was about 50 years old. One day Art was really pissed off when he showed up to play. He had been trying to sell his 14-foot aluminum boat that had a 15-horse engine and came with a trailer. Remember, this was in 1972 so the $250 price was about right for what it was, maybe a bit on the low side. Of course, everyone who stopped by to look at it would try to get it for less.

"I'll give you $150 for it."

"Will you take $200 for it?"

"It's not worth more than $175."

"OK. $225 is my final offer."

After fielding offers over a weekend, Art finally had enough. One too many "What would you take for it?" comments put Art over the top.

Art finally yelled at a guy, *"JUST TAKE THE F**KING THING, YOU CHEAP ASSHOLE!"*

The guy said, "OK," and hooked up to the trailer and took off. The lucky winner got a boat, motor and trailer for nothing.

There at the Elks, most of the members had their own power carts. Cart sheds accommodated at least 150 carts. The rows of sheds had separate doors for each cart, which members provided their own padlocks for. Most of the members also had lockers in the clubhouse which they had secured with their own padlocks.

Another member who played golf quite frequently with Art was called "Leather Head." His actual name was Les Carr, but Leather Head kind of fit his hairless skull. Anyways, Leather Head casually watched Art open both of his padlocks and memorized the combinations to both locks. Then he proceeded to swap the locations of the locks from cart shed to locker and locker to cart shed.

The next day Art came to play, he virtually wore the skin off his fingers trying to open them. Finally, he proceeded to get bolt cutters and cut them off.

The biggest tournament each year at the Elks is a tournament for couples. It is called the "Indian Summer Tournament" and it is held every September. There is a waiting list to get into it. Most of the couples at the Elks play, but others come from all over Washington and even Oregon.

One day something happened at the club that disturbed Art—*go figure*. Anyways, Art stormed into the office at the club and withdrew from the tournament that was about a month away. The next day Art tried to get back in. Apparently, Mrs. Schneider felt quite differently about playing in it and talked some sense into the "Pickle Salesman's" head.

At that point the committee put them down at the bottom of the waiting list. After making Art stew over this for a couple of weeks, he and his bride were put back into the field to play.

One other event involved me and Art. On December 23, 1972, I was sitting at the bar at the club. I was there because Liz and our five-week-old son were at her parents' house in Kirkland. I'll explain why shortly. There was snow outside, so no golf was being played.

Behind me the famous game between the Raiders and Steelers was being played. That was the game where the immaculate reception took place. I'm casually sitting there talking to "Choppy" the bartender. I wasn't much interested in the game as I didn't like either team but looking at the mirror behind the bar I could see the TV.

Art was watching the game along with about ten other guys. With just under two minutes left, Oakland scored to go ahead 7-6. Art was jumping up and down in excitement, because he was a Raiders fan.

So, just being myself, I turned and said, "Hey, Art, I'll still take Pittsburgh for five bucks."

He said, "That's stupid. No way they can win now!!"

I said, "I'm not looking for a lecture, I just want a bet. Take it or leave it."

He said, "If you don't want your money, I'll take it."

My reply: "Good. Done deal."

I've got this itch, where on the right occasion with the right guy I will make a bet that is not too bright. If I lose, so what. But if I win against a hot head like Art, it is flipping priceless!

So, when Bradshaw drops back to pass from more than 50 yards out I am facing away from the TV talking to Choppy. After scrambling and almost getting sacked, Bradshaw's pass flies about 25 yards downfield. The ball hits off Jack Tatum of the Raiders and flies back toward Bradshaw. Franco Harris of the Steelers snatches it up just before it touches the ground and romps some 40 yards for the Steelers touchdown to go ahead 13–7. Time ran out as there was only 5 seconds left when the play started.

Behind me Schneider went nuts. He was jumping, stomping, screaming and howling all at once. I had watched it in the mirror, so I knew exactly what happened, but this was just too good!!

After a few seconds, I casually turned and said, "So, Art, you celebrating your win? Here's your $5 bucks."

Art said, "You son of a bitch! You know what happened."

"No, I don't. Tell me," I replied.

I was surprised—he did actually pay me about a week later.

There was another guy named Floyd Kent, who earned the name "Nasty." He was a tall, fairly thin guy who had beaten lung cancer the year before I came to Yakima. After his surgery he was playing golf before his doctors wanted him to. Most guys would have still been in bed recovering. Several years before that Nasty, Art and many others in the Men's Club were building a footbridge to take from the 2nd green to the 3rd tee. Art accidentally dropped Nasty's hammer into the small lake.

Nasty said, "Get it!"

Art said, "I can't swim."

Nasty then picked up Art and threw him into the water. Fortunately, the water wasn't more than 5 or so feet deep. Art came to the surface and climbed out, but not with the hammer.

Nasty asked him, "Where is the hammer?" and then threw him back in the lake. Art managed to come back up again, and this time he had the hammer.

Basically, every time Nasty came into the pro shop, he had a complaint. Something was always wrong. After about two months of this I had grown tired of it. So on this one afternoon he came barging in complaining that someone was teeing off before they should have.

Before I could stop myself, I said, "Nasty, just one time this year could you please say hello before you start bitching about something?"

He looked like someone hit him over the head with a baseball bat. Stunned, he turned around and left the pro shop without saying another word.

Hours later Don, my boss, came in from the bar and asked, "What did you do to Nasty?"

I told him what I had said to him earlier.

Don said, "Don't worry about it, but Nasty is trying to get guys to sign a petition to get you fired. It's all OK because no one will sign it."

The next day Nasty called me and invited Liz and I to come to his place for dinner. He managed and lived at a nice apartment house in Yakima. Along with his wife we had a nice dinner and visit. Afterward he told us we could use the laundry facilities there and we were invited to use the pool anytime. He also tried to play golf with me on Wednesday afternoons whenever I could. I guess I was about the first guy to stand up to him and after the initial shock he respected me for it.

Jack Burns was a guy of about 45 years of age who dressed and had the look of an accountant or businessman. He was too nice to be a lawyer and too honest to be a car salesman. He was a reverse sandbagger. Gentleman Jack tended to report his best scores and not his worst. Consequently, he seldom won events and wasn't the best partner to get in team games. However, Jack was a nice guy who was fun to play with.

Jack actually worked in a plywood factory. Several years earlier Jack had inherited a big chunk of money. From all reports, he probably could have retired, but Jack had a different way of looking at it. He managed to take about a year's worth of leave from work and took off around the world. He did everything he dreamed of doing while he spent his entire windfall. Jack then went back to work in the plywood factory. He told me he would do it exactly the same if he had it to do over again.

I can't leave out Don Quist, who was called "Mumbles" by all, because he always had a pipe in his mouth, and he sounded like he had a mouthful of rocks. Besides giving me a lot of good advice, he always told me, "Stick with me, kid, and you'll be wearing zircons!"

There was another guy named Les Welker, who was a neighbor of Don's. He wasn't an Elks member and he never played golf, but he liked to hang around the pro shop and talk with me. Occasionally he would putt a little bit on the putting green, but most of the time he would just hang out. He was the manager of a local K-Mart or something like that. It was like a small version of a Walmart today, but they had everything a person could want.

Les liked to talk to me about business and how to treat employees. Although I never complained about what I got paid, I'm sure he had my situation sized up. Most lectures boiled down to taking care of your employees so they will take care of you. He taught me a great deal and I have tried to practice what he preached.

On two different occasions, Les had Liz and I come down to his store. He would go around the store with us and a shopping basket. He mainly was trying to supply me with a better wardrobe. He pretty much filled the basket with slacks, golf shirts, sweaters, sox, shorts and belts for me. At check out, I didn't even pay 10% of the sales price on the items.

Les is another person I had the good fortune to know; not for the money he saved me, but for the lessons he helped me learn. Thank you, Les!

CHAPTER 38

A New Opportunity in Golf

As the year went on, Liz kept getting bigger, but I did get an air conditioner. In early November I got a call while I was working in the pro shop. The call was from Jan Sorenson. You remember Jan, the secretary in the middle school where I had taught. The one who I tormented and made prank calls to. Jan and her family lived up above Snoqualmie Falls Golf Course on the outskirts of Fall City, Washington. Jan was calling me to give me a heads up on the head pro job at Snoqualmie Falls GC. The job also included buying 20% of the golf course. Wow, it does pay to play pranks on people.

I met the guy I was to buy out in Ellensburg the next week. He put me in touch with Bill, the principal owner of Snoqualmie Falls GC, and Liz and I met with him a week after that. I was really excited, because I didn't want to be an assistant pro any longer than I had to be. Also, with a baby on the way, $450 a month pay and living in a one-room apartment just didn't cut it!

So, on November 15th, 1972, I met Bill Porter and played golf with him at Overlake Country Club, where he was a long-time member. Afterwards, he took Liz and me to dinner, and we signed the papers to buy 20% of Snoqualmie Falls Golf Course and start work on January 15th, 1973.

I learned that night from Bill, why the so-called pro was leaving Snoqualmie Falls GC. He was never an actual PGA member and he had never entered the PGA apprentice program. Plus, he was being forced to leave because he had been selling land that didn't exist. The non-existent property was in Oregon. He would get people to invest $3,000 to $5,000 that he was going to match, and they would buy the land. He promised big profits in a short period of time. Of course, he would use this new money to pay off someone else he'd taken money from before. Simply said, it was a ponzi scheme. He and his wife liked to live higher than the money he legally earned would allow. The

$20,000 I paid went to the court to be distributed to some of the victims. Between that and his parents donating money, Terry was able to stay out of jail. Later I learned that a few years earlier he was living in Oregon and selling non-existent land in Washington. His parents had sold their house to bail him out of that.

I was supposed to be back to work at the Elks by noon on November 16th. We were staying with Liz's parents in Kirkland. When we got up Liz said she felt funny.

I said, "Like in ha ha funny?"

That wasn't it, so she called the doctor. We had coverage with Group Health and the only facility at that time was in Seattle. He asked her to come in so he could check her out. We did and within a couple of hours Jeff was born. Had we headed to Yakima that morning he would have come into this world in a Chevy Vega going over Snoqualmie Pass.

I had to get back to Yakima two days later, so Liz and Jeff stayed in Kirkland. Mom and son were both doing fine. Shortly after returning to the Elks, Yakima was hit with a freeze in the lower teens. Since I had nothing better to do than be stupid, Don and I decided to play 9 holes. The temperature was close to 10 degrees and with the wind chill factor it was approaching zero. We put on as many clothes as we could fit into and still be able to swing. We even found gloves for both hands and stocking caps. We decided to play the back 9, so we would be seen teeing off on #10 by the 20 to 30 guys drinking in the bar. When we teed off, they were all lined up along the windows to watch the two stooges. We finished on the frozen turf and had drinks bought for us afterward.

A week later I drove over and picked up Jeff and Liz to bring them back to Yakima. After two weeks in our little apartment, Jeff was throwing up after eating all the time. We took him to a doctor in Yakima and tests indicated that Jeff was jaundiced. The doctor lectured us for not taking proper care of him. Jeff actually had a yellow tint to him, but in the poor lighting of our apartment he looked fine. The doctor thought he might have pyloric stenosis blockage and that surgery would be necessary. I'm pretty sure he called over to Group Health to ready them for our arrival. We dropped by the Elks to inform Don, pick up stuff, and hit the road. That had to be the longest three-hour drive of our lives. The time between our arrival at Group

Health and Jeff's operation wasn't long. The valve from the stomach to the intestines wasn't working; consequently, he would eat and then vomit.

When Jeff came out of surgery, he looked so small and pathetic. On top of that, his IV was in his head and covered with a small plastic cup so he couldn't hurt it. Through the night we were instructed to hold a little mirror under his nose to see that he kept breathing. That was almost 50 years ago, and it feels like yesterday.

Jeff recovered in great fashion, but after several days I had to return to Yakima. Don and Linda had a trip coming up and I had to tend the shop. I wasn't scheduled to start at Sno Falls until January 15th.

Besides the pay in Yakima that couldn't support us, and the shoe box we lived in, an event took place in September that really put me off.

Arnold Palmer and Kermit Zarley came to Yakima for a golf exhibition at Yakima Country Club. Lester Moe, the head pro at Yakima CC, and Lloyd Harris, the pro at Suntides, were to fill out the foursome. Virtually every person in Yakima who knew what golf was, were going to be there to watch. Don went up to watch and Linda stayed at the Elks doing paperwork. There were no golfers there and no reason for me to be there. I asked if I could just go up to watch Arnold Palmer for just a couple of hours. Linda said, no, she had too much to do.

I explained that she could lock the door and it wouldn't matter.

She still said NO!

That day soured my feelings about staying.

On the bright side, two days before I left Yakima the members held a going away party for me. They presented me with a fancy pen holder trophy inscribed with: "To the best assistant pro we know—Yakima Elks Golfers." Doing this for an assistant who had been there for less than a full year was unprecedented. That gift is one of my most prized possessions.

I finished the year and stayed until January 14th. That afternoon my friend Gary Castagno showed up with the same truck he used to take me to Yakima. So after only eight months of full time in Yakima, he was taking me back to the Snoqualmie Valley. Liz, Jeff and I had an apartment in Fall City, WA across from the King County work shed. Oh yes, Moosey and Boom Boom were headed back to the west side of the state as well.

CHAPTER 39

Almost Ruined by the PGA

When I took the job in Yakima as an assistant golf pro, I had no idea it would lead to one of the most stressful situations in my life.

If you want to be a "real" golf professional working at a golf facility, you must enter the PGA program. When you sign up you are given a program you must follow to become a member of the PGA.

When I entered the apprentice program, I was to work 40 months at a golf facility and get one credit per month. I was to attend two PGA business schools that included tests to complete the requirement. I was also going to get 8 credits toward my required 40 credits for my college degree. At the end of my 32-month apprenticeship, I had to pass a test and then go through an interview with the PGA section officers. Upon passing the final and passing the interview, I would be elected to membership and become a PGA member.

My program was set, and I knew what I had to do to become a member, or so I thought. After all, when I attended college, a program was set and completion of it led to graduation. If requirements changed, they did not affect a student's established requirements. Well, it turned out that this was not how the PGA did things. Any changes were applied to all apprentices working on their path to membership.

After I had taken the job at Snoqualmie Falls Golf Course, the PGA decided that any apprentice not working for a PGA member would only get half of a credit a month. I was now called a non-member head professional, because I wasn't working for a PGA pro. At that point I went from having a little over one year left to complete my program to now having nearly three years to finish my credits.

The PGA then decided to require all apprentices to pass a playing test before they could attend the second PGA school. Changing me from 1 credit a month to a .5 credit per month lengthened my time to where I had to take the playing test, and there was no playing test required at all when I started the program.

The playing test basically required that the player shoot within 5 strokes of the course rating over 36 holes of play. If the course was rated at 70, then the player would have to shoot 150 or better for 36 holes. The player was to be allowed three tries to pass the test, but if he did not pass after three tries, he would be out of the apprenticeship program.

Since the test was a new thing, the PGA didn't have any qualifying events scheduled. I was hoping to attend school two that year, so I was told that they would use the first two rounds of the Northwest Open as my qualifying event. It was held at Illahee Hills CC in Salem, OR. Illahee was rated at 70.5, so I needed to shoot 151 for 36 holes. Unfortunately, the course was set up to play tougher, because it was the Northwest Open Championship. The tees were set back to make the holes play longer and the holes were cut close to the edge of the green or behind sand traps.

I also had more pressure on me than most. I had three chances to pass, or I would be done in golf. I had $20,000 invested in Snoqualmie Falls that I would have to sell. I had a wife and a one-and-a-half-year-old, and Liz was pregnant with #2—soon to be Willie. In addition, my golf skills had declined as I rarely had time to play in my new head pro job. Eighty hours a week of cooking hamburgers, taking green fees, washing carts and mowing greens didn't exactly improve my golf game!

The first day, with favorable weather conditions, I shot a lousy 78. I would need a 73 the next day to make it. Day two brought steady rain and wind to add to the difficulty. I managed a 74 under lousy conditions for a total of 152, one over the score I needed. The Pacific Northwest Section Tournament Chairman told me that under the circumstances of tougher golf course set up and challenging weather conditions, he was going to try to get me approved.

A week or two later he called to inform me that the board wouldn't pass me. However, since I wanted to attend school #2 which was being held in El Cajon in a couple of months, they created a special playing test for me and one other guy. We were to play 36 holes at Rainier Country Club in Seattle with the president of our section. To complete the foursome, Ted Naff played along. Ted was one of the better playing club pros in the Northwest. He was also a nice guy, who was fun to play with. I had been paired with him about six years before in the Seattle Amateur. Ted had also attended WSU, so we were fellow Cougars. So, Ted was the positive factor for the day. On the flip side were three negatives.

First, the course rating at Rainier CC is lower than it should be. Course rating is based almost entirely on distance. The size, speed and undulation of greens means virtually nothing. The narrowness of the fairways means very little. To pass the test I had to shoot 147 for 36 holes. On that course with that pressure, it was a tough assignment.

The second negative was that Billy, the section president, was about as much fun to golf with as a hemorrhoid. He said little and seemed to be studying my every shot.

Third, the other potential qualifier had no business even trying to pass the test. He failed miserably and dragged down the mood of the entire day of play, which lasted nine hours.

I missed the number by two strokes, so my entire future in golf hung on one final event. I was a nervous wreck every waking moment until the next event. I didn't know if the PGA was going to spring another "special qualifier" on me or make me play in another tournament like the Northwest Open and use the first two rounds.

Finally, several weeks later, our section actually came up with a real qualifying tournament. The field was made up entirely of apprentices trying to pass the playing ability test. That is what is still done today. The difference is that over the last 30 years or so, players can try as many times as they wish. It is no longer three tries and you are out.

This qualifying event was to be held at Tumwater Golf Course. Tumwater is at the other end of the spectrum from Rainier CC. Tumwater is long which makes for a higher rating. The greens are not severe, and the fairways aren't narrow. If I could ask for a course to have to qualify on, it would be Tumwater.

However, with all the pressures I had heaped on my shoulders, it was to be one of the most draining days of my life. The score necessary to pass was 152. I shot 74 in the morning round, so all I needed in the afternoon was a 6 over par 78.

Another plus I had that day was my three playing partners were all great to play with. For all 36 holes we encouraged each other and kept the mood as light as we could with friendly chatter. One of those players was Dan Puetz, who is a friend of mine still today, and that was in 1974.

Anyways, standing on the 18th tee that day, all I needed was an 8 to qualify. An eight would give me a 78 for a qualifying score of 152. On top of that, #18 was medium in length for a par 4 and had no out of bounds. I was so messed up that I stood there on the tee with my whole future staring at me. I didn't know if I could do it!

After a decent drive and somewhat lousy iron shot, I was on the green, but unfortunately about 30 feet away. One putt later I had a 3-foot putt for a par and a total of 74. To qualify now I only had to get the ball in the hole in 5 more putts and I still didn't know if I could!

I somehow made the 3-footer to shoot 74 with a 36-hole total of 148. I had qualified, so I could finally go to school #2. I could stay in the program, and I could become a PGA member. I wouldn't have to go back to teaching school. Over the last few years, I have thought on occasion that I should have stayed in teaching. I wouldn't have made nearly as much money, but I would have gotten more of a feeling of accomplishment. As mentioned, the classes from my two years teaching at Tolt High School have had their 50th anniversaries of graduation. Both the classes of 1970 and 1971 keep me posted and invite me to any of their functions.

But now back to golf. I attended school #2 in El Cajon and passed the test to graduate. The last day, after taking the test, we all listened to Gary Wiren speak to us about what the PGA did and does for us. He then asked if anyone would like to say anything. Guess who couldn't hold back.

I rose and went through the whole thing. That the PGA made changes retroactive and that the .5 credit a month then led to my having to take a new requirement of a playing ability test and on and on and on. When I was finished, I got a standing ovation from the class of over 100 apprentices.

Gary Wiren then stepped up to the microphone and said, "I agree with everything you said."

Wow—Wow and WOW! Several of my Northwest Section PGA

buddies who were there, figure that I am still on tape somewhere in the PGA archives in Florida.

I finished my months at .5 credit a piece and passed the final exam. Someone in our section decided that the school #2 test I had taken wasn't tough enough. Again, because of the .5 credit rule it took me longer to complete the requirement than others. During that time the school #2 test finals had been made more difficult. Consequently, before they would interview me for membership, I was forced to take another examination. Our branch executive secretary, George Haas, felt that this was total bullshit, as did I. I had to take the test in George's office in Seattle. He as much as gave me all the answers ahead of time.

I was a good little soldier at my interview, since I didn't wish to muddy the waters and thus suffer another setback. One of the questions asked was, "What does the PGA do for you?" and I don't remember what favorable bullshit I replied.

However, years later a fellow professional actually told the truth. He answered, "They get me a 5% discount on car rentals from Avis."

He was reprimanded for his answer, forced to apologize, and required to get several letters of recommendation from PGA members before he was elected to membership.

I was finally elected to membership in July of 1976.

CHAPTER 40

Finding My Way at Snoqualmie Falls GC

The last year I was teaching school, Liz and I played a round at Snoqualmie Falls GC. The first clue to poor course conditions and lacking course maintenance came on the first green. My putt rolled up to the hole and bounced away. The cup wasn't dug deep enough so the insert rose up about an eighth of an inch above the putting surface. As we played on, I observed that the greens and fairways were in lousy shape. The tees were just rubber mats. There were no sand traps to make it more challenging. Basically, it was a cow pasture that had 18 circles that were mowed down short and a hole with a flagpole inserted was on each of these circles. On top of that, there were lots of cotton-wood trees in bloom, which made my hay fever go nuts.

The course had been built in 1963 by the guy who had start-ed Cascade Golf Course in 1955. Yes, it had been a dairy farm. Fortunately, this guy did keep the greens in close to decent shape. They had one sprinkler outlet per green, but no other watering. By midsum-mer, the course was brown with 18 semi-green circles. At that time, the other courses in the area were pretty much the same, including Mount Si where I had worked.

In 1969 three guys bought Sno Falls for the fun of it. None of them knew squat about golf course management or maintenance. The money guy was Bill Porter, who had owned a car dealership. The so-called pro was Terry, and his main skill was running ponzi schemes, although he was 0-2 on those. The third guy, Art, was to be the super-intendent. Art had been Bill's head mechanic at the auto dealership.

A logical question would be, "Why would I buy 20% of this?"

I was so anxious to get out of Yakima and live in something bigger than a closet that I would jump at anything. I also needed to make more than $450 gross a month. When I tell people that I bought 20% of a golf course for only $20,000 they can't believe how lucky I was. Of course, Terry had only paid $2,500 for his 20%, as had Art. Bill had put $50,000 into the corporation but did it as a loan. Bill the business-man got back every penny of that with 10% interest tacked on.

The reason Bill let me in for only $20,000 was because I had 11 years' experience working at golf courses. I could play well enough to become a PGA pro and I was in the PGA apprentice program. I could also give lessons, mow greens and tees, cook hamburgers, merchandise, keep the pro shop clean, handle bookkeeping duties, and make customers happy. I was also dumb enough to work 80 to 90 hours a week. For several years my normal Sunday had me mowing greens at 3:30 AM so I could open the building by 5:30 AM. I would then work inside running the pro shop and helping in the kitchen all day. This included getting carts out to rent and washing them at night before putting them away. My last duty was cleaning the grill in the restaurant at 10:00 PM. That comes to a tidy little 18 or 19 hours in one day. Most days I only worked 15 or 16 hours. These were only during the busy season. November through February my hours weren't bad at all.

My pay started at $900 a month. However, I had rent to pay, not like the free housing in Yakima. The apartment in Fall City was only $120 a month so I was ahead of the year before. The $20,000 investment was made up by a $5,000 gift from Mom. I borrowed another $5,000 from my grandfather, which I paid back in full. He was the one who got me started playing golf. I borrowed $5,000 from the Seattle First National, Snoqualmie Branch, and paid that off in a couple years. The remaining $5,000 I got selling most of my remaining shares of Texaco stock I'd bought over the years.

So, we are living one mile from the golf course, but only have one car. I can't leave Liz stranded with baby boy Jeff and two cats, so I man up and walked one mile each way to work. This of course started in January where it typically rains in Western Washington. In addition, to get by financially I had to work on my one day a week off from the course. The first year I worked as a gopher (go for this, go for that) for a carpenter who played golf at Sno Falls. The second year I tended bar one night a week.

Another bonus of the job was that Liz and Art's wife, Jane, were required to help in the restaurant for no pay. This was in the busier months of the year. April through September they each worked three days a week from 10:00 AM to 3:00 PM. When Liz worked so did Jeff.

Jeff would be put in a playpen and get lots of attention. That could account for his friendly outgoing personality.

Art and Jane had three teenage sons. They helped outside on occasion. Art and Jane lived in Bellevue, over 30 minutes away. Early maintenance work wasn't part of Art's work schedule. Closing at night also wasn't a big part of Art's schedule. Art and Jane had been involved for three years and at this point, felt trapped, and really didn't want any part of the "damned place." They decided to sell their 20% and get out at the end of the busy season.

My experience at golf courses was such that during the busy season, courses were open for business during daylight hours. That meant having greens mowed or swept by 6:00 AM. It also meant not locking up before 9:00 PM.

Art and Terry didn't open until 7 or 8 AM and they wouldn't mow greens until noon. Once we got into late March, I would walk to work by 6:00 AM weekdays and 5:00 AM weekends so I could sweep the dew off the greens and open an hour later. We started getting golfers to start earlier and play more frequently. Business increased as the playing conditions improved, and the service went from awful to the best I could do.

On occasion when Art or his kids did work, it would be as little as they could get by with. Whenever I asked why something wasn't done that should have been, Art would use his favorite phrase, "It's good enough for who it's for."

Looking around the maintenance shed I came across an aerifier. Part of a regular maintenance program includes aerifying greens at least twice a year. When I asked Art how often they aerified greens, he said, "What is that?"

During that first year at Snoqualmie Falls I overstepped my bounds. The clubhouse had the kitchen at one end with the pro shop at the other. The building is about 120 feet long. The seating for the restaurant is in the middle, with a wall dividing off the pro shop. The wall had only a 4-foot opening to allow back and forth entry from restaurant to pro shop. Being the only person inside for a good portion of the time, I couldn't keep an eye on both ends. Somebody could be waiting to pay for golf while I was cooking a hamburger. They also could be stealing something without my seeing them.

I had been dealing with this problem from January through November. One of our regular players, who was a carpenter, hung out there a lot in the winter. On a rainy day in November when Bill wasn't around, I asked Joe if he could remove the wall. Sure, he said, and he proceeded to do it. He was going to come back to finish it up a couple days later.

The next day Bill showed up. Once he settled down, he realized that it was an improvement. Mainly he was pissed that I did it without asking him first. He was right, I shouldn't have done that. I guess he didn't fire me because someone would have to take over most of the hours I was working, and I had already virtually doubled his business.

To get the next season under way we had to get a replacement for Art.

Do you remember the backup catcher who was a freshman when I was a senior? He used to preach to us on the team bus, and we called him Deacon Dowd. He was the one whose hat was placed at the top of the goal post at Mount Si High, and I climbed up and got it for him. So, the Deacon, *aka* Chris Dowd, had worked on a King County maintenance crew for five years. Also, he had helped do maintenance at Si View Golf Course for several years. More importantly, he loved golf and wanted to work at a golf course.

I managed to get him and Bill together to figure out how Chris could buy out Art. Chris had a wife named Mary who could help in the restaurant.

CHAPTER 41

New Partner: The Superintendent

A fter that first year at Snoqualmie Falls GC, the rest of my years could be divided into two parts. First, the Chris and John years. Second, all the years after Chris. From 1974 to 1991 Chris and I took care of everything. The only thing Chris couldn't do was give golf lessons. The only thing I couldn't do was fix things, although I learned a bit of that. We both did maintenance work, cooked and worked in the pro shop. Chris could work for me when I took time off and I could cover for him.

As time went on and business grew, we hired people to work in maintenance and to work in the pro shop. We also hired gals to work in the restaurant. However, Chris and I were ultimately the backbone of the business.

Chris was able to start working in February, and that made my life much easier as well as making the golf course much better. We now had early morning mowing, regularly changed cups, and freshly cut fairways. Chris could also cook and got along great with the golfers. Plus, we started making improvements to the course with added sand traps and brush clearing along the edges. I actually had a "working" partner for a change.

Chris and I started having a men's night with golf starting after 3:00 PM and dinner afterward. After dinner we had card games for those who liked poker. There was even the occasional dice game. Chris and I had become a team who worked together and played together.

After several months of walking back and forth from the golf course, I did give in and buy a car. It was a 1959, ugly-green Chevy Biscayne. I bought it for $70. There is a chance that it burned more oil than gas, but it did get me back and forth to work.

Liz and I also bought an acre of property located on the hill looking over the golf course. The property cost us $6,000 and that was somehow allowed as a down payment on the house we had built. The house was a precut or pre-fab house with two storeys and three bed-rooms. It cost $22,000 and had all the room we needed plus some.

The location of the house helped keep our family together. We already had Jeff and his brother was to arrive on 7/11/1974. As with Jeff, we had no idea what gender our second child was going to be. Whatever the case, the house was less than half a mile away, and most of that was the driveway into the golf course. Starting at six years of age, they could ride their bikes there whenever they wanted to see good ol' Dad. Most of their summers were spent hanging out, playing golf, and even helping with things they could do.

I was entered to play in the Washington Open to be played at Glendale CC. My time was 8:00 AM for the first round. At 11:00 PM the night before, Liz went into labor. We packed up Jeff and a few things for Liz and headed for the Group Health Hospital in Seattle. On the way, we dropped Jeff off at the grandparents' house in Kirkland. I sat bedside with Liz until 5:00 AM with nothing happening. She and I decided that I might as well go play, since it appeared that nothing was going to happen. I had to drive to Fall City, change clothes, pick up my golf clubs, and then head back to Glendale CC in Bellevue.

I barely made my starting time. Between rushing, no sleep, and worrying about what was happening I was a wreck. I topped my drive on the first hole and it rolled into the bushes some 20 yards short of the ladies tee. After shooting in the mid-'40s for the first nine, I went into the pro shop and called the hospital. It was determined that Liz had false labor. Her father had picked her up and taken her back to Kirkland. I was emotionally drained and physically exhausted. The back nine was just as bad as the front nine. I missed the 36-hole cut af-ter the next day's round was in the upper 70's. Of course, after the first round I would have needed a 62 in the second round to make the cut.

Two weeks later the doctor decided to induce labor and get what would be Willie's life on the road. Liz had spent the two weeks in Kirkland to make things easier for the real deal. Her dad took her in for the induced labor and delivery. I headed in from Fall City in almost plenty of time.

When I walked into the hospital room, they were getting ready to take her into delivery. One of the nurses asked me if I wanted to watch. I had never heard that such a thing was ever done unless it was in a car on the way to the hospital. Liz and I hadn't discussed it or gone to classes or anything. Being a coward, I said, "No thanks."

It seemed like 10 minutes, but within an hour a nurse brought Willie out to see me. She walked up to me and handed over this little red screaming thing that looked like he was sprinkled with powdered sugar. He was born on 7/11 and weighed 7 pounds 11 ounces. Born seven/eleven, Willie was bound to be lucky. Best of all, Liz was fine as well.

Chris vs. The Bread Man

When Chris started in February 1974, his wife helped in the kitchen. Liz, although pregnant with Willie, worked a month or two. By mid-April Liz was retired and we got a neighbor girl to help out in the kitchen. In reality, most of the time Chris and I handled it ourselves.

Shortly after Liz was retired, due to the pregnancy, Chris's wife started a relationship with the Gai's Bakery bread delivery man. Chris picked up on this and soon determined when and where they would rendezvous. My first knowledge of this came one day when I was working in the pro shop and I heard the driver yelling, *"John, help me!"*

Chris was using him to destroy the railing on the small porch off the kitchen.

I will give Randy some credit though. He continued delivering to the golf course, even after Chris threw him over the meat counter one day at the local grocery store. Two county sheriffs even came by one day to explain to Chris that he had to stop doing this to Randy. Chris explained to them that he was going to kill him.

They said, "Please don't say that!"

Finally, one day Chris caught them in the Gai's truck at their hiding spot rendezvous. While his wife tried to help Randy, Chris grabbed him by his hair and delivered a good right cross to his face. The blow put Randy to the floor and left a fine pelt in Chris's hand. Randy had a wig!

Chris jumped from the truck and ran back to his car. On the way, he stopped to bury the wig in the roadside gravel.

My brother, Hiram, was kind enough to be Chris's attorney. At that point my brother was a public defender in Seattle.

Several months later, I got a call from Chris, who was at his parent's house, where he was living at this point. It was 10:00 PM and two cop cars had pulled up to their house. They were taking him to jail at the King County Courthouse in Seattle. Chris asked me to please come in and bail him out.

I went down to the clubhouse and scrounged up about a thousand bucks and then headed for Seattle. When I approached the counter to pay the bail, I was told he wasn't there. I said that I knew he was there, but they still said no. I really didn't want to walk around that part or any other part of Seattle after midnight with over a grand in my pocket. After at least two hours, they let me bail him out. They just wanted him to cool his heels for a while before they released him.

Several more months later, but before Chris's court appearance, Chris thought it would be helpful if we found Randy's wig and got it cleaned up. I said it would be ruined by now, but I decided that such a hunt would, if nothing else, be worth the laughs. So, Chris and I, along with a shovel and rake, went on the "Great Wig Hunt." It is hard to believe, but we never found it. I did however get many laughs out of this tale!

Hiram got Chris off with no jail time, but he did have to pay for a few hundred dollars' worth of dental work that Randy required.

CHAPTER 43

The Art of Cooking

The kitchen was set up with a table in the center. The stove and grill were up against the outside wall of the kitchen. The table was 3 feet from the grill. Then it was 3 feet more to the wall where the opening to the food area was located. The table was roughly 3 feet by 8 feet. Without the aid of a 4x4 block under each leg, it would have been too low. It wasn't fastened to the blocks; it just sat on top of them.

There was a cutting board in the middle of the table. All of the platters and dishes were on the left side. There were at least a dozen platters for breakfast orders. We had at least 20 regular plates for burgers and sandwiches, and more than ten bowls for soup.

On the right of the cutting board were containers of chopped lettuce, sliced tomatoes, chopped onions and pickle slices. The sauce we used for hamburgers was made with mayo, mustard and relish. It was in a big bowl on the table as well. Separate containers of the mayo, mustard and relish were there also.

One day Chris and I were working the lunch rush. Four-year-old Brenda was hanging out that day with her dad, Chris. She was playing around in the kitchen even after being told to cool it before something bad happens. Well, something bad happened when Brenda bumped the table too hard. The legs at one end fell off the 4x4 blocks. Everything, as in everything, slid in what looked like slow motion onto the floor. Close to half of the plates broke and all the goop and veggies covered the floor. Chris and I couldn't save a thing from falling.

We operated the restaurant my first 18 years at Snoqualmie Falls GC. Liz helped for one and a half seasons and Chris's wife worked half a season. Like I mentioned earlier, a neighbor girl started helping out as well. However, for the most part it was just Chris and me. Most days I took care of the pro shop and the restaurant until 11:00 AM. Chris would work outside until ten but would then come in to help in the kitchen.

I would have a hamburger cooking while getting a cart out of the shed, then collect a couple of green fees and hustle back to finish the hamburger and serve it.

After three years for me and two years for Chris, thanks to the increased business, we were able to hire more help in the restaurant, although Chris and I still handled the brunt of it, especially on the weekends.

We allowed tournament groups to bring their own food if they wanted. Some groups did, but a lot of them had us feed them. We offered cheeseburgers or a steak dinner. One tournament group of 80 players had us serve as many as any person in their group wanted. We just kept count of how many we served. Guys who normally would only eat one would eat three, because they didn't have to pay for them. Eighty guys ended up consuming about 150 burgers. I'm sure our count wasn't padded.

We had 12-oz. sirloin steaks that the people would cook themselves. Our barbecues were 55-gallon oil drums cut in half, with a metal grate that the charcoal sat on. A regular grill sat on top of that, upon which the steaks were cooked. Each dinner came with a baked potato, salad and rolls.

The dressing we served was Uncle Dan's. It was sort of like a ranch type of dressing. It came in a powder form that we mixed by the gallon with mayonnaise and, I as remember, milk. Usually, it was just Chris and I taking care of feeding 50 to 100 people, so everything was done as fast as possible. One time I was stirring the Uncle Dan's mixture rapidly with a long-handled metal spoon in a glass gallon jar. That day I couldn't find the whisk or a plastic jug. It seemed like I wasn't stirring too hard, but suddenly, a hole blew out of the side of the gallon jar that was about the size of a tennis ball. The entire mixture flew out in two bursts and hit me just below the waist. I had a huge mess, but fortunately we had more Uncle Dan's and the rest of the ingredients. We also kept more plastic jars and whisks around after that.

Weekdays I quite often made homemade soup. Sometimes I would make chicken and rice, but my favorite was what I called beef barley. I would make it with hamburger, beef flavoring, barley and whatever vegetables I threw in that day.

I enjoyed making grilled sandwiches with combinations of different things. I would add tomatoes or onions to tuna and cheese. Ham and cheese lent itself to various additions. I would even cook a hamburger patty and then make it into a grilled sandwich with cheese, onions and green peppers. At that time, I had never heard of a Philly Cheesesteak sandwich, I thought I was inventing something myself.

A good part of working in the restaurant was that Jeff and Willie would hang out in the kitchen with me when they weren't playing golf. They would try to grill something that I wouldn't eat. The only requirement was that it had to be real food, and not old or rotten. Fried lettuce with mustard and ketchup with an egg and onions is not really that bad.

Chris was better at cooking breakfast than I was, or at least faster, but I was more creative with omelets. Chris would come in with a dirty shirt from working outside and just turn the shirt inside out and start cooking. Some people think that sometimes things happen in kitchens that aren't up to health department codes or standards. I really don't know if that is true. However, I did figure out that if I dropped something on the floor while cooking, like a hamburger patty, I didn't look up to see if someone is watching. Just pick it up and put it on the bun like nothing happened. Never look guilty.

My worst experience cooking came when we were hosting a statewide public links ladies' tournament. Ladies' tournaments always must have a theme. At this time, Redmond Golf Course had closed, and their Ladies' Club chose Snoqualmie Falls Golf as their new home. This was a huge plus to our business and image. Through Chris's hard work outside and mine inside we were really growing. But, back to cooking. Sometimes I referred to myself as the PGA cook, which I'm sure attracted more customers.

The third and final day of the Hawaiian themed tournament included Hawaiian music with Hawaiian dancers. The dinner, which I got to cook, was barbequed salmon fillets. Our ladies also came up with a grass skirt that they got me to wear as well. The temperature on that sunny July day was about the same as the number of players that I had the pleasure to serve. Both were over 100.

Standing in the sun cooking over two large grills was absolutely awful. I totally hate the heat, but that was completely absurd. Adding to the fun, was barbecuing in a grass skirt. The frosting on the cake for me came after the ladies finished eating. Out came the Hawaiian dancers and I was forced into dancing with them.

Not only did I have burned arms and hands from the barbeques, but I was also on film looking like a fool dancing in a grass skirt.

Another interesting cooking experience came when we bought a machine to cook the new Canadian Jumbo Hot Dogs. Prongs that were about 5 inches long protruded out and the hot dogs were skewered onto them. The apparatus turned inside this glass box-like container and cooked the hot dogs. Buns were stored in a metal bin above them, where they stayed warm.

The first year we had these there were several players, usually men, who liked to comment on them. This machine was displayed on the counter so everyone could see them and hopefully have one.

Amongst those who enjoyed consuming, as well as commenting on the jumbo hot dogs, was a guy named Don. He often played with a couple named Jim and Joyce. Although I had never witnessed Jim at a urinal or nudist camp, apparently Don had. While sitting at a table with both Jim and Joyce, Don would say, "Hey, John, bring me one of those Jimmy Burgers."

He would then pick it up, study it, and say in the accent W.C. Fields used, "Oh, it's a Jewish one!"

Of course, Jim and Joyce would be totally embarrassed.

Don had other talents too. He could yodel, sing opera, and blow bubbles with his own saliva. After a pro-am that I had taken him to, along with my main partner Bill and a friend of Bill's, we went to a fancy restaurant in Tacoma. Don decided to start singing opera. He was spurred on by the applause he got after his first offering. The waitress asked him to stop, but he wouldn't. She threatened to get the manager, but he sang on.

At this point, I'm eating my steak as fast as I could because I knew we were going to be tossed out.

Finally, a guy came up and was virtually yelling at him to stop, but Don continued to his finish that he did with great flair right in the guy's face.

At completion, Don said in his best W.C. Field's voice, "And how can I help you, my good man?"

"YOU ARE GOING TO HAVE TO STOP YOUR SINGING!" the man screamed.

Don, still as W.C. Field: "And may I ask who you are?"

"I'M THE MANAGER!" he shouted

"Well, I guess that's good enough for me," Don replied.

To this day I don't know why we weren't kicked out, probably because the others in the restaurant had actually enjoyed his singing.

Back to the Canadian Jumbo's. We had a foursome of guys in their late 20's that would almost always get one after 9 holes. One of the four of them would say, "Hey, John, I'll take one of them *blue veiners*!"

So, this one day I spotted them coming up the 9th hole. I took one of the dogs off its prong and used a blue marker pen to draw veins on it. I then put it back on a rotating prong. When they came in, the order was placed for a blue veiner, and he got what he wanted!

I did replace it with a non-toxic one, but only after we all had a good chuckle. Even though he always kept his order the same, that was the only time that I fixed one up.

One day I came across a small electric fan. I wondered if it might be of use when I was cutting and chopping onions to help prevent my eyes from watering and stinging. I set the fan on the table so it would blow air away from me across the cutting board while I chopped away. Sure enough, it worked!

However, I found another use for the fan that was even better. Until 1981 there was a dairy farm by the golf course. Cows grazed, digested and eliminated their food less than 100 feet from the restaurant back door. At times there were a lot of flies around and some of them periodically found their way to the kitchen.

Fly spray was not allowed, nor anything else that might cause a fly to drop into the food. The one thing that was allowed was fly strips. Those were tacked to the ceiling and hung down in a spiral. They were quite sticky and whatever flew into them was stuck. I hung six of them to the kitchen ceiling, mainly over the table that had all the stuff on it.

After a week or so, many golfers who came into the kitchen noticed them.

I casually inquired to some of them, "Which strip do you think will collect the most flies?"

Of course, I would end up betting on a particular strip. Then when the bettors were not around, I would set up the fan to blow toward the strip of my choice.

Strange as it may sound, I never lost on that bet. It didn't take long before no one would bet on it anymore.

CHAPTER 44

Humphrey Joins the Club

M y next building remodel came when I had a friend wall off part of the storage room next to the kitchen to make me an office. After six or seven years at Sno Falls, I had taken over the bookkeeping part of the business, and an office made that work much easier to accomplish. Unlike my removal of a wall without permission from Bill, I got him to approve of this first.

Anyway, not too many days later, many golfers reported hearing a kitten meowing in a tree by the 5th tee. Those that saw him described him as about half grown and black in color. Later in the afternoon when business had died down, I went out in a cart to the 5th tee to investigate. I armed myself with a small bowl of tuna fish. Gradually the long-haired black kitten climbed down to see what smelled like tuna. Unlike a couple of abandoned kittens I found years later, this guy was quite tame. After a quick tuna snack, I took him back to the clubhouse with me. I decided to name him Humphrey. This was the first thing I could do to honor Senator Hubert Humphrey who had looked out for me when I was a page some 12 years before.

After closing I took Humphrey home. That would have been great, but Boom Boom didn't care to share his house with a newcomer. Moosey was more understanding, but that didn't matter. Therefore, I took Humphrey back to the course where my office was the one place he could stay overnight and not set off the alarm. See, that's why I mentioned the office.

Humphrey was lovable and became a friend with the golfers. While I did get him some cat food, he still feasted on tuna quite often.

We had a pile of towels that we intended to sell to golfers for wiping off their clubs. Humphrey claimed this pile for a bed. Basically, Humphrey did what Humphrey wanted to do.

I had a couple of shelves I had put up to display hats for sale. See, I could do something! One day I noticed this black furry thing that looked like a Russian winter hat on one of the shelves. Humphrey had somehow jumped up there and curled up to sleep with his back facing out.

One of our regular senior players asked me if we had any new hats. I said no, and then I remembered this new Russian winter hat we had gotten in.

I said, "Bob, I forgot but we did get in a couple of new winter hats. One of them is over there on that shelf."

Bob went over and touched the Humphrey hat. Humphrey bolted away, and Bob jumped. Fortunately, Bob didn't suffer a heart-a-stroke.

According to health codes, Humphrey was not allowed to be in the restaurant, let alone the kitchen. The health inspector was in the middle of inspecting the facilities one day when Humphrey strutted across the kitchen floor. Needless to say, she was slightly alarmed. She told me that I had to always keep him out of the restaurant.

I explained that I had taken him home, but we had a cat that beat him up. A couple years later that bully cat had passed away and I had taken Humphrey home again. Humphrey, having a mind of his own, walked the half mile back to the golf course by himself.

I pleaded that I had done everything I could, but the course was the only place he would stay. I explained that the only alternative would be to shoot him. I was hoping the lady had a heart.

She said, "No, don't do that, but please try to keep him out of the kitchen."

On several winter nights when we went to watch hockey games in Seattle it would be raining very hard. Back then, there was no warning system for floods in the Snoqualmie Valley. Upon arriving back home and seeing how high the river was, and it was still rising, I felt I had to go to the course to make sure Humphrey was in the building and in my office where he wouldn't set off the alarm. There was a 50-yard stretch of the golf course road that was almost three feet lower than the rest. On those nights I waded through 2 or 3 feet of water to check in on him. Every time he was safe in my office.

When I would get calls from the alarm company that the golf course alarm had gone off, I was supposed to go to the course. I was not supposed to enter the building until the police arrived. However, the alarm could have been tripped by Humphrey. If I had closed, then

I knew Humphrey was safe in my office so he couldn't have set it off. The nights I didn't close I couldn't be sure. After several false alarms we could be fined.

On one of those evenings, I got the alarm call and headed for the course as fast as I could. I entered the building and found Humphrey walking around outside my office. I put him in the office and headed for the door so I could get back to my car and look like I had waited for the cops. As I stepped out of the building, I met two police cars each with a policeman pointing a gun at me.

Some people have had loaded guns pointed at them, but I had not. It is not a good feeling. I raised my hands as instructed and answered questions. Fortunately, neither of them coughed or sneezed before they lowered their weapons.

Humphrey was my buddy and the golf course mascot for about 10 years. One night the closer didn't make sure he was inside, and he disappeared. I'm afraid the coyotes got him.

CHAPTER 45

Fixing the Driveway

The driveway to the course is about a quarter mile long. When I started there in 1972 it was all gravel. Over a 10-year span, we had it all black-topped, the final section being the lower parking lot.

Back before black top, since the drive was all gravel, we would periodically have it graded. One time after the grading we had oil sprayed on it. The layer of oil was much heavier than we ever dreamed of. Oil was dripping off the cars, over their hubcaps and spraying on the fenders. Fortunately, we had a pile of sand left over from aerifying greens. All by myself, I shoveled sand into the work cart and by hand cast it over the entire quarter mile of driveway. It took me most of a day to do it all. However, it worked fantastically well, and it kept the road in good shape for over a month. During that time, we were informed that we were too close to the river to spray with oil. The only legal substance we could put down was called pulp liquor. It cost us $500 to grade the road and spray pulp liquor on it, and that only kept the dust down for a week.

One morning a guy with a briefcase and suit coat came in and asked me who owned the road/driveway? I told him it was Willis Campbell who owned the farm next to the golf course. He asked where he could find him and I told him where his office was. Ten minutes later I got a call from Mr. Campbell and was told not to ever send anyone to his office again and that the driveway was our responsibility. At that point, I was a bit put out when Mr. Suit coat returned.

Here is how the conversation went:

Him: "I have been sitting at the top of your driveway for the last hour and I have come to the conclusion that you are in violation of Code #9.45 of the *Puget Sound Air Pollution Statutes!*"

Me: "Oh no, not #9.45. Anything but #9.45."

Him: "So you know what that is?"

Me: "F**K NO!"

Him: "I'm serious!"

Me: "Don't I look serious? So, what is #9.45?"

Him: "You are in failure to prevent the fugitive particulate matter from becoming airborne."

Me: "Oh, you mean the f**king dust, and it only took you an hour to figure that out?"

Him: "I'm serious!"

Me: "I'm serious too! So, what do you want me to do about it?"

At that point I explained to him that it cost us $500 every ten days to put something on it. I explained that the particulate matter came from the dump trucks hauling rock out of the quarry that was not ours, etc., etc., etc.

He proceeded to write out a ticket stating how we were guilty.

After I signed it, I asked him, "What would happen if we didn't pay the ticket?"

He informed me that, "We would then have to go to court."

So, then I said, "It will take weeks before we would go to court, won't it?"

He replied, "Yes."

Then I asked, "If we lose in court, we can appeal, can't we?"

He again said, "Yes."

Then I stated, "By the time that happens summer will be over, it will be raining, and there won't be any more f**king dust!"

With that he started to leave but stopped at the door to ask me what my name was. I had signed his ticket, and my handwriting may not be beautiful, but it is certainly legible.

Therefore, I replied, "I can tell you work for the government because you can't even read!"

Then he proceeded to stomp out of the building.

It turned out that there was a hearing that my boss attended. When Bill returned, he asked me, "What did you say to that guy?"

I said, "Nothing really, we just had a little chat about the driveway."

They decided we would get a fine, which was then suspended once we black-topped the first third of the driveway. We sold five memberships, each good for five years at a reduced rate to pay for the work.

A couple years later we did another third, and several years later finished it along with the lower parking lot.

CHAPTER 46

The Watering System

When I started at Snoqualmie Falls the water system amounted to one outlet per green. A quick-set coupler that was attached to a hose could be inserted into the fitting. Inside the fitting was a spring sort of thing that would release the water. At the end of the hose was a sprinkler mounted on a stand. The fitting/pipe was just below ground level so mowers couldn't hit it. When they were new, they had a cap that kept them from getting dirt, grass, or anything else that would plug them up. The course had opened in 1963 and ten years later at least half of these caps were gone.

The sprinklers were normally used from late March until mid-October. From October to March these fittings would get grown over or covered up with dirt or grass clippings. When the system had to be fired up someone had to locate these plug-in pipes.

Chris, being a hard worker, battled a bad back and on occasion had to spend days in traction. When the greens needed water, they didn't care what the status was on Chris's back. About his third year at Sno Falls, the greens were screaming for water when Chris was in traction at home. No problem, John to the rescue. This was probably about 1976.

Chris had gotten the pump set up and all the hoses out, so I just had to locate all the fittings. I think he messed up his back setting up the pump and suction line.

Of course, it was completely pitch dark when I was out trying to locate the fitting at each green. Some were easy to find, especially those that still had their caps. I knew within about a four-foot diameter where they were. Fortunately, I had watered enough times to have an idea of where they were all located.

I had found most of them and I had the sprinklers going on the front nine. My friend Stan Harris was with me. He was mainly watching and visiting. Our lighting was from the lights of the golf course pickup truck. The method of locating these outlets was me crawling around and stabbing a screwdriver into the ground hoping to hit metal.

I just couldn't find the one on number 16 green. I had been crawling, stabbing and cussing for probably 10 minutes. *Wham*—instantly muddy river water that had been rushing through at least a mile of dirty pipe at 120 pounds of pressure hit me directly in my wide-open eyes. Since my face was only a foot from the ground, it got me full force.

Thankfully Stan was with me since I was out of commission. He got me loaded up in the truck and back to the clubhouse. I couldn't see anything. He took me to the kitchen sink where there was a hose with a spray handle. After several minutes of Stan washing out my eyes while I held my eyelids open, I was able to see a little bit. Another several minutes with me bent backwards over the sink with water running into both eyes helped improve my vision a bit more.

Doctor Stan then fixed us each a couple of Canadian whiskey cure-alls before we went back out to finish the job.

The screwdriver had gone directly into the opening and had hit the spring device just right to release the water. I couldn't have done that in the daylight, even if I had been trying to.

As time and money allowed, we were to put in an automatic sprinkler system in two stages. The first took care of the greens and tees, the second watered the fairways.

CHAPTER 47

The River Battle

The word I hate the most starts with an "F". In the singular form it has five letters, and the plural form has six. The word is FLOOD!

My first flood experience took place in 1959. For us to get from our home in North Bend to the print shop in Snoqualmie, our shop foreman took us part way in his fishing boat. My brother Hiram and I then went around parts of Snoqualmie in a rowboat to take pictures for the paper.

After that flood, King County started a flood control department. Their first order of business was to build dikes along the tributary branches of the Snoqualmie River where they went through North Bend. No thought or care went into what all of that water was going to do to everything and everyone downstream from there. Consequently, in future floods the town of Snoqualmie flooded worse, as well as the towns and everyone else living below Snoqualmie Falls.

At this point in my life, I would advise against buying and/or building anything on a river. Unless you want to buy a beautiful riverfront golf course from me for a fortune. It comes with a lot of stories and history at no extra charge. When I bought into Snoqualmie Falls GC in 1972, I didn't give flooding a great deal of thought. I was told that the clubhouse floor was built up three feet higher than any flood had ever reached.

My first flood at Snoqualmie Falls GC came in 1978. While we have had much more damaging floods since, I was amazed at how much damage that flood did. The fourth green, which was then located within 75 feet of the river, was destroyed. The sod was peeled off it and distributed in chunks almost all the way to the clubhouse a mile away. We gathered the chunks up and laid them back like a jigsaw puzzle. There was sand and silt distributed over close to half of the greens.

Chris and I were shoveling off the practice green when Warren showed up. Warren Childers was the guy who had signed up Gary

Barter and me to work on the railroad in the winter of 1967. Since that time, he had retired.

Warren disappeared into our maintenance shop area and 10 minutes later came back with a squeegee he made from two by fours. It had about a five-foot handle and a three-foot blade, both 2x4s. It was heavy and awkward, but it scraped mud off faster than a shovel did. Chris then hooked up the pump and with added water it really worked OK. For subsequent floods we bought squeegees that had regular handles and about 4-foot rubber blades.

That flood took us less than a month to get the course playable again. Even back then, we got some volunteer help from golfers who considered Snoqualmie Falls their home away from home.

Warren was a good friend. He wasn't a very good golfer, but he did play a bit. Most days he would just hang out and visit. I used to have Warren go to the bank for me to take deposits and get me change. That was the good old days before credit cards. To me, credit cards are the worst thing ever invented, yes, even worse than video games. Besides causing a recession that bordered on another great depression, they cost business owners thousands and thousands of dollars. Banks thrive on the weakness of people to spend well beyond their means.

Anyway, enough of that. Warren would also go to the Post Office for me. He even mowed fairways a few times, until he caught one of the gangs on a metal fence post. The post got bent into an L-shape, the gang mower wheel got damaged, and Warren was almost thrown off the tractor. Fortunately, he wasn't hurt.

One day Warren headed for the bank with four deposits, each deposit for a different day's business. At that time a deposit for a weekend day would typically have about $3,000 in cash, $200 in checks, and NO credit cards. Between the four deposit bags, Warren had at least $10,000 in cash. About 30 minutes after Warren left, a guy came into the pro shop carrying the four deposit bags. He had found them on the tank cover of one of the toilets in the men's room. All of the money was still in the bags. The finder was thankfully one of our regulars. Warren had used the toilet and left, forgetting what he was sent to do. That was his last banking job for me.

Warren still went to the Post Office for me, but not for very long. One day a resident of Fall City brought me a handful of mail that he

The clubhouse is in the background. The golf course has switched from "waterfront" (top photo) to "river bottom" (lower photo).

found on a sidewalk in town. They were bills and things I had sent with Warren to mail. Somehow, he dropped them on the sidewalk before he could mail them. Then when I went to the Post Office, he had failed to pick up our mail as well.

Top photo: Baxter and I check out the 5th green after flood waters recede.
Middle: damage to the 6th tee.
Bottom: damage to the 4th green
Not pictured are fairways and tees that had 6 inches to 2 feet of sand and silt over them.

I had to get my PO Box key back, which I hated to do to him. It turned out that the reason he was failing at his regular tasks—that he did out of kindness to make my job easier—was due to the fact that he was starting to suffer from Alzheimer's disease. Fortunately, he still remained my friend and he did continue to hang out at Sno Falls, until he wasn't able to drive. Warren was a really great guy!

But, back to the "F" word. The first truly devastating flood hit us in 1990. Since the flood in 1978 we had several similar high-water levels, but we found out in 1990 that they were nothing by comparison. By 1990 we had built a new #4 green over 75 yards away from the river. The 4th hole remained the same length as it had been, but moving the green gave us space to build a new 5th Tee. This lengthened the 5th hole from 425 yards to over 500 yards.

The 1990 flood waters tried to make a new river channel through the golf course that took out the front part of the new 5th tee. It also created a new bay that was 15 feet deep, over 50 feet wide, and extended 100 yards into the course from the former riverbank across the 5th tee, the 4th fairway, and partially into the 8th hole.

Fortunately, one of our regular Sunday morning players worked for the Army Corps of Engineers. He gave us the green light to rebuild the riverbank. It took close to 200 dump truck loads of large rock to build it back up. Then we had to plow up parts of the 4th, 5th and 8th holes to fill in the bay.

All the material that the river dug out to leave the bay got washed over the 17th, 18th, 9th and 1st fairways. It also covered the 1st and 9th greens. Mud was over 2 feet thick on the 4th and 9th fairways. We had to grade and seed both fairways.

The squeegees also came in handy because every green had some silt and/or sand on them. In fact, some greens needed shoveling first, because they had over a foot of material on them.

This flood closed us for over three months and the course wasn't back to normal for over a year. We probably never would have made it through and survived if it weren't for our loyal golfers. Every weekend we would have 20 to 30 guys and gals show up with their own rakes and shovels to help. Most weekdays there would be close to 10 volunteers. It wasn't just the physical help that made us survive; it was the moral support as well. I would always feed them and give them a beer, but that was only a token of what I owed them. Of course, I did and do give them my love.

There have been a number of these volunteers who have helped flood after flood. I would list them, but there are too many for my small brain to remember. Plus, I would hate to have someone feel unappreciated because I accidentally left them off the list. Mike Hovey, the Men's Club president, deserves to be a star. Not only is he always there to help, but he helps organize work parties and get more people there to help.

However, there is a superstar. Joe Loranger is the heart and soul of the volunteer squad. Joe calls guys to get them to show up. Joe brings a dump truck and a backhoe and leaves them until the entire cleanup is done. Joe, the owner/operator of Loranger Automotive Repair, also helps repair any equipment that either broke down or got caught in the flood. Plus, at least every other weekend during the cleanup Joe will bring food he has prepared to feed all the volunteers. All the while, Joe is digging in physically to do everything he can to get us back open. Without him I don't think we could have made it through several of the floods.

By the way, the clubhouse that was built 3 feet higher than any historical high-water level, got water in it. We had to repair some walls and replace all flooring and carpet.

Oh yes, North Bend had virtually no water—their flood control had screwed everyone downriver.

The town of Snoqualmie got blasted badly by the 1990 flood along with us, and that started to set the stage for more unfair and misguided projects to reduce flooding. In November of 1995 and then again in January of 1996 there were two more major floods. They weren't as bad as in 1990, but somewhat close. What made them really bad was they were like a one-two punch. When we were almost ready to open after the first flood, then we got hit with the second. The town of Snoqualmie got hit by both of these as well, so something had to be done.

Unfortunately for everyone below the Falls, they had more tricks up their sleeve.

At this point, I guess the powers that be realized that diking was not the answer. The next trick was to reduce restriction points on the river to open the channel, so that water could escape Snoqualmie faster. I guess the powers weren't convinced yet that pushing more water out of the upper valley and into the lower valley would create a downstream flooding problem on another level. They needed more proof and they got it.

In reality, they probably weren't that incompetent, although that is sadly possible. The more likely answer is that they were criminally negligent, and there is no doubt that they just didn't care about the lower valley. Their logic was, sure the lower valley would suffer, but there was more money in North Bend and Snoqualmie pulling their strings. The lower valley was just farming, and a couple of bergs named Fall City and Carnation. Well, there was Duval and others too, but they were smaller yet and really didn't matter.

So, two river widening projects later, one at the crest of Snoqualmie Falls itself, plus the lowering of the water retention dam at the top of the falls, and now the lower valley was (and still is) set up for disaster any time it rains hard or snow melts. On the bright side, North Bend still doesn't flood, and Snoqualmie has seen a nice reduction of their flood levels.

It took the hard work of the Army Corps of Engineers partnering with King County Flood Control, the town of Snoqualmie, and Puget Power to make it all happen. Their projects did an excellent job of dumping the water over the falls faster so that the lower valley has less time to prepare and far higher water levels to deal with.

In 2006 we got hit by our highest water level yet. The water got into the clubhouse for the first time since 1990. The actual upstream flow of water going through North Bend was less than it was in 1990. However, thanks to their river projects, the flow of water through the lower valley was the highest yet, and the flow through Snoqualmie was much lower. Our damage was significant. Fortunately, I got lots of help from our devoted family of golfers.

My son Jeff, who was working full time for me as a golf pro himself, warned us that these projects and this flood were an indication that flooding was probably going to be even worse. Our superintendent at the time told Jeff he didn't know what he was talking about and that he shouldn't be so negative. Unfortunately, Jeff was just being realistic and did know what was going on because 2009 brought the biggest flood we have ever had by a landslide.

The water was over a foot deep in the clubhouse and nothing on the course was spared. Most of the building had to be repaired. Many greens, tees and fairways had the turf torn up. Sand and silt covered almost every square inch of the property in depths up to 4 feet deep in places.

Besides a major overhaul of the building, this flood took weeks of bulldozers and dump trucks moving the deep debris off the course. It took months of our loyal golfing family members and staff working daylight to dark 7 days a week. I can't even imagine the number of total work hours that went into cleaning it up. We were closed for over four months before we got 9 holes open. A few more weeks and we opened 18 holes.

Sadly, the only normal looking part when we opened was the cup the ball fell into at the end of each hole. We gave out pieces of Astroturf for golfers to hit off of while they played. Not surprisingly, we had about 20% of our normal business that summer and we had to borrow money to stay afloat. It was well over a year before the golf course started to look like a golf course again. However, with the help of so many amazing people and an incredible amount of work we once again survived.

Flood control is a joke. Flood watch would be closer to the truth. Actually, they do give flood warnings. We are notified and given access by computer to information about how bad the high water is going to be. Plus, I obviously have to admit that the upper valley has received flood control, but it has been at the expense of the lower valley.

After one of the bad floods, King County even set up a place where people could bring flood-damaged items they needed to throw away. So, they screwed the lower valley, they told us when we would be getting screwed, how bad we would get screwed, and where we could dump the resulting ruined items once we had been screwed.

I also learned at one of the meetings why the only real solution for the whole valley had never been approved. After the flood of 1959 when flood control got started, there was a discussion about putting a dam on the Middle Fork east of North Bend. A dam there would have no negative effects on fish migration and could even be used to keep water levels higher, cooler, and better oxygenated year-round for the fish. Plus, fish tend to struggle migrating up the 278-foot Snoqualmie Falls.

It turned out that the powers-that-be actually thought that the building of a dam would cause the farms to go away in the lower valley. They reasoned that if those properties didn't flood, they would be developed into houses and industry. The problem is, because of the flooding most of the farming in the lower valley has gone away. With a dam, flooding could have been eliminated or reduced, but with their other projects we now have more flooding in both frequency and severity. There could have been a dam that either only reduced flooding, or, if it was designed to eliminate flooding, they could have been smart enough to zone the lower valley as agriculture only.

The last couple of years we have had several floods of significant height, but the amount of silt and sand has diminished. It is still somewhat bad, but we're surviving.

Another problem is that dredging has not been allowed for more than 50 years. I don't know exactly how long, but I have been at Sno Falls Golf for 50 years and there has been no dredging. Islands have formed in the river on both sides of the course. A sea plane used to land and take off by the clubhouse. Now there is an island there large enough to build houses on, and rafters have to walk across it to get to water deep enough to float on an inner tube in the summer.

Years ago, when dredging was allowed, river boats (paddle wheelers!) would come up to Snoqualmie Falls. On top of that, there were far more fish spawning and coming up the river to spawn.

The department of ecology came to visit me one day because a fisherman turned us in for having a one-inch drain pipe into the river. What we found when we went to the site was a piece of rebar stuck in the bank that we didn't put there. At the same time, there is a culvert pipe on the opposite riverbank facing us that is over 10 feet wide. It is carrying the run-off from Snoqualmie Ridge, which was developed by Weyerhaeuser. When I questioned them about it, I was told that it is only used during extremely rainy conditions.

I said, you mean like the conditions that flood us and that this run-off 10-foot wide drain pipe is adding more water to? That made it better?!

Basically, if Snoqualmie Falls Golf had big money, we could pour anything in the river. Maybe not anything, but certainly as much water as we wished.

CHAPTER 48

Keeping the Grass Green

Before we could build grass tees and change the design of several holes, we needed to install a new irrigation system. At this point we only had one lousy outlet per green.

When Chris joined me at Snoqualmie Falls, he had been a road crew grass cutter for King County. He quickly picked up knowledge in golf course maintenance. He decided to take on the task of installing a system that would water 19 greens and at least 18 tee boxes. We didn't have the money to install fairway watering, but what we did install had to be adaptable to future fairway irrigation. It needed to have a large enough main line and a strong enough pump to later handle everything.

We couldn't afford to have the system installed, so we had to buy all the pipes, joints, heads, wiring, glue and tape to do it ourselves. Oh yes, and buy and set up the pump, suction line, and electronic operating station. All Chris had were written instructions and an old ditch witch that a friend had loaned us.

This would have been about 1979, but even back then we had a few volunteer helpers. Of course, I helped too, but I didn't volunteer. Chris led the troops and in about six weeks he had the system ready to fire off.

He pushed a few buttons on the control panel and we heard the pump start up. A minute or so later, once the pipes filled up with water, we saw the three sprinkler heads around #1 green start sprinkling. Farther down the course we saw the heads on #2 fire up. Then we heard a loud bang coming from the pump station and watched all the sprinklers stop sprinkling.

We ran down to the pump station to see what had happened. The pump had blown back off the slab and flown over 6 feet, almost landing in the river. Chris called the outfit that we had bought everything from to find out what went wrong. In the installation instructions they failed to mention that the pump had to be bolted down to an immovable object or the back pressure would do exactly what it did. That was sure nice to know, but why wasn't it in the instructions?

We proceeded to spend a week pouring concrete to make a rock-solid foundation for the pump. Large bolts were built into the concrete to fasten the pump to. Concrete was placed around the pipe leading through the ground and out onto the course to feed the 6-inch main line.

Once again Chris fired up the system and we watched as sprinklers started sprinkling. After about five minutes of success, it looked like "Old Faithful" moved from Yellowstone Park to behind our 9th green. Chris ran to the control panel and shut down the pump.

Chris called again and they told him, "You have to back-block all 90-degree elbows and should do the same on any 45-degree elbows as well."

Behind the 9th green was the first 90-degree elbow. Once again, there was nothing in the instructions about this.

Over the next few days, Chris dug up and back-blocked all the 90 and 45 degree couplings on the course. The next time we fired it up, it went well and we now had a system that could, with the punch of a few buttons, properly water greens and the tees we were going to start building.

CHAPTER 49

Legendary Laurie

There was a guy who guided us when we decided to install the irrigation. He is the guy that insisted on the 6-inch main line to accommodate fairway watering later. This guy's name was Laurie Evans. Laurie owned a number of things including Evans Construction Company, Bellevue Bulldozing, Skate King and Evans Plaza. I'm sure there were other entities as well. He had also built Glendale Country Club and I believe Bellevue Municipal Golf Course.

Laurie had started before the depression selling *The Star* newspaper in Seattle. Somehow, he worked his way into having a dump truck and then a caterpillar tractor. At times during the depression people couldn't pay him for his work. Some of these people would sign over a small portion of their property to Laurie as payment. Most of these properties were in what is now called Bellevue, WA. Obviously, he was hard working and shrewd, and it all worked out for him.

The first time I met Laurie was at Mount Si Golf Course in 1964. I had a match against a buddy of his named Bruce Watson. Bruce had Laurie join us and for me it was quite an experience. Laurie didn't let my golf swing interfere with his talking. In fact, Laurie could time tossing beer bottles into the metal garbage cans in the middle of my swing too. Despite his efforts, I still won the match.

Over the next seven years while I worked part-time at Mount Si G.C., I would see him on occasion, but I don't remember playing with him again. Then, after a couple years at Snoqualmie Falls Golf, Laurie started playing with an early Sunday morning group we called "The Barbers". The group had started with Norm and Ward Russell, who had a barber shop in Bellevue. Another member of the group was Dick Berg. Dick was the Army Corps of Engineers guy that saved our butts after the 1990 flood.

Anyway, Laurie guided us on the irrigation system and then

brought in equipment to move dirt. He built all the elevated tees over time, and we smoothed them out ourselves.

He shaped a new green for us on #4 and later dug out and created ponds on #13 and #15. He did these projects over a 5-year period and didn't charge us a fourth of what it was worth.

We also had Evans Construction do a remodel of our clubhouse that both improved the layout and best of all added a heating and air conditioning unit. Before that the open beamed building would get extremely hot and hold the heat overnight in the summer. The building had no air circulation either, so it would be unbearable on hot days. Plus, if it was 85 degrees at night when I closed, it would only drop to 84 degrees by the time I opened. I don't think we got a hometown discount on the remodel, but it was a good deal, and they did a good job.

I played golf with Laurie occasionally, but not much, because I didn't have time to play very often. During the Chris years at Snoqualmie Falls, both Chris and I were working most of the time.

Laurie did a lot of things for me over the years. I was working one fall afternoon when Laurie drove in with his Lincoln Continental. He came into the pro shop and announced, "Hey, kid, you and your wife are going to Sun Valley next week and staying in my condominium. I already cleared it with Porter, and Chris is going to cover for you."

Then he threw his car keys on the counter and said, "And you're taking my f**king car and just shut up, because you're going!" Laurie dressed, looked, and acted like a bulldozer operator.

Liz and I went on the trip and had a great week.

Another time Laurie came in about a week before Christmas and gave me $200. He said, "Take this, kid, and get something for your wife and kids for Christmas, and shut up about it, I don't want to listen to your crap!"

Laurie also had a house in Phoenix on a golf course. I went there four years in a row in the spring. Two of those times, Laurie paid for my flights. Each time there were two others, so we had a foursome for golf. I still don't know how Sno Falls survived without Chris or me there, but we both went at the same time once.

Laurie absolutely loved to heckle me on the golf course. He loved to get me pissed off and he was quite good at it. The year Chris and I went together to Phoenix, we were joined by Ward Russell, one of the barbers. We had played a couple of rounds in the Phoenix area and then were going to drive over to San Diego to play Torrey Pines. We left Phoenix at 2:00 AM in order to arrive at Torrey Pines early enough to get a good tee time. While we were driving, it rained 4 inches in San Diego. Upon arrival, we discovered that every golf course was closed that day due to the rain.

Laurie suggested that we drive to Borrego Springs and play, so that's what we did. We played an old course named DeAnza Country Club, and it was beautiful as well as fun to play. The next day we played a new resort course named Rams Hill GC that was beautiful. At this point I had taken three days of Laurie's heckling and I couldn't take much more.

Since Laurie had played the course before, he would give us directions on where to hit for blind shots. I think it was about the fifth hole that was a long par 5 that went uphill and then dog-legged back downhill. I had hit my drive into a perfect position to be able to get home on my second shot. However, since I couldn't actually see where the green was, I asked Laurie where I should aim this blind shot to the green.

He gave me a target that was in the background well behind the green to hit towards. I hit the shot exactly in the direction that Laurie had pointed to.

He started laughing and I said, "What's so funny?"

He said, "You are screwed, you're in that deep sand trap by the green."

"But that's where you told me to hit!" I said.

"I know," he replied.

Not only was my ball in the trap, but I was up against the back side of it, and I couldn't hit the ball anywhere but sideways just to dislodge it. Therefore, it took me two shots to get out and I was livid! He was yakking at me that it was a poor showing for a golf pro and that I should be ashamed of calling myself a pro (which I never did).

Anyways, I finally snapped. I was standing close to him while holding my sand wedge like a baseball bat. I truly came within a split second of hitting him in the head with it. His eyes got as big as saucers when he saw I was teetering on nailing him. I turned and threw my club against the trunk of a palm tree that was ten feet away. The shaft of my club got bent slightly, but at least I didn't kill him in a fit of rage.

By the end of the round, we were speaking and by dinner we were even friendly. After that, Laurie would occasionally kid me a bit while playing golf, but he would never heckle me again.

In the years that followed I took Laurie to pro-ams and played with him other times for fun. When my son Jeff, who was born the day after I signed to buy in at Sno Falls, became a PGA professional he would take Laurie to pro-ams too. There were a couple pro-ams where Jeff had both his younger brother Willie and Laurie on his team. Laurie always loved to bother his playing partners, even if they were on the same team. At one of the pro-ams with Jeff and Willie, Laurie kept rattling the change in his pockets to interfere with the concentration of the other players on the team.

After Willie was sick of hearing it for a number of holes, he asked Laurie while he set up and hit, "Can I help you find whatever it is you are looking for in your pockets?"

Apparently, he finished his question at impact and the golf ball sailed off into the bushes to the right of the fairway. Laurie heard him and chuckled. He was probably both happy that his technique bothered Willie and amused at how Willie demonstrated it while in the actual process of trying to hit his drive.

Jeff also told me how Laurie would constantly say, "I'll tell you one thing!" before every story, anecdote and piece of advice he would share with them. It was all they could do to keep from telling him to stop saying, "I'll tell you one thing" when he was actually going to tell them about a hundred things.

When Laurie was down to his last few days, he was in a hospice in Bellevue, Washington. At this point he was in his mid-nineties. I called him and talked briefly, but he said he didn't want visitors. Two days later, Liz and I were going to drive to our vacation/retirement home in Ocean Shores. I decided to stop by and see Laurie on the way.

Liz dropped me off and went to do a few errands while I visited. I went up to his room and his son Len met me at the door. He said that Laurie had been asleep for the last two days and had talked to no one. I asked if I could go in and say goodbye to him, even if he couldn't hear me.

I leaned over the bed and said, "Laurie, this is John Groshell. I just wanted to thank you for all the things you have done for me."

He blinked a couple of times, then opened his eyes and said, "Groshell, you son of a bitch, I told you I didn't want any visitors! But since you are here, help me sit up so we can talk."

Len and I got him sitting up with his legs hanging over the side of the bed and his tray table in front of him. We talked for at least 20 minutes about the golf course and people we both knew. I thanked him for things he had done for me. We kidded about a lot of things we had done together. But his main message was, "Groshell, you could have been the best player I ever knew if you had your head on straight!"

After about 20 minutes he said, "I'm tired, help me get laid down here and get the hell out of here."

Len followed me out and said, "Dad hasn't talked to anybody in two days. I don't know what you ever did, but that was amazing!"

Laurie passed away the next day without waking up and talking to anybody again.

I think Laurie identified with me. While I certainly never succeeded financially like he did, I did do alright by working hard and we had both basically started with nothing.

CHAPTER 50

Tough J.K. Moore

A round 1980, Jack Moore came into the picture at Sno Falls. He was the superintendent at Tall Chief Golf Course. Tall Chief was a 12-hole course for the last 10 to 15 years before it closed, about five miles away from Sno Falls GC. However, when Jack was the superintendent, it was an 18-hole course with 6 holes on the side of a steep hill. Jack, who preferred to be called J.K., loved to hang out at Sno Falls and drink beer, B.S., and play cards when there was someone to play with.

When Jack was growing up, his father wanted to make him tough. He would bring home guys from the tavern and make Jack fight them in the backyard. Apparently, it worked, because Jack went on to graduate from Montana State, where he was the starting quarterback. He was also the starting right fielder on the baseball team. Upon graduation, he went to work for Weyerhaeuser. Most of his time there, he was a timber cruiser. From a plane he could look down and estimate the board feet of timber and the type of trees below. Jack was a very talented man, but after a few years Jack and Weyerhaeuser parted ways.

J.K./Jack wanted to help Chris and me anyway he could. One day I ventured out into our shop and saw something I will never forget. Chris and Jack had a hand mower upside down. They were trying to take the blade off of it. Jack was holding a big wrench that was on the bolt holding the blade on the mower. Chris had a large hammer that he was going to hit the wrench with. On the third or fourth blow his aim was off and he hit Jack in the back of the hand. It sounded like when Mom pounded veal to make wiener schnitzel. *"SPLAT!"*

It hurt me just watching it, but Jack didn't even let go of the wrench. All he said was, "Ooooooooooh, Chris, if I can take one more of those, I think we'll have it!"

Jack wanted to meet my father. My father also wanted firewood. So being the helpful guy Jack was, he cut down a tree and cut it into chunks, which I then split with a splitting maul. We loaded up the wood in my pickup along with my sons Jeff and Willie. At this time, Jeff was five and Willie was three years old. This meant my dad was getting firewood and a visit from his son and two grandsons, plus a guy who wanted to meet him and have a drink with him. My pickup was a 1968 Chevy ¾ ton. This was well before 4-door pickup trucks or even crew cabs. I was driving, Jeff was in the middle, and Jack was holding Willie on his lap on the passenger side.

By the time we headed for Seattle 30 miles away, Jack had already consumed quite a few beers. Regardless, he brought along a fifth of McNaughton's to share with my dad. Jack's connection to my dad was that my dad had grown up in Montana and Jack had gone to school there. He brought McNaughton's because I had told him that was what Dad used to drink. At this point Dad didn't really drink anymore.

Anyways, we got the wood unloaded and stacked in Dad's basement. Then we sat down for a fairly long visit. Jack got Dad to have one drink, I had a couple drinks, and Jack polished off the bottle.

On the drive back, Jack talked some, but by the time I got back to his house he had fallen asleep. It was after 7:00 PM, so that was to be expected. Jeff and Willie were both asleep as well. I should have gotten out of the truck and gone around to Jack's side and lifted Willie out, but I didn't think fast enough. Jack opened the door and simply tipped over and fell out. He landed on the top of his head in the gravel. By some miracle Willie landed on Jack and wasn't hurt a bit. Willie could have been crushed. Jack was picking gravel out of the top of his head for weeks.

Jack also liked to make bets and he would try to stack them in his favor. Plus, he was a good card player. He could be so drunk that he hardly knew his own name, but he would know every card that had been played.

One winter, when things were quiet, I decided to clean up and paint all our benches for our tee boxes. Chris had made them years earlier out of 2x4s and 4x4s and they were heavy. There were 18 of them, since we only had one set of tee boxes at that time.

Chris and I hauled them all in and put them on the deck out of the rain. Each bench had to be sanded and then painted twice. First with a primer coat and second with a finish coat. I decided I would do at least one thing a day. I would sand one, primer one, or finish coat one. Of course, I was still collecting green fees and cooking hamburgers.

Jack would drop by every day and want me to play cards with him. Most days I couldn't because I was busy with normal work or working on the benches. When I was about halfway through my duty painting the benches Jack asked, "When are you going to be done with those F–ing benches?"

I said, "I should be done by March 1st."

He said, "I'll bet you a half gallon of McNaughton's you won't."

I said, "OK, you're on."

Early in February, I was getting close to completion. Jack was badgering me about when I would be done, because he wanted me available to play cards with him. We agreed to move the deadline for the bet up to Valentine's Day, February 14th.

About a week before Valentine's Day, I went to Jack's house to borrow a ladder. There in his garage was a partially hidden unpainted bench. I took the ladder and left the bench without saying a word about it.

On February 11th I had finished every bench at the golf course. Knowing that Jack was at work, I loaded up a finished bench and took it to Jack's garage, so I could switch it with the unpainted one. The day before Valentine's Day I was finishing the final coat on that bench when Jack dropped by.

He said, "So is that the last bench?"

I said, "As far as I know, I've done all of the benches that are here."

The next day he came barreling down the driveway with the painted bench in the back of his pickup truck. He drove straight to the 2nd tee box, where he threw the bench out. Then he stopped at the pro shop on his way back through and came inside to say, "You son of a bitch!"

Jack went on to become the superintendent at Mount Si Golf Course. There he did a great job of making the course beautiful. Jack also spent the rest of his life helping people whenever he could.

CHAPTER 51

A Bad Bet

At the point I had been at Sno Falls for about eight years, we had a couple gals that helped in the kitchen. We also had a couple of guys who helped Chris outside as well as two other young guys to help out wherever needed. One youngster was Karl Albrecht, who was the nephew of Karl Albrecht, the guy I had coached basketball with at Tolt High School. Karl, age 17, mowed fairways and did various other jobs. The other young guy was Gil Shaw. He was 14 years old, and he washed carts as well as other duties we would assign him.

One duty I assigned Gil occurred when we were out golfing. I had him climb a tree on #15 to retrieve a club. The club had been thrown by Forbes Baker, who was a regular player and the Men's Club president at Sno Falls GC.

Forbes was notorious for having temper tantrums and throwing clubs. On a number of occasions, I had told him that he should knock it off or nobody would want to golf with him, but he kept on doing it anyway.

Forbes bought a new set of Titleist irons from me. They were the top-of-the-line pro shop model irons. He had used them about a month when he came to me and admitted that he threw his pitching wedge into a tree on #15. He told me this so if anybody turned it in, I would know it was his. I said fine and got him to tell me which tree it was stuck in. So, obviously that was the club I had Gil recover from the tree.

I then swore Gil and my other playing partners Karl and Jack to secrecy, and I hid the club in my office. The next time Forbes played he saw that the club was no longer in the tree. When he finished the round, he asked if his club had been turned in and I said no. Technically I wasn't lying, it hadn't been turned in. Gil had helped me get it.

I did tell him that sometimes a person will find a club and intend to turn it in, but then forget to do so by the time they finish their round.

This was also true, but obviously not the case this time. I then assured him that if it got turned in; I would give it to him.

After over a month, I asked him if he wanted me to order him a new pitching wedge to match his set. He said yes and I ordered him his replacement. When it came in, I sold it to him at a slightly reduced rate.

I then waited at least another month before I gave him his original pitching wedge that Gil had retrieved from the tree for me. I told him that a guy had picked it up almost two months before and had forgotten to turn it in and he hadn't been back to play Sno Falls until now. I can't claim that wasn't a lie.

I kept telling myself that I did this to get him to stop throwing clubs. He didn't totally quit, but he did cut back on his frequency of club throwing. Beneath the surface, I think I did it to be mean, because I thought he deserved it.

Anyways, Jack and I would play golf with Karl and Gil at least once a week. Both Karl and Gil were about 10 handicappers. Jack was about a 17 and I played to about a 4, so the matches were even. We usually played a game called bridge where one team bid a number that would be the total of both players' scores on the hole. The other team would then have to either bid a lower score or say, "I doubt it." The team that won the bid would have to match their bid or lose the hole.

Karl and Gil had extra pressure on them because Jack would constantly make side bets with them, always betting they could or couldn't do something. He'd bet, "I bet you can't hit the green from here," or "I bet you miss this putt," or "I bet you can't chip it within 10 feet."

The bets were usually for dimes, so it wasn't the money, but the idea of winning. For Gil and Karl, there was nothing they wanted more than to beat Jack.

One night I was working in the clubhouse tending both the pro shop and the restaurant. It was late enough that most of the business at this point was selling beer in the restaurant, and there was hardly any of that either.

Uncle Karl was there hanging out and so were the kids, Karl and Gil. A guy came in and got a beer and a polish sausage. Using a fork, I took the sausage out of the jar, placed it in a napkin, and handed it to the guy. After he paid and left, I noticed that the jar had no more sausages, only the brine remained.

Sometimes I don't know why I do what I do. Instead of dumping the brine out in the sink and throwing the jar away, I poured the brine into a 16-ounce cup. Without saying anything about it, I just set it on the back counter. After about five minutes of shooting the breeze, young Karl asked why I saved the brine instead of dumping it.

I replied, "I've always wondered if a guy could drink that stuff? After all, the polish sausages are good, why wouldn't it be?"

The four of us discussed this for a while. Finally, it was decided that we could make a bet on whether someone could drink it or not. Before such a bet was made, whoever was going to do it would have to pass a practice session. Uncle Karl came up with the idea that either nephew Karl or Gil would bet Jack that they could drink it. I said that whichever one of them wanted to do it, I would back them so they couldn't lose anything, only win.

We decided to make the bet $50. If whoever did it won, they would get $50 from Jack, if they failed I would pay Jack $50. It was agreed that the person would have to drink the full cup in five minutes. He would then have to keep it down for another five minutes.

Nephew Karl jumped at the chance. Throughout the entire discussion period of approximately 30 minutes, Gil had looked at Uncle Karl and me like we were a couple of jerks. While Gil was only 14, he was more streetwise than 17-year-old Karl. At this point, Karl was anxious to get started with the trial run, but Uncle Karl and I stalled him. Uncle Karl, being a basketball coach, was preaching guts and winning attitude. I was explaining that he should hit it hard out of the gate and then just coast in. He was about to start when I advised that it would be better to do this out on the deck where there was fresh air. In case of an eruption, I didn't want to do the cleanup.

Finally, we got him outside and started the countdown like he was an astronaut. 4 - 3 - 2 - 1 *GO!*

Karl took my advice and attacked. He got down more than half before he took a break. His face was getting red, and he started sweating. He then started sipping, sip-sip-sip, before he suddenly started projectile puking. After a minute or so of this he was empty. He ran down to the bathroom and put his head in the sink letting cold water run over his head. He also drank a lot of cold water.

After 10 minutes of that he came back to the lunch counter where

Gil, Uncle Karl and I were gathered. Gil had been telling us what jerks we were before Karl came back. Even so, the first thing Uncle Karl said to his nephew was, "You didn't even try, you were just sip-sip-sip. You didn't even have your elbow up!"

Young Karl replied, "I did try, I DID!"

I said, "I think you can do it; you just need to practice. I'll save the brine in the future and when you come in from mowing you can just drink a little bit each day. You probably will get where you like it."

Karl said, "Yes, I think I can."

Fortunately, he never did try it again. There weren't any ill side effects from the brine either. Gil went on to become a jet plane mechanic. Karl became an accomplished musician, specializing in the viola. He played it as a member of the Los Angeles Philharmonic Orchestra, and he also gives lessons for all the string instruments. Fortunately, his uncle and I only caused him temporary discomfort, not permanent damage.

In case readers think I am a heartless bastard, I once did something nice for a young kid...

About 20 years ago we were in the market for new tee signs on the golf course. Jerry Baker from Missoula, MT sold us on Jerry Baker signs he made out of cedar with a routed-out design of each hole and all the needed information.

The signs cost us nothing as he got businesses to pay to have their names hanging below them for advertising. Jerry and his wife, Bernice, parked their trailer in our lower lot and plugged in to our electricity while they canvassed businesses for advertising. They spent the better part of a summer doing this.

During the summer I got to meet their adult sons Mark and Doug. For a couple weeks their grandson Brandon was there as well.

Brandon was a 12-year-old and was a burn victim from a boating accident when he was about 8. He had suffered through many skin grafting operations.

I had four tickets for an upcoming Seattle Mariners game, so I invited Doug, Mark and Brandon to go with me

The morning of the game I got an idea to get the Mariner Moose (the team Mascot) to come up and visit Brandon. I remembered that one of my former 8th grade students worked in the Mariner ticket office. Lyla and Twyla Smith were twins and both in my class. I'm pretty sure it was Lyla who worked for the Mariners.

So, I called up the ticket office and got a hold of Lyla and made my request. She said she would check in to the possibility. A couple of hours later she called to tell me the Moose would come to our seats to see Brandon between the 5th and 6th innings.

I told Doug and Mark about it, but we didn't tell Brandon.

Right on schedule the Moose appeared along with a cameraman and a couple assistants. With him he brought a bag full of Mariner stuff. There was a hat, a pennant and shirt. Also, an autographed picture of the Moose. Brandon and the Moose even got put on the big screen for all to see. Brandon was totally thrilled by it all.

A week later I was at another game, and low and behold I appeared on the big screen as the "Fan of the Game." I think the recognition had something to do with my arranging the Moose to visit Brandon.

CHAPTER 52

Our Financing Situation

It took me about eight years after starting at Sno Falls to get Bill Porter, the majority owner, to let me do the bookkeeping. During the first five years he would get one of his young friends to write things down while he would dictate to them. Of course, we weren't very busy back then. Next, he would get a kitchen helper to help him, while I would be stuck cooking and serving by myself. Finally, I said I should handle all the paperwork and the kitchen helpers could stay in the kitchen. In addition, I could do it all without dictation from him.

I then, with Bill's permission, had the storage room divided up to make an office for me. There I took care of paying all bills and payroll. I took care of payroll taxes. I kept the check register balanced and did the monthly spreadsheets.

The accountant we used had been Bill's accountant when he had the car dealership. Every month I had to take all our books to him. He would keep everything for a week to 10 days. During that time, I would keep track of checks on notebook paper and then transfer the information to the check register when I got it back.

Finally, I talked Bill into switching to an accountant who would come to the course every month. This enabled us to keep everything on site. One of our golfers suggested his accountant and I was able to get him to add us as a client. Bill Jacobs took care of our accounting needs until two years after I retired. That amounted to close to 40 years.

Business wise, golf is seasonal unless you are in Hawaii. In the Pacific Northwest you lose money in November, December, January, and February. For Sno Falls Golf those are the months when flooding is the most likely. March, April, September, and October are the months you hope to break even. Now, thanks to flood control and the Army Corps of Engineers, we can flood in March, April, and October too. So, there are four months to make money, and they are May, June,

July, and August. Consequently, you must save up during those months to get through the rest.

Bill Porter liked to buy equipment on time and make payments where we had to pay interest. For instance, we had a lease on our rental power carts that we had to pay monthly.

When I taught at Tolt High School there was a teacher on the staff named Vivian Randlev. She had just bought a new car and had paid cash for it. She'd planned ahead and saved enough money, and she also was getting paid interest on the accumulating amount while she saved. Therefore, instead of buying on time and paying interest, she paid up front with savings that included interest she'd made. I remembered that.

In our situation, where floods are a certainty, we can't afford a number of monthly payments. Floods have shut us down for more than three months five times.

I talked Bill into letting me start a separate savings account for equipment and power carts. I also started paying off all contracts as fast as possible. Within three years we owed nothing to anybody and had over $50,000 in the special savings account. We wouldn't have survived the floods of 1990, 1995, 1996, 2006 and 2009 if we'd bought things on credit. We save in the good months and get through the bad. Other golf courses run lines of credits to the hilt and hope to pay them off during the good months. Our method is much more relaxing.

CHAPTER 53

The Shot Heard Around the Valley

O ne night when Chris and I were cleaning up the kitchen and dining area at about 9:00 PM, Chris decided to hit a couple balls out
of the clubhouse and over the river. He took his stance as close to the
door opening as possible without hitting the door jamb with his club.
There was a ramp that came up to the door and plywood that hung off
the handrail on the ramp. Chris had to hit the ball through the door
opening and at least 3 feet high to clear the railing and the plywood.
He selected an 8 iron to handle the task. After hitting five balls out
and over the river, he stopped. He said he was practicing for the next
morning to make bets with the Sunday morning Men's Club guys on
whether he could hit a ball out the doorway and over the river. The
Sunday morning crowd played early and was always in the clubhouse
by 11:00 AM drinking beer.

Sunday morning with 25 to 30 guys in the clubhouse, Chris proposed his bet and at least 10 of the guys bet him he couldn't do it. After
plenty of hoop la, Chris swung away. The ball hit the right door jam
and bounced around inside without hitting anyone or breaking anything. Chris had choked, but he then hit one out without any bets on it.

So dumb ass John then said, "Anyone can hit it out from right
in front of the door opening, what about from the other side of the
building?"

Basically, where Chris hit it from was less than 4 feet from the door
opening with the only real obstacle being the handrail with plywood
siding to hit it over. The other side of the building required a shot of
about 20 feet before the ball reached the door opening. The backswing
and follow through needed to navigate missing the glass sliding door
to the porch as well as the L-shaped counter. The shot was also at a
slight angle to the door opening, because of the counter and there was
a 6-inch diameter metal support post in the middle of the building that

I needed to avoid hitting the ball into. The post was just barely right of the line I had to take to the door.

The consensus was that no one should even try it because the odds were someone would get hurt. Regardless of logical thought, we put intelligence aside, and almost everyone there bet me I couldn't do it. In preparation for the shot, several of the dining tables were turned on their sides to serve as shields for the gallery. All that could be seen to the right of the open door was eyes and foreheads watching the action over the lunch counter. The rest of the gallery were on the floor peeking over the turned-over tables.

I picked a 3 iron. Not only did the shot have to miss the steel pole, it had to be 4 feet high to clear the plywood and under 6 feet 6 inches to go below the top of the door jam. Obviously, it had to go through a 3-foot-wide opening as well. And, it had to go clear over the river. I knew if it got through the opening it would easily get over the river.

As I was getting ready to swing, my hands were sweating. Besides the difficulty of the shot itself, a three iron is one of the tougher clubs to hit. The only thing going through my mind was, "What am I going to tell Porter if I break something or worse yet injure or kill someone?"

When I took my stance, everyone was yelling and cheering. I swung away and hit what was without a doubt the best 3 iron shot I have ever hit. The ball went screaming out through the exact center of the 3x3 opening, cleared the railing and soared way over the river out into the distance. That was 35 years ago, and that ball might still be flying!

It's funny, but there were about 30 guys at the event and yet there are at least 100 guys who claim to have been there to see it.

That one shot was instrumental in changing my name. I had been "Johnny G" for several years. From "Johnny G" it had changed to "Johnny G Spot." When I successfully hit an almost impossible shot that endangered about 25 people I was rewarded a new name of greater importance. That name was "Captain G Spot."

CHAPTER 54

River Wreck-Reation

Knowing what I know today, I would never again buy anything located beside a river. If there were something like a guarantee that you would get back ten times your money if you ever had a flood, then I would consider it.

Yes, a river is pretty. Yes, sometimes you can catch fish in it. Yes, a lot of wildlife can be seen in it and close to it. Yes, the sound of the water flowing is very soothing and peaceful. Yes, in the summer one can swim in it to cool off. But the biggest "YES" is that it can flood and destroy everything in the water's path. It doesn't care if you are a good person who helps others and rescues dogs and cats. It doesn't care if everything you accomplished over 50 years gets wiped out. It just does whatever damage it wants to do!

I know I already went through my crybaby story of flooding. I explained that flooding was a minor problem when I actually bought into the course, and thanks to King County Flood Control and the Corps of Engineers it has become a major problem for us and the entire lower valley. So now I am going to tell you some other not so great things about being next to the river.

Even in the summer when it runs tamely alongside the course, thanks to ignorant people, it can be dangerous.

Earlier I mentioned that a seaplane used to land in and take off from the river right next to our clubhouse. That was before the river bottom filled up too much from floods and a lack of dredging.

Anyway, on a sunny day in the late spring of about 1978 a seaplane swooped down and landed on the river. It cruised slowly upriver and got turned around for takeoff. As it was revving up the engine to take off it got hung up on some rocks. Chris and I happened to be watching, so we walked down to see if we could help. The pilot asked if we would climb in the river and push him off the rocks so that he could take off. Being the good ol' hicks from the country, Chris and I couldn't refuse help to a city boy with his fancy plane that he got hung up on where anybody with a brain wouldn't have landed in the first place.

After pushing on it for 10 minutes and slowly getting it to move off the rocks and sand into deeper water where it was finally floating, I stood up to catch my breath. I was waist deep in water when suddenly something hit me in the back of my head. It made my knees buckle and it almost knocked me out. I had forgotten about the stabilizer, *aka* the back wing. As I was fighting to keep my balance in the river current, all that went through my mind was, "This is the stuff you read about in newspapers."

The jackass pilot let it drift on down the river and tied up to something on the riverbank. The right pontoon had a hole in it and he couldn't take off. The next day three guys came out from Renton to retrieve the plane. One of them was the owner of the seaplane flight school that the plane belonged to. The trainer who would bring students out to land in the Snoqualmie no longer had a job. He was supposed to stick to lakes.

To get the plane buoyant they stuffed inner tubes in the pontoon and then inflated them. After that, they were able to fly it back to home base.

Before I continue about other joys of being on the river, I want to quickly share my other airplane story. One foggy morning a plane took off from the small neighborhood airstrip next to the golf course. I had learned years before that a rule in flying says you can take off in the fog, but you can't land in it. Laurie Evan's son Len had flown me and several others in his seaplane to go play golf at Port Ludlow and it was clear there so we could land safely.

On another outing Len had flown us in his helicopter to Yakima to golf. On the return flight, when we were flying over Snoqualmie Pass, we could see that the Snoqualmie Valley was fogged in. Len explained that you never fly into fog to land. He set the chopper down at the summit and Chris's wife drove up and picked us up.

Back to my story about the pilot that took off in the fog. He probably shouldn't have taken off in the first place, but once he did, he should have followed the rule of not trying to land. Unfortunately, he decided to try to land instead of flying on to his planned destination or at least to somewhere clear from fog. He circled around a few times at several hundred feet trying to get his bearings, before he came down to land.

Unfortunately, he wasn't over the air strip at this point and instead was over our golf course. His plane first hit a tree on the side of our 11th and 18th fairway. This happened just above Kevin, a member of our greens crew who was out mowing greens, and one of the plane's wings was torn off by the tree. The plane then squarely hit a tree between our 18th and 9th fairways. The pilot was launched through the windshield several hundred feet into our 2nd fairway. While he obviously didn't survive, fortunately no one else was killed or injured. The course was closed and emptied for the rest of the day so the FAA could both investigate the accident and collect all the evidence that was scattered across four of our golf holes. Fortunately, this is the only time in over 50 years that something like this has happened at our golf course.

Back to the joys of being on a river. Sometime around 2005 floating the river became a popular thing to do. Local kids had floated the river for many years, and they only did it if they knew how to swim. They also wouldn't leave the river on the way to Fall City to destroy people's property or harass golfers on the golf course. Plus, they wouldn't litter in and around the river with their beer cans and other garbage and there might be about 20 of them on any given day. Once they got to Fall City, they wouldn't harass citizens there or shoplift in the stores. Most of them were 14- to 18-year-olds.

Today's rafters are mostly 17 to 24 years of age. They come out from Seattle, Bellevue, Redmond and other populated areas. They aren't prepared for a 5- to 6-hour float down the river, and they don't know what they are doing. They are strictly coming out to drink, have fun and enjoy the water for free. Their rafts aren't designed to handle the challenges of the float. In some cases, they barely know how to swim if at all. They drink too much and make terrible decisions like tying their rafts together. They start too late in the day to finish when it is still safe, daylight and warm enough. They park in dangerous places for themselves and others using the roads as well as parking on private property and filling up parking for the local businesses. Plus, you have probably figured out that there can actually be thousands of them on busy days.

These floaters have simple desires that the local government, for some unknown reason, doesn't want to stop them from enjoying. So what if having fun involves getting drunk, harassing homeowners and local businesses, destroying property, littering, damaging the river ecosystem, and endangering their own lives? Who cares if the result of this behavior is tying up the police, firemen, aid cars, fire engines, helicopters and rescue boats?

One summer evening after dark while working in my office at the golf course I heard someone knocking on the outside door to the porch. This was well after dark, because I like to do most of my bill paying and other paperwork at night when no one is there to distract me from being able to get it done. Anyway, I opened the door to find a wet rafter in just his swimsuit. He was in a panic that some of their party of 13 rafters was still in the river at after 10:30 PM. They had stupidly tied five cheap rafts together to float the river and they had drifted into trees across the river from our 5th hole. Four of the five rafts had been ruined by underwater branches these city dwellers hadn't noticed. This had happened after 6:30 PM and they had no idea how far they still were from reaching Fall City.

They were over 2.5 miles from town and the golf course clubhouse is the only building on the river for this entire segment of the river. Several others from his group started showing up, but many were still somewhere out in the river.

I had called 911 when the guy first knocked at my door. By the time it was over, there were three aid cars, two police cars, one fire engine and one helicopter called into action. It took over an hour to locate and save all of them. I fixed coffee and hot chocolate to warm them up and provided donuts and sweet rolls for food.

What was the makeup of this ignorant group? First of all, they were from Seattle, and they had come out to enjoy a fun family float in this little river of warm water called the Snoqualmie. Most of them could hardly swim, but you don't need to when you are floating on rafts. Nobody had told them that after dark it gets really cold, because the water is run off from snow melt and spring water. None of them knew how early they needed to start to finish safely before dark. They also didn't realize there were things like tree roots and fallen trees that could pop cheap rafts, nor did they realize that tying the rafts together would ensure that all the rafts would be doomed if only one or two got popped or snagged.

None of them had done this float before. They figured family fun was best for all to enjoy, so why not include some little kids too. There was a four-year-old, a two-year-old, and a six-month-old baby to enjoy a fun little river float. REALLY!!!!!

To cap it off, the aid cars and police had to take them back to Seattle to get spare car keys, because they lost all their stuff in the river. This meant that three aid cars, two police cars, a fire engine and a helicopter were tied up with them for over four hours. If some chubby guy like me had a heart attack in Fall City during that time he would have been out of luck.

Every summer now there are many rescue missions on the river where aid cars drive across the golf course to help a rafter in danger and of course people sometimes die. In fact, one year a young man died because he tied his cooler to his leg to make sure he wouldn't lose it. When it accidentally fell out of the inner tubes it took the young man to the river bottom in a place that was too deep for him to stand without drowning.

There is a simple solution that would save lives, protect the river's ecosystem and fish, stop problems for local citizens and businesses along the river, and save the county and taxpayers money for police, fire and other rescue crews. *Ban rafting on the Snoqualmie River!*

CHAPTER 55

Master Eater!

Chris was a hard worker and a nice guy. Chris also liked to have fun, play golf and eat. Chris's father, Orv, said he came by it honestly. While his mother was pregnant with Chris, she loved corn on the cob. Orv simply said that Chris was corn fed. If Chris was going to have a hamburger, while he was cooking it he would eat a tuna fish sandwich. Of course, several bags of chips would accompany the sandwich and hamburger, which he would follow with a couple bags of almonds.

One year I was playing in the Washington Open at Gold Mountain GC in Bremerton. The first day of the tournament, Chris came along to watch. I brought John Krona along to caddy. At this time, John was about 17 years old. He had been a student of mine the last year I taught. He had played on the high school golf team that I coached as well. John ended up becoming an accountant and is still our family accountant today. Liz also came along to watch.

It turned out to be a difficult day. Warming up on the driving range I shanked several iron shots. I hadn't hit a shank since my sophomore year in college. Quite possibly more people have committed suicide over getting the shanks than did during the Great Depression. I warned my playing partners not to walk ahead to the right of me whenever I was hitting a shot. On the 9th hole, one of the guys moved ahead of me about 20 yards. The nine-iron shot was a pure shank and just missed his head by inches. After that no one went out ahead of me.

On the way home, we stopped at the Spaghetti Factory in Tacoma for dinner. Their servings there are humongous. When our platters arrived, we all dove in, because we were extremely hungry. It had been a long day and walking six miles on a hilly golf course can build up an appetite. We all ordered spaghetti and meatballs.

I attacked my dinner like I hadn't eaten for days. When I was about ½ of the way through my pile of food, I came up for air. The first thing I spotted was the look on John Krona's face. He looked both shocked

Chris Dowd was my "working partner" from 1974 to 1991. He is holding his son Matthew who is now over 40. Chris was the hardest-working person I have ever known.

and amazed. He was staring at Chris finishing off his plate of spaghetti and meatballs in both a fashion and speed he had never witnessed before in his life. Chris also made packing up to go home after dinner easy, because he helped us all finish anything we couldn't, so we didn't need to get any doggy bags.

Our Men's Club used to have an event called the Potluck Tournament. Wives played with the men and then there was a potluck feast afterward. That morning Chris mowed greens and I took care of the pro shop and the restaurant. Chris finished mowing by about 7:00 AM and he came in to fix his own breakfast and cook for others. He fried three eggs, several strips of bacon, a big slab of ham, and a huge pile of hash browns. Along with that tasty little meal went four slices of toast and at least a pint of milk. Although he had used the greens

My "working partner" Chris Dowd from the early years. Here he is getting his bronco ready for the Calgary Stampede.

mower to mow, you would think he had crawled around and cut the greens by hand with scissors by the size of the meal he was having.

Shortly after his breakfast, the couples began arriving with their contributions for the potluck to be held after golf. I thought most of their offerings would be safe since Chris had already eaten enough for three starving loggers. I was wrong! Chris did hold off until they all teed off, but that still gave him about four hours to graze before they would be finishing their rounds.

I will say that the salads were safe. One gal brought in crescent moon shaped pastries that were at least 2 inches thick. There were four of them and they were about 8 inches long and 3 inches wide. Chris ate one of them! There was a huge tray of lasagna which Chris put a good dent in. Since Chris enjoyed pasta, he also put a hurting on the pan of ravioli someone else brought in. With about an hour to go before the golfers finished, Chris started coasting as he casually grazed through other dishes.

The ladies did notice a reduction of the size of their offerings, but they took it all in stride. Once the golfers had loaded up their plates and were enjoying the food out on our deck, Chris went out and joined them. I don't know if he was still hungry or if he was trying to make them think he hadn't tried any of it earlier.

For a while we sold cinnamon rolls as well as donuts. The cinnamon rolls were large and yummy, and it was easy for Chris to polish off a couple of them at a time.

I don't know or care why I do some of the things that I do, or how I ever think of doing them in the first place. One day I was looking at these cinnamon rolls and thought, "It would be fun to watch Chris eat one in three bites."

The average hungry guy would probably take 10 to 12 bites to eat one, but Chris was WAY above average. So, I said, "Hey, Chris, I bet you five bucks you can't eat one of these in three bites."

He said, "Hell, that would be easy!"

Well, it wasn't easy, but he did it. He looked like a chipmunk loading up nuts for the winter. There were several people in the clubhouse that had fun watching. While he was in action, I made fun of him and got him to laugh, which made him choke a bit, but he kept on breathing and chewing. That may well have been the best $5 I have ever spent.

One other skill that Chris was blessed with was the ability to recognize beauty in a woman and the ability to remember quite a few of them. He demonstrated this skill numerous times, but one of those times was extremely memorable and impressive.

In those early years one of our members was a magazine salesman/distributor. He had all varieties from *Time* to *Better Homes & Gardens*. He had *Popular Mechanics*, *Life* and *Playboy*. In fact, he had lots of magazines with girls who didn't have much clothing. His name was Roy, and about twice a year he would bring us a stack of magazines with the covers torn off. I guess that was so we couldn't sell them. The stack would be about 8 inches thick and include *Playboy*, *Penthouse* and various other magazines not recommended by the Boy Scouts of America. The stack did not include triple X magazines, just tasteful girls with little clothing.

I won't say that I never peeked at them, but Chris studied them. We also kept the stack out of reach and sight of our kids and the general public.

In some of these magazines, there was a "Girl Next Door" segment, where amateurs sent in pictures of so-called neighbors.

Anyhow, one nice day an elderly guy and his granddaughter came to play a round of golf. When they finished their round, they came in to report that he had lost a sweater on the golf course. It was warmer than when they had started their round and the granddaughter had removed a garment or two. She was still decent, but more skin was showing. I wrote down a description of what they lost and told them I would call them if it got turned in.

Believe it or not, she had lit up Chris's radar when they first checked in to play. When they came back in after the round, the radar really fired up. After they walked out, Chris came up to the pro shop. He had been working in the restaurant. Of course, he had been watching her closely. He declared that he had seen her in one of the magazines. Talk about finding the needle in the haystack.

Anyways, we let it go at that. The clothing item had not been turned in, so I hadn't called her. The next day, she showed up to see if she could go around the course looking for it. She was wearing shorts and a skimpy shirt. After she went out to hunt for it, Chris declared that he flat knew he had seen her in one of those magazines. While she was searching the course, Chris was searching the magazines.

She was still out on the course when Chris ran into the pro shop waving a magazine in the air and exclaiming, "I told you! I told you! Look at this!"

By golly he did find it. He was rewarded for his memory and hard work searching the magazines when she returned from her search. She had taken off the skimpy shirt and short shorts and was wearing a bikini. To this day, neither Chris nor I remember whether she found her grandfather's sweater or not.

CHAPTER 56

Big "O"

Chris's father, Orv, was a retired truck driver who was used to getting up by 1:00 AM to drive. Orv liked to open up the building for us early in the morning. He normally arrived at about 4:00 AM to do this. He would unlock doors, make coffee, and get a few power carts out for us to rent later. Other than food and beer, Orv wasn't paid for his volunteer help. He had fun doing this and being around the golfers. He would also help with anything else he could, including repairs of things in the clubhouse. He could also help in the kitchen as well as serve beer.

At one point, Orv got into collecting pop and beer cans to recycle for money. When Orv started a project like this, he would dive right in full force.

One morning at about 5:00 AM I got a call at home from the alarm company. It seems some strange noises were taking place at the course, and they wanted to know if they should call the police. I said don't call them yet, I'll go check on it.

I got up, threw on some clothes, and headed for the course. Upon arrival, I find Orv driving back and forth over a small mountain of cans. Granted, this was a good way to flatten them out, but it was also a good way to set the alarm off. I explained to him that if he decided to do this again, it would be nice if he turned the alarm off before he started. It was the perfect time for the activity because the parking lot was empty. I just didn't want an early wakeup call from the alarm company.

The flood of 1990 really got us, and I have talked about that already. I didn't mention that it jailed Orv. Back then flood control really had no warning system to speak of. We knew we were going to be flooded, but we had no real idea of how bad.

Orv drove in that morning and went through about two feet of water for 150 feet of our driveway. A few years later we raised that stretch to almost the same height as the rest of our driveway. As Orv drove through it, he knew he had to continue all the way as there was no room to turn around. Realizing that he was damn lucky to have made it through, he knew he shouldn't go back through it again to try to go home. Orv was stuck at the course.

He opened the clubhouse and turned the alarm off. He then opened our cart/maintenance shed and made room for his small pickup truck. The floor of the cart shed was about 18 inches higher than the parking lot. After locking the shed back up, he went into the clubhouse and got settled in without having any idea how high the river was going to get. The clubhouse building was built so that the floor was more than 3 feet higher than the highest water level in history.

So, there was Orv, stranded inside and warm with lots of food and beverages. And no idea how many hours or days he would be there until the river receded enough for him to get back out. He even had running water and toilets.

There was some apprehension though as the river kept rising. Nobody knew if the clubhouse could handle the pressure if the water got high enough to get into the building. Also, with the river flooding came debris and even trees. Could the building be dislodged, and if so, what would happen to Orv?

The water did continue to rise, and it even got into the clubhouse, but only by a couple of inches. Sadly, we have had floods reach heights of over 18 inches in the building, like the one we had in 2009. Fortunately, the building has survived them all. After this flood of 1990 we did have the structure checked and secured better in order to make sure it could withstand whatever might come.

But, back to Orv. He was quite happy in his solitude. At the peak of the flood only an inch or two of water got on the floor with some areas in the building staying dry. He had everything he needed, plus one thing he didn't need. That was the telephone, and it was working just fine from the clubhouse to his house, where his wife, Peg, was calling him regularly. According to Orv, Peg even told him he didn't comb his hair the right way.

Whatever the case may be, Peg finally got Chris to arrange to have Orv taken out by boat. Not "taken out" like Luigi, the guy with the violin case would do, but moved to drier ground. Chris and our neighbor next to the golf course picked up Orv with the neighbor's fishing boat. Orv had spent just over two days in his island getaway.

We couldn't access the course by car or truck for five days. There is only one good thing about one of these floods. Sometimes a good steelhead will be left behind by the receding waters. If an eagle doesn't get to it first, we can have a nice BBQ. This flood left a beautiful bright steelhead near the 18th green. Orv went fishing for it with a pitchfork and he was successful.

The flood of 1990 provided Orv with a couple of relatively peaceful days and one nice fish to eat. Sadly, his pickup truck didn't do as well. The cart shed got over two feet of water into it and that caused Big O's truck to be damaged.

CHAPTER 57

Superintendents

The person in charge of maintenance at a golf course is called "the Superintendent." When I started at Snoqualmie Falls Golf Course, one of my partners, Art, was considered to be that guy. However, he was just an automobile mechanic. In fact, I was closer to being an astronaut than he was to being a superintendent. The guy I replaced was a self-proclaimed golf pro, but he never even entered the PGA program. He did know how to sell property that didn't exist though. Bill Porter was the businessman, because he had money. None of them knew the golf business.

Regardless, Art acted as the superintendent the first year I was there. As I recounted, he and his wife wanted to get out, so I arranged for Chris to take over Art's share of the partnership. Chris then became the superintendent and filled that role for the next 17 years. I have already covered a bunch of stories about Chris, and I could go on and on.

Ok, just one more adventure. Chris and I, along with one of the beer delivery guys, were sitting at the counter shooting the breeze. Chris happened to spot two fishermen stealing beer out of the beer truck. They had pulled their boat over to the riverbank and climbed up the bank to grab a case of beer. As we came charging out of the clubhouse screaming, "Don't steal that beer!" and "Leave it on the riverbank!" they managed to get back into their boat and push off.

I looked to my left and Chris had a boulder the size of three bowling balls and lobbed it at them. I thought it was going to reach them, but it barely fell short. As it fell, it seemed like slow motion and the fishermen's eyes looked as big as manhole covers. It would have gone right through their boat or if it hit one of the guys it could have killed him.

Chris was also yelling, "We will follow you downstream to the boat launch and get you there if you don't give back that beer."

They had a drift boat, so they couldn't go fast, nor could they go upstream. They managed to get back to the riverbank and hand the beer back without anyone getting hurt. Chris's technique had recovered the beer for the driver.

Although Chris had been a great partner and worker for many years, I think the flood of 1990 got to him. It would be hard to see something be virtually destroyed that you'd spent 16 years making beautiful. It was, and still is with each and every flood, difficult to climb back on that horse and ride.

Whatever the reasons, Chris lost interest, got sidelined with some personal problems and bad decisions, and we had to buy him out. Therefore in 1991, I was down to one partner, Bill Porter.

Harry Frantz had already been working on the maintenance crew and he became the superintendent, though with no share of ownership. He continued as such for three years and was fortunate that during that period no major floods took place.

In 1994, Bill Porter passed away. Some years before, we had started a buyout program of Bill's shares, so that I could work towards becoming the sole owner. Even though I still had about five years left of paying off Bill's heirs, with his passing I had Bill's salary to use to pay a new superintendent a reasonable salary. At this point, I had become the sole owner of Snoqualmie Falls GC.

After a great deal of thought, or at least as much as I could stand, I came up with two names. One of them was Dale Sim, my fishing buddy and ex-classmate at Mount Si High. Dale was the right-hand man at Fury Construction. Dale could handle anything that required dirt, landscape, building or catching fish. I will fill you in on the fun times with Dale later in my stories.

The other candidate was Lee Baldwin. He was one year ahead of me at Mount Si High School, but we had different friend groups. I actually knew his younger brother Jim better than I knew Lee. However, I got reacquainted with Lee when we both worked at Mount Si Golf Course. I believe it was 1970 when Lee came to work on the maintenance crew at Mount Si GC. I had been working summers on the crew since 1962. I got to teach Lee how to operate a greens mower and mow fairways. It didn't take much teaching as he was already capable of handling equipment.

Hughie showing me love – his wife Glenda trying not to watch while Suzy and Lee look on.

Lee also worked under Chris at Sno Falls in the late 1970s for a couple of years. He also worked in maintenance at Meridian Valley Country Club before he created Baldwin Construction Company.

I ended up selecting Lee because he had the background to handle the job. Plus, he was ready to hang up the construction business. Lee and I were also friends from the years at Mount Si Golf and partying with our mutual old pal from Mount Si, Hugh Peterson.

Upon leaving Mount Si Golf, Hugh ended up in Las Vegas after working two years at Kellogg CC in Idaho. After he had been in Las

My smartass buddies, Hughie and Lee, squatting to look my height and me on my tiptoes.

Vegas for several years, Lee and I would visit him for three or four days playing golf daily. We did this for at least 15 years.

Among the interesting people we played with was a guy names Jim Aldred. Hughie said about Jim, "He used to have red hair and a white nose but now has white hair and a red nose."

We always played Las Vegas Country Club but also played other great courses,

Two other players we played with were the twin brothers to Mickey Mantle. Their names were Ray and Roy. Ray played left-handed and Roy played right-handed. As you remember, Mickey was a switch hitter.

Roy was more serious and fairly quiet while still being a nice guy. Ray was funny and outgoing. Once when he introduced us to the club's assistant pro he said, "Gene might not be the ugliest man in the world, but he is in the top five." Gene—who was really quite handsome—laughed with the rest of us at this back-handed joke.

Another time when the cute waitress in the bar served us drinks, he told her, "If I was riding a mule and you were walking, you'd like me." I don't know what her name was, but he called her "Daisy Mae."

One day I started with a double bogey on the first hole at Black Mountain Golf Course and still shot a 72! Afterwards, in the bar, Ray said, "It's about time you left town."

The next day he told Gary Hawthorn, who was going to join us, that he should give me a "good leaving alone." In other words, don't bet me. Gary was another character who could get up and down out of anything. He had a great short game. Hughie called him, "Catfish" because you couldn't catch him.

When Lee started at Snoqualmie Falls everything was great. Lee was instrumental in cleaning out trees that covered the course with leaves. He put in drainage that made wet areas much more playable. Along with the fellow employees and a few volunteers, Lee put in the fairway watering to make us the only golf course in the Snoqualmie Valley to have lush green fairways in the summer. He modernized the watering system so it was more efficient, and you could specifically water the areas that needed it more without overwatering other places. He survived and helped us recover from the two highest floods in our history, the floods of 2006 and 2009. He also moved and built a new 4th green to withstand flooding without getting torn apart like it had in those two floods.

Lee, being a carpenter by trade, took care of the maintenance of the clubhouse. As I already mentioned, Lee was not as lucky as Harry had been in regard to flooding. He got stuck cleaning up after many floods. After being there only one year, we had a bad flood in November of 1995, and then another one just two months later in January of 1996. To get hit with another flood before you are done cleaning up the first one is totally discouraging, but Lee handled it.

Lee's wife Suzy also worked outside on the crew doing everything the guys did. In addition, Suzy put in gardens throughout the course and really dressed the place up. The first several years that Lee and Suzy were there, they had the outside crew workers over to their house for dinner too.

As years went by, Lee got more critical of the people on the crew. Employees reported that quite often he would tell them to do something and then tell them that they did it wrong or that he never told them to do it in the first place. Lee would also come inside and criticize and/or tell my pro shop assistants what to do. He never did that when I was around though. One of my assistants even quit, because he couldn't stand Lee's criticism or bossiness anymore.

Lee even criticized me behind my back. I had several employees and golfers tell me that. His main criticism was that I was too easy on people and thus I was a poor leader. According to Lee I had no leadership ability.

Looking back, he was correct, especially when it came to him. I should have let him go years before I did. In fact, I even let him stay for one more year than we had agreed to and even then, he tried to get me to go another year, but finally I moved on.

During Lee's years we attempted to get a permit to build a new maintenance building. The entire golf course is in what is called "floodway." That is worse than flood plain.

We wanted to build something up on stilts that would not get flood water in it. Of course, this would displace less water than the building we already had was displacing during floods. It would have made life better for us and it would have made flooding slightly lower for everyone down river from us.

Early on in our project to get a better maintenance building, it was discovered that the boundary line to our north was off by about 15 feet. Even though that boundary had been established in 1962 when the property was broken up to become a golf course and a fence was put in to mark it, we still ended up with a legal battle with our neighbor. It seemed that our old well, which had been abandoned for over 25 years at that time, rested in this 15-foot strip that was in question by the new surveys. Possibly our neighbor thought he could obtain some sort of water rights if he could take the property with the abandoned well.

We ended up going through two lawyers, two surveyors, one architect, numerous meetings, and even one official arbitration all in trying to get this new maintenance building. The whole thing ended up costing over $125,000 before I said screw it. I finally pulled the plug when

No posing here: live picture of me taken by either Hughie or Lee when playing in Las Vegas. I didn't know it was being taken or I would have choked. Notice circled ball going straight down the fairway.

I was told that we could get the permit to build it if we took all the blackberry bushes off the riverbank. First of all, the river goes around two sides of the golf course amounting to 1.5 miles of riverbank to clear. Secondly, taking blackberries out would create erosion and the golf course could conceivably be lost to the river.

During this process, I had to attend two county meetings where I listened to and answered questions from various department heads. I had to pay $147 per hour for each of these governmental geniuses to attend and comment. There were about a dozen of them in attendance.

Probably the most interesting question one of these brilliant county workers asked was, "Are any of the vehicles that will be stored in this building gas powered?"

Before I could stop myself, I replied, "HELL NO! They are all wind up! Did you know there are wind up golf carts, mowers, tractors and other maintenance vehicles?"

At this point, I was told that if gasoline-powered vehicles were going to be stored there, then a special floor had to be built. This floor would gather any drips of gasoline and these drips would run down channels and be captured in barrels that would then be hauled away.

First, any leak that was noticeable would be fixed immediately. Second, small drips and drops would evaporate before they ever made it to the drain into the barrels. There would never be any reason for a special floor to collect gasoline spills and we have never had a gasoline spill make more than a small spot on the floor in the 50 years I have been there. To engineer and install such a system would be both ludicrous and extremely expensive.

In hindsight, I should have asked her if every automobile agency showroom had these floors. How about every garage that worked on cars or every home garage where people kept their cars and lawnmowers? Maybe she didn't know that cars and lawnmowers used gas too.

Another $147 per hour genius oversaw impervious surfaces. An impervious surface is one that does not absorb water. A roof is an impervious surface if it is waterproof which, the last time I checked, keeping water and other things out of the inside of the building was one of the main reasons to have a roof. A floor could also be considered an impervious surface if the building did not have a roof and the floor did not allow water to penetrate.

In our case, we had to make a building that had an impervious surface footprint that was only 10% larger than the existing building. The genius lady in charge of impervious surfaces insisted that the roof and the floor combined to push us over the 10% increase. The other county lady sitting next to her tried to stop her from showing her stupidity, but she couldn't be stopped. She was a real bulldog, and it was very difficult for the person running the meeting to get her to realize what she was saying.

All in all, it was a valuable $125,000 spent. I learned a great deal from the whole experience. I learned that lawyers take your money and tell you that you can't lose, because legally you are in the right. Then they drag it on as long as possible to collect more money. Finally, when they are tired of milking you, they tell you to settle and pay money, because you never know what a jury will do. Pardon me, but I shit you not! This is how it went down.

In case you wanted to know the best part about all of this, we could have bought the 55 acres, the house and the barn where this strip of land was for $110,000 in 1981. This would have meant no neighbor and no legal battle. It also would have meant we would own the driving range and private cart shed next to our golf course. The barn could have served as a better maintenance building. Unfortunately, that didn't happen, because Bill Porter said no. He didn't want us to buy it because the golf course itself was just a little toy for him and something to play on when he felt like it.

Once Lee retired, I lucked out and hired Eric Verellen. Eric had been the superintendent at Elk Run Golf Course. Elk Run Golf Course had just closed, and Eric was available. Lee was leaving, but he wanted to be part of the hiring of his replacement. In fact, Lee had already interviewed Eric, before I knew anything about him. This followed the normal operating procedures. Lee had to run everything that he possibly could.

I told Lee that before anyone was hired, I had to talk to them. Therefore Eric had to make another trip out to the golf course to meet with me.

Fortunately, I hired Eric and he has proven to be an absolute asset to the golf course. He knows grass. How to make it grow and even how to slow down its growth. He knows the soil needs to be at a particular Ph level and he knows how to test the Ph balance himself. I can't begin to tell you everything Eric knows about course maintenance. This year he even won a national award for excellence in his field. Best of all, Eric is a mild-mannered nice guy who takes care of his crew. They all seem to love working for him. Even though I am now retired and my son Jeff and almost son David Doty are operating the course, I hope Eric stays on with them for many more years.

I must jump back in time to when Chris was still at the course, to talk about one other important member of our maintenance staff for many years. Roger Erickson was hired as an assistant superintendent/ mechanic about four years before Chris left the golf course. Roger was a good ol' boy, who could fix almost anything and operate any equipment you would ever want him to run.

Roger did have a couple small downsides. One was a bad back that would act up on him periodically. He came by it honestly though, because years ago he had a small tree fall on him while he was working at a tree farm. The other problem was that Roger was not really good at reading and writing. He wasn't illiterate, but his skills were definitely limited. He could order parts by looking at pictures and he could put almost anything together. He also liked to build things and had the vision to create things. Roger was a good guy with a kind heart. I think the only cruel things he ever did were to set a pigeon free in a friend's garage and ship a box of manure to a mutual friend of ours, Keith Iacolucci, that he disguised as a college care package. Both things were done to be a funny prank though, since he liked both of them.

Sometimes Chris would do something on a given day when he knew I wouldn't be around to stop him. On one of those days, he and Roger constructed what looked like a rock snowman in the middle of the 18th green. They made it by stacking three boulders. It was easy to see from the clubhouse, and it was definitely unique. The problem was that golfers didn't see the value or humor in having to putt around their rock snowman. They REALLY didn't like their good approach shots bouncing off it and down into the valley of death to the left of the green. It took me a month to get them to move it to the back left part of the green, where it was still visible but not in the way of play. A little over a year later I got them to remove it altogether.

Roger also built a paddle wheel boat that was about 4 feet long. He installed a generator in it that hooked to the paddle wheel and illuminated a light inside the boat. It was cute and it could be seen in the river from the clubhouse. Unfortunately to really enjoy the light, you would need to see it at night and most golfers go home before it gets dark. I don't know what happened to it. It may have been stolen or a log may have knocked it loose and taken it down the river.

Roger also rigged up a long measuring post that he painted lines on to indicate water depth. He used a 6-inch diameter steel post. Somehow, he used metal strapping and attached it to a stump in the far side of the river. People also enjoyed looking at it to see the depth of the river at any given time. The problem with this cool invention was that it could disappear under water in the winter when the water levels got high. A fishing boat on the river could have been wrecked by it because they could have accidentally hit it when it wasn't visible. Because of that, I got Roger to remove it when the water levels came down in the late spring. Fortunately, nobody ran into it before then.

Using his ability to visualize and build things, Roger designed a device for the back of our aerating machine. It gathered the plugs brought up by the aerator and piled them. These saved hours of raking and shoveling plugs for all the crew members.

For whatever reason, when Lee became the superintendent, he was harder on Roger than others on the crew. I doubt that Roger ever got any kind of atta boy from Lee, and I know Roger didn't feel Lee appreciated him. Even though I had no leadership qualities, according to Lee, I wrote letters of appreciation to everyone who worked for me and helped us through the bad floods. Later I learned that Roger kept my letters on the wall in his shop at home.

I have no idea why, but Roger's wife left him. At approximately the same time, his son Ben had grown up and was moving out. Roger's whole world was crashing down around him. Knowing he was quite limited when it came to reading and writing, I went to his house and told him I would be happy to go through his mail daily and pay bills for him or handle any other paperwork. He took me out to his shop and showed me his shotgun that he had sawed off. Sadly, I wasn't smart enough to put 2 + 2 together and didn't think anything of it. Several weeks later, he climbed in Lee's van at the golf course and used it on himself.

Probably only minutes after he did it, I drove in and parked in my usual spot right next to Lee's van. Thankfully, I didn't look at or into the van. I had already been through something similar with my dad when I was a kid. Approximately an hour later, someone ran into the pro shop and reported it to me, and I then called 911.

Due to all the investigating and processing of evidence, we were told not to say anything to anybody about what was going on. It was hours before Roger's body and Lee's van were removed from the premises. I was told not to contact his family, because a clergyman was going to talk to them.

His son Ben called and wanted to talk to his dad. I lied and told him Roger had left and I didn't know where he went. I couldn't stand the thought of Ben driving in and seeing his dad in the van.

Days later Ben had called and was upset that I had lied to him. A couple of weeks later, at Roger's service, he told me he understood and said he was sorry. I was the one who was sorry for not making Roger's work situation tolerable. I just didn't realize how bad it had been for him.

CHAPTER 58

Cooking at the Golf Course

We started hiring help in the restaurant once Liz was pregnant with Willie. The first such person was Jeannie. She was a middle-aged hardworking gal who could cook, serve, clean and, most important of all, put up with Chris and me.

In today's world she could probably report us for harassment or at least mental cruelty. There was nothing that was sexual harassment, just joking around. The truth was that Jeannie could handle herself and she gave it back in spades. Jeannie had worked in taverns as well and she was a perfect fit for us.

Over the course of about the next three years, we had help from the Storaasli girls. The Storaasli family lived about a mile from the course. Nancy, the girls' mother, was the best golfer in the Ladies' Club. She was also nice, beautiful and fun to have around. Doug, the father of the girls, was a decent golfer (Nancy could kick his butt at golf) and he was a character. I took him to several pro-ams because he was fun to golf with.

Chris and I were a bit more refined around the girls, but we were still ourselves. We respected the Storaasli family.

The girls were named Teri, Lauri and Sandy. All three of them worked hard and were pleasant all the time. The golfers loved them (who wouldn't) and they just made the place more alive.

Teri, the oldest girl, went on to marry Rick Fehr, who was an accomplished PGA tour player. Rick is now working as a teaching pro in the Seattle area. It's a small world. Years earlier I had been paired with Rick's dad, Jerry Fehr, in the Seattle amateur.

The middle daughter, Lauri, worked for us longer than either of her sisters. Lauri ended up marrying John Whims, who is now the insurance agent for Snoqualmie Falls Golf Course.

Sandy, the youngest sister, didn't work for a long time at the course, but she was a great addition when she did.

One day I got a call at the golf course from Doug Storaasli. He had been driving past our house on Fish Hatchery Road and he had been shot at and hit by some kid with a BB gun. He was pretty sure it was my son, Willie. It sounded *possible*; no, make that *probable*, actually I'll go with *for sure* that Willie bagged a moving vehicle. Thankfully, Doug was good natured and there was very little damage to the car.

The Storaasli family ended up opening a Dairy Queen and they did well with it. I think once they retired from it, they moved to Texas.

The main reason I brought up the Storaasli family was to fool you into thinking that I was a balanced and responsible man. Certainly, such fine upstanding parents wouldn't let all their daughters work for someone who wasn't.

Once the Storaasli girls moved on, it was only a couple more years before we started leasing out the restaurant. We went through a couple of leasees, and all did fine but decided to move on after a couple years. Then, for close to 20 years, Mike Salgado, otherwise referred to as Gato, ran the restaurant. Gato kept the place staffed with competent, hardworking, pleasant and beautiful young ladies. His parents, Ray and Cora, also helped through the busy months when they were dodging the heat of their home in Las Vegas.

Thanks to Gato and his staff, the course was able to maintain a family run atmosphere. The pro shop people, outside crew and restaurant staff all worked together and had fun together. The backbone of Gato's staff was Vanessa and Megan. They, along with Gato, would even come out and help with flood cleanup.

Besides operating the clubhouse restaurant full time, Gato helped run the Kingman Open for 20 years. It was a great golf tournament with an auction that raised over $25,000 annually for cancer research. Vanessa and Megan also helped with this.

All work and no play would make Gato, Vanessa and Megan dull little campers. Consequently, fun was always close whether at work or other activities.

One year, Gato bought eight tickets for the annual WSU Cougar football game to be played in Seattle. The rest of their home games were played on campus in Pullman. I think the game in Seattle was for recruiting purposes and, yes, to make money.

Amongst the eight to attend were Gato and his wife Pam. Vanessa

Mike Salgado, aka "Gato," showing his tough side.

Good Guy Gato with wife Pam, and daughters Gabby to his right and Meghan to Pam's left. When Gato took over the lease, Meghan was 3 and Gabby was not born yet.

and her boyfriend Cody (now her husband) were part of the group with Megan and me.

Of course, we had to meet for brunch and beverages before the 1:00 PM game. We met at a restaurant/bar in Pioneer Square about four blocks from the stadium.

After a good breakfast and several beers, we headed for the stadium on foot. We had a full football game to sober up since no alcohol is served at college games. No one had to worry about a DUI while driving home after the game.

My sick mind came up with the idea of holding hands with Megan as we walked just to watch the look on people's faces. Megan was a bit

Megan forgives me for making her hold hands with me in public.

Vanessa at her wedding reception. "So Vanessa, there was this groom who put a jelly bean in a jar every time they made love in the first year of marriage. After that he took one out of the jar every time and they never emptied it."

hesitant, but I convinced her that she wouldn't see anyone she knew, and it would be fun watching people's reactions.

At the time I was about 65 and Megan around age 22. Megan is also several inches taller than me. On top of everything she is cute, and I am chunky.

I have to give Megan credit. She lasted for two blocks before she bellowed, "I can't do this!"

Some of the looks we got were priceless. I saw at least ten wives elbow their husbands and point at us. Megan managed not to throw up and since that was years before COVID, she didn't even ask for hand sanitizer when we got to the stadium!

Three years ago, Gato decided he had done the restaurant thing long enough. He now works in the pro shop and on the outside greens crew as well. I'm just happy that he is still part of our Sno Falls family.

CHAPTER 59

Pro Shop Crew and Other Characters

Well, it's time to move up front to the pro shop. You all remember Bill Porter, the principal owner. I have mentioned some of the business aspects regarding Bill, but behind the scenes are some lighter anecdotes.

When he was working (at least that is what he thought he was doing), I had to make sure there was another person or two there to help him out. Bill would quite often forget to turn off the microphone after calling groups to tee off. The speaker would then broadcast to everyone the conversations taking place in the pro shop. I can't vouch for every pro shop in the world since I have only worked in four of them. However, my experience has been that the conversations can be a bit *interesting* at times. They can even involve discussions about people on the first tee or practice green that the employee or customer in the shop may not have wanted them to know anything about.

If it was at all busy or if one customer showed up, Bill couldn't handle it. One day when we had no golfers, I went outside to give a lesson. I stayed close by so Bill could get me if something happened. Before I knew it, Bill was yelling for my help.

I came running in to find two people in the building. They were Bill and the guy who asked for a hot dog. It turned out that the only buns that Bill could find were frozen and in the original plastic wrapping. Bill had decided to throw the entire package, with plastic wrapping, onto the grill to thaw them out. I can honestly tell you that it is exceptionally difficult to get melted and burned plastic to come off a 375-degree grill.

It was also entertaining to watch him run the starting sheet and call people to the first tee. On more than a few occasions he would pick up the microphone and say, "Hello. Snoqualmie Falls Golf Course,"

Shawn Thornton – aka "Side Show" or "Freaky". He is a very good golfer who won the Club Championship again this year. I think he putts so well because his eyes are different colors.

into it for all to hear. He would also reverse the process and pick up the phone and call a group to the tee box.

One day, when it was very busy, Wade came back into my office and said, "Come look at this!"

Wade Iacolucci was the second person I ever hired to be an assistant golf pro for me. We had previously hired his older brother Spencer, who had worked on the greens crew. We also hired his younger brother, Keith, to work for us. All three brothers had grown up just down the street from our house. Wade liked to use the word "helmet" when referring to someone that was stupid or doing something stupid or looked stupid to him. Helmet, of course, was in regard to the appearance of the end of a man's thingy. OK, I'll try to appear grown up and say in reference to the end of a man's penis.

Wade Iacolucci aka "Mutt" – the creator of the "helmet foursome" with his understanding wife, Leslie.

On this day, Wade had opened, and Bill had come in to "work" along with a retired schoolteacher named Bob Albrecht. I was in my office at this point, but I had been working with Wade before Bill and Bob came in to work. Having Bill and Bob take over for Wade and I on a busy day was not a wise move, but it was potentially entertaining.

I followed Wade back into the pro shop and he said, "look at the starting sheet."

There in the starting slot for 12:15 was the name "Helmet." Behind the name were four check marks to indicate that all four members of the group had paid their green fees and were waiting to be called to the tee box. Of course, Wade had fictitiously done the whole thing, and there was no such group around. It did make me wonder if anyone

Keith Iacolucci aka "Spanky." I named the boulder behind him "Mount Spankmore" since it looks like him.

actually had that last name, but I was ready for some sort of show to occur.

About then Bill announced over the PA system, "Jones on the tee, Smith on deck, Helmet in the hole."

If I were calling those groups to the tee I would have said, "Jones on the tee, Smith on deck followed by Collins. I didn't announce groups "in the hole" whether they were named Helmet or not.

After the Jones group teed off, Bill announced, "Smith on the tee, Helmet on deck, Collins in the hole."

About then, Bill and Bob began discussing if either of them knew who the Helmet group was or if they remembered checking them in. Wade and I were around the corner in my office laughing so hard that

Keith (Spanky) and his wife Andrea holding up their day's catch – it looks like they caught many more. Andrea was the starting point guard on the WSU Cougars basketball team.

we were crying. It was quite obvious that neither Bob nor Bill under-stood the other meaning of helmet as used by Wade.

Therefore, the next thing we knew, Bill says to Bob, "I'll go back to the restaurant and see if I can find the Helmet group."

We have never had speakers in the restaurant because the an-nouncements every seven to eight minutes would get annoying. As Bill waddled through the pro shop to get to the restaurant, Wade and I went out the back door and into the side entrance to the food area. I said waddled because Bill really and truly walked like a penguin.

Bill first yelled out, "Is the Helmet group here?"

Then he went table to table asking individuals, "Are you a Helmet? Have you seen a Helmet?"

Fortunately, Bill was old enough and feeble enough that nobody hit him. He got back to the front desk in time to make the next call, "Next on the tee the Helmet group, on deck Collins, Carter in the hole."

Bill then went out on the deck in search of any Helmets and once again made it back unscathed. He and Bob then concluded that the Helmet group must have teed off earlier and they hadn't noticed.

I am fairly sure I have never laughed any harder than I did that day. In retrospect, if Doug and Nancy Storaasli had witnessed our behavior, their girls may not have been allowed to work for me.

Before I dive into another Bill Porter story, I need to introduce a number of young guys who either worked for me or just hung around and played golf during that era. I'm just going to give you names and their nicknames, along with how they earned their nicknames. As the book goes on, they will pop up in stories here and there. That period ran from the last three years we ran the restaurant until about four years after Bill Porter's death, or about 1985 to 1998.

My first assistant pro was Mark Roberts. Mark was with us for barely a year. He was one of two people who I actually fired. He tended to have loud phone calls with his wife that featured four letter words. These calls often took place in front of golfers. Also, when he gave putting and chipping lessons, he would often sit on the deck and sip 7 Up. He would then yell directions to his students as they putted or chipped down below at the practice green. This is the only time I mention him, although there is one funny story about him losing a bunch of bets with our golfers that I should at least mention. He told the group of about 10 guys that he was going to pay them, but he must have dropped his wallet on the course. He then pretended to go out to look for it, but instead got in his car and left as quickly as possible to avoid paying his bets. Unlike the rest of the guys, I am about to discuss, Mark never got an official nickname.

Wade Iacolucci, the creator of the "Helmet Story", was the second person I ever employed as an assistant pro. I named him "Mutt" and quite often he was referred to as "The Mutt." The original origin of the name came from a note he had written about someone in which he referred to this person as a Helmut. Due to his misspelling it and his love for the word, I just had to name him "Mutt." The Mutt has worked at several different clubs since he left us, but "The Mutt" has stayed with him. There is more to come about The Mutt, but he now works at Swinomish Golf Links in Anacortes, WA.

David Doty became my next assistant professional. Sometimes I refer to him as "our own Don Rickles." Mutt, David and I were fishing in Eastern Washington one day in Mutt's 13-foot metal boat. One could even call it a confined space for three guys. After at least five hours of fishing, it struck me that David had kept up a steady stream of jabs at both me and The Mutt.

I then said, "David, you just have to ignite things. You are like a spark plug. I don't know whether to call you Sparky or Plug. Personally, I prefer Plug and to add emphasis it needs two G's. Let's call you Plugg."

Therefore, David became Plugg until one day his mother heard him called that. Due to her Japanese accent, she said, "Why you call him Prugg? That's a funny name."

Shortly it became Pruggy because that was more affectionate.

Dave "Prugg" Doty and my son Jeff "Radar" Groshell were the only two to start and finish becoming PGA Members under my tutelage. As a PGA member it was my responsibility to help teach them. I have always felt that it was my responsibility to take advantage of any potential learning experience. One fine afternoon at Snoqualmie Falls GC, Pruggy and I were there when an opportunity hit us in the face.

Bill Porter was leafing through his personal mail, like maybe two envelopes. One of them contained a new credit card. He took the new card out of its envelope and studied it closely. He then got his old card out of his wallet. His next move was to get scissors out of the desk drawer where he was sitting.

After studying both cards for a bit, he swung into action. Just as he was about to slice and dice his card, Pruggy jumped in. "No, Bill, that's your new one."

Bill stopped, put that card in his wallet and proceeded to cut up the old one after Pruggy checked it out.

I waited a few minutes and then invited Pruggy out on the porch for a teaching session. It went something like this:

Me: "What were you thinking?"

Pruggy: "What do you mean?"

Me: "Chances like that only happen a few times in a lifetime!"

David Doty aka "Pruggy." I'm not saying that he is a smartass, but I do call him our own Don Rickles.

Pruggy: "What?"

Me: "We could have watched him cut up his new card and you ruined it!"

Pruggy: "I should have let him, really?"

Me: "No shit, little Beaver! You will never have that chance again!"

Pruggy: "You would have let him do it?"

Me: "Did you hear me stopping him?"

We still talk about that on occasion. The next time I get a new card I should take it out in front of Pruggy and act like I'm going to cut up the new one and see if he stops me.

Keith Iacolucci, the third Iacolucci boy to work at Sno Falls, got his name "Spanky Boy" and/or "Spanky" from his older brother The Mutt. I'm sure there was something to inspire it, but I couldn't possibly imagine what that would be.

Bob Clark was a retired military guy who played golf at Sno Falls and hung around there a lot. Bob was also a Men's Club officer. When the Men's Club got their first computer to calculate handicaps, Bob was the guy called on to install it and get it running correctly. Bob spent days and days of sitting on a stool bent over and staring at the screen. While doing this he was wearing glasses that sat down on the end of his nose. After watching him hour after hour, it struck me that he looked like Mr. Peabody, so that is what I started calling him. You know the little white dog on *Rocky and Bullwinkle* that knew everything. That quickly stuck and became just plain "Peabody", which is what everyone including his wife calls him to this day.

Shawn Thornton grew up down the street from us. He was in the same class as my son Jeff, which is how he ended up becoming a golfer in the first place. Besides playing almost every sport with Jeff and brother Willie, he would come golfing with them quite often and is still a golf addict and very good player to this day. Shawn was hanging out one day shooting the breeze with Pruggy and me. Shawn just happens to have two different colored eyes. I think one is green/hazel and the other brown. Pruggy was doing his usual Don Rickles job of attacking both of us verbally.

I was doing all I could to get Shawn to fire a comment back at Pruggy, so I could then go after him. Finally, he weakly muttered something like "You Jap" back at Pruggy.

Immediately I seized the opportunity and turned on him by saying, "Who the hell do you think you are talking to David like that? Just because his sweet mother is Japanese, and he is half-Japanese doesn't give you the right to say something like that! And look at you, two different colored eyes, you're a freak. You belong in a circus in the sideshow. That's going to be your name here, *Sideshow!*" To this day, 30 years later he still goes by Sideshow or Freaky.

Our older son Jeff accidentally gave himself his first nickname while golfing with The Mutt in a pro-am at Everett Country Club. He was apparently having a bad round and had to play out of the woods on several occasions. In an effort to make light of it, he said to Mutt, "I feel like a squirrel going to collect nuts instead of a golfer today."

About two weeks later his new golf bag showed up with "Squirrel" in bold block letters on it. That name still resurfaces occasionally, but his other nickname "Radar" is the one that more people call him. He got that name from Lee Baldwin, who thought he looked and sounded like Corporal Radar O'Reilly from the TV show *M*A*S*H*.

Our younger son, Willie, was given the name "Cleeto", also by The Mutt. He earned that name by constantly wearing his soccer shoes in the pro shop. Willie did play goalie for Mount Si High School's soccer team and Linfield College's soccer team.

John Irvive, who helped in the pro shop, was on the putting green one day practicing. There was a light rain coming down. I had never noticed that he was losing a bit of hair, but the light rain was making it obvious. Spanky was standing on the small deck by the pro shop, and he most certainly noticed. Spanky hollered, "Hey guys, come look at Island Head! Wow, Look at the island!"

Thus "Island Head" was born. Spanky was a couple years older than Island Head and tended to be mean to him.

Erin Ginnell was one of the hockey players for the Seattle Thunderbirds that we were billets for. Erin, being Canadian, soon was referred to as "Cheese Head." There wasn't much creativity to that name. There are a number of things to still come up involving him.

All of these young guys were within six years of age of each other with my younger son Willie (Cleeto) being the youngest. This era, as I called it, took place during a 10- to 12-year period when they ranged from 15 to 30 years of age.

Island Head grew up and moved to the East Coast many years ago. Whenever he returns to visit his parents, he calls or comes by to visit.

Peabody has moved to Lynden, WA about a 3-hour drive from Snoqualmie Falls GC. We still hear from him periodically.

The Mutt is at Swinomish Golf Club, as I mentioned earlier. Liz's sister, Eileen, lives in La Conner, which is a stone's throw from his golf course. Eileen hits range balls there on occasion. Every time she does, she calls Liz to tell her how nicely Wade treated her. Eileen's granddaughter Jessica even worked as the beer cart girl at his course.

Cheesehead went into scouting for hockey clubs and is presently the head of scouting for the new Las Vegas Golden Knights of the NHL. I still hear from him occasionally.

Son Willie, *aka* Cleeto, lives in Milwaukie, Oregon and delivers mail. Yes, I still hear from and see him!

Spanky lives in Seattle and has retired from being a carpenter to "come home" and take over the lease for the restaurant at the golf course. During his carpentry years he has helped us clean up after floods and he has done a number of building projects for the golf course and for me personally.

Sideshow is still nearby, living on Vashon Island with his family. While all these guys were good players with single digit handicaps, he was the best of the group who didn't become a PGA pro. He and I share the course record at Snoqualmie Falls having both shot 60, 11 under par. To be fair to Shawn, he shot 60 when the course was harder. I did it in the mid-'70s before the trees got bigger and sand traps were added. When I did it, I lipped out a four-foot putt on #18 that would have given me a 59. Freaky comes out to help clean up after floods and he is there to win the Club Championship most years too. He just won the 2022 Club Championship a couple weeks ago.

Of course, my son Jeff (Radar) and Pruggy are there and running the place since I retired.

One more guy, Ken McConkey, should be included. Little Kenny worked on the maintenance crew for several years, and he is still around. He is front and center to help with flood cleanup, and he is the Commish for the fantasy football league that Radar, Cleeto, Pruggy, Sideshow, Spanky, Gato and I compete in along with three other guys. With the exception of Gato and Peabody, the rest of that group grew up at the golf course. To me they are all family. Those who grew up there are like sons to me. If I ever need or needed help, they would be there for me.

I guess I need to include my nickname during that period, as well afterwards, to all of these guys.

When my parents had the newspaper, they would print and send out annual family reports. This was a combination Christmas card and family newsletter. There were pictures and articles covering the Groshell family's year as that year was ending. Both Hiram and I hated these reports.

Since the valley was small, everyone knew each other, and these reports were delivered to all of our classmates' houses, these reports often led to embarrassment at school for my brother and me. When I was about eight years old, one of these newsletters contained a picture of Hiram and me walking in a field. It was a big picture taken from up close, so there was no way to claim that the picture wasn't of us. The best part of the picture was the caption underneath: "Two little punkins in a field." Oh, soooo cute! Many kids brought these to school, which was a real joy! After a month or so of harassment I thought it was over, but as I have learned since, nightmares never seem to end.

Fast forward 30 years later, and one of my classmates prances into the pro shop with one of these cards. The person had good intentions and thought I might want it as I actually did want it and it was very kind of them to bring it in. Mutt happened to spot it on my desk later and of course found the picture with the caption. Starting that day and continuing forever, I am Punkin or Punky to that whole crew.

CHAPTER 60

Toes Knows

There was one person who was a big part of my golfing life—both in my 10 years working and playing at Mount Si Golf Course and many of my years at Snoqualmie Falls.

Within a couple of years of playing at Mount Si and getting lessons from Harry, I was a four handicap or less. My fellow maintenance worker and buddy, Gary, had been a four handicap or less since he was 14 or 15 years old. He and I would work eight hours outside then tee off around 3:00 pm several days a week. We liked playing alone so we could give each other a bad time and practice extra shots as well.

We were just about to tee off when Hughie, the assistant pro, leaned out of the pro shop window and yelled, "Hold on, brats, I've got a single coming out to join you."

We looked at each other with an "Oh, crap" look on our faces as an old man of 45 to 50 years of age approached. He introduced himself and we teed off. As it turned out he was a low handicap player and funny to boot.

Gary and I had more laughs that round as Trig Ambjor joked and gave us a bad time all around the course. He may have even beaten one or both of us. For the rest of my years playing at Mount Si, I played many rounds with Trig. During my school teaching years the usual foursome was myself, Jim North, Hughie and Trig.

During that span I did more betting with them on golf than I ever have since. My last couple of years teaching was when I played the best golf of my life. I actually counted on my winnings for my spending money and was seldom without enough.

Jim North was the ex-Washington Redskin tackle who was my freshman basketball coach. He was also a very good player and character who got a bee in his pants in the Washington Amateur. I went through all of that earlier.

Hughie was the assistant pro and PGA Member who was also a ladies man and a real character.

Trig Ambjor was an excellent singer, joke teller and fun-loving guy who played well enough to beat me twice in the Men's Club Championship finals at Mount Si. The two years I won it, I beat Jim North in the finals.

Always, when we played as a foursome, Jim and I were partners against Trig and Hughie. The summer before Hughie took the job of head pro at Kellogg CC in Idaho, the boys cut back on the amount of betting with me, I was winning too much.

These three "wild, golfing, beer-drinking fellows" became my mentors after my family went poof. They never pushed me to be an Eagle Scout.

After I had been at Snoqualmie Falls Golf several years, Trig started playing there on occasion. He had gotten divorced and lost his job. I ended up hiring him to marshall the golf course and help out in the pro shop. After a number of years, he even moved into our basement where we had plenty of room for him. As an employee he was fun and added life to what was already a lively bunch. He fit right in with my "kids".

As you have read, we all had nicknames. One had to have thick skin on occasion to survive. Trig battled diabetes for years. Finally, due to an infection that wouldn't clear up, the docs amputated his right leg below the knee. Soon he went from Trig to "Five Toes". The Mutt has to be given credit for coming up with that name. We all got stuck with names we may or may not have liked. Most of the time we would streamline it to simply "Toes". Often when Trig made a statement or answered a question one of the "kids" would say, "Toes Knows."

Once recovered from surgery and used to his new leg, Toes went right back to golfing. He had played many pro-ams with me with ten toes and continued to with five. While he obviously wasn't as good, he was still quite competitive.

There was a two day pro-am in Sequim, WA every year that I would take three amateurs to. Toes played in it with me several years. It was one of those years that he came up with a new name for me. As we were walking off the 18th green, after one of the rounds, he said, "Good round, Fluffy Stumpf**ker."

I kind of liked it. It has a friendly ring to it.

Several years later after several setbacks with his diabetes, Toes passed away. A large crowd wanted to send Trig off. Of course, I attended. Trig has been a friend since I was 17 and helped me during my formative years.

A number of people got up to talk about Trig. One after another they spoke of this fine family man who had found God. Trig was a good person for sure, but they were painting a picture of someone else. I felt it was necessary for me to say goodbye to the Trig I knew and liked. Keep in mind that the crowd was mainly composed of well-dressed couples from 60 to 80 years of age.

So, as I was looking up to wherever heaven might be, I said, "Well, Trig, I can forgive you for beating me twice in the Men's Club Championship. I can also forgive you for turning me into what I am with your influence during my formative years. In fact, I can forgive you for everything except for naming me "Fluffy Stumpf**ker."

Well, the house came down. I have never seen that many "Old Ladies" of 60 to 80 laugh so hard. Oops, I am 77 now—I meant "young ladies."

CHAPTER 61

More Bill Porter Stories

Lest you feel that I am cruel or heartless based on stories regarding Bill Porter, let me give you a bit of background.

Bill was a nice man, but he was always a businessman who looked after number one. When Bill, Terry and Art bought Snoqualmie Falls GC, Bill put in $50,000 as a loan to the corporation that they formed. Terry and Art each put up $2,500 as an investment, not as a loan. Over the next eight years, Bill received full payment with 10% interest on that loan. Art and Terry each got $20,000 for their shares when they sold. The $20,000 I paid bypassed Terry and the courts paid off people he had scammed.

While Bill, Chris and I were there, we drew equal pay. That was fine, but the money I received for giving lessons went into the regular revenue. Also, Bill didn't even work half of the time that Chris or I did. Although I can understand not getting the money for lessons I gave when Chris was working, it seemed unfair because most of the lessons were given late in the day after Chris and Bill had gone home. During the day when Chris was working, I had to run the pro shop and restaurant, which made it impossible to give lessons until the last couple hours of daylight.

Once we started a buyout of Bill, it was done by retiring his shares as he was paid. This buyout started while Chris was still there. When we bought out Chris, his shares were retired as well.

At the point that Bill passed away, there was still a sizable amount left to finish retiring his shares. Bill had also given 13 of his shares to two of his friends. Once Bill died, the remaining part due to him, went to these same two friends. Once all of the payments were made, the number of shares remaining was 25, and they were all mine.

Over the entire process, all the buyout checks to Bill, Chris and Bill's friends were done with golf course checks. Once Bill and Chris were gone, golf course checks were from me alone.

Now I have been informed that if I were to sell the golf course, as far as the IRS is concerned, I only paid $25,000 for it. In actuality, I have paid close to $800,000. How much money in taxes do you think Bill and his heirs had to pay? If I were a betting man, which we all know I am not, I would want the under on his tax burden. If I were to sell it for one million dollars, I would owe tax of over 50% on $975,000. Basically, I can't sell. What I get is a dividend payment monthly and I will for about 10 years.

Let's say a guy buys a hardware store for one million dollars, and he pays $100,000 of that as a down payment with his own money. The remaining $900,000 plus interest he pays with his new hardware store checks. When he sells will he only get credit for his original $100,000? I think not! Every move Bill ever made was made while looking after Bill's finances.

With that in mind, I think I earned the right to tell "true" stories that are factual accounts, even if they involve Bill!

I admit that being able to buy part of a golf course for an initial $20,000 was an opportunity that would be hard to find. The best opportunity went to Art and Terry, who got the same thing for $2,500, and they both blew it.

The lucky guy was Bill, who got a person who had worked in golf for ten years and could do everything from mow greens to give lessons. That guy was also willing to work 80+ hours a week and his wife was willing to work in the kitchen for nothing. Then he got a guy named Chris, who busted his ass like John did and could handle golf course maintenance, cooking and pro shop work as well.

So anyways, many times Bill tried to open a pro shop window that wasn't made to open. He would answer the microphone instead of the telephone. He would try to make announcements on the telephone instead of the microphone. He would forget to turn off the microphone, which would lead to all sorts of PR problems when people heard conversations taking place inside. At this time, Bill was in his upper 60's. I am now 77 and work part-time in the pro shop at Ocean Shores Golf Course, only causing mayhem when I intend to.

Bill liked to check the cash register periodically to see how much money he was making. He seldom operated it, because we preferred to have an accurate accounting of business for each day. When he was there working, oops I meant making an appearance, he would sit at the desk playing starter and phone answering guy.

One day when he decided to travel the five feet from his chair to the register to check our current earnings, something funny (for those watching) happened to Bill. He pushed the buttons to get a reading and then bent over to check out the safe that was in a cabinet under the register. Apparently, he forgot that the cash drawer came out when those buttons were pushed. Being bent over the drawer lightly bumped him in the head when it opened. This disturbed whatever sense of balance that he had, and he began flailing his arms while yelling, "*Whoa-whoa-whoa!*"

He then fell to the floor landing on his wallet area. See, I didn't say something less classy like his butt. Anyway, there he was on his backside flapping and flailing his arms like a turtle on its back. Pruggy and Spanky were the two working with him at the time, so I unfortunately didn't get to witness the event. However, I was told that Spanky got the jump on Pruggy and darted to the restaurant, which left Pruggy to get the turtle righted. I don't know if someone else helped Pruggy or not, but he got Bill back on his feet. Thankfully Bill wasn't hurt. It turned out that the wallet was a good enough cushion.

One day Bill took Spanky, Cheesehead and me to play Overlake Country Club, where he was a member. Bill was being nice to invite them, and they really wanted to play the course. They asked me to go along as well to add to the fun for the day. I had played Overlake in a number of tournaments, so playing it wasn't a big thrill. I did want to go golfing with Spanky and Cheesehead though.

Bill always had a couple of Jim Beams before golf, and he didn't want to drive from Sno Falls to Overlake or home to his apartment after golf either. This meant someone would be his driver. On top of that, someone would need to ride with him in the golf cart when we played. Plus, someone would have to be his partner in team games, which would be a bit costly.

I established that I would be Bill's betting partner. Keith and Erin were both about 6 handicappers. My pro-am handicap was about a 3 or 4 at the time, and Bill was somewhere in the twenties. There was virtually no chance that I wouldn't lose with Bill as my partner, but this way I established that I was not his driver or cart partner.

Therefore, Spanky and Cheesehead had to determine who would drive him in his car and who would ride with him in the golf cart while playing. They decided that rolling dice was the best way to settle it. Before they started the roll off, they both decided that riding in the cart was the better option, since they could get out and walk for some of the round.

They started the dice rolling in my office, while Bill and I were just outside of it working at the counter in the pro shop. Every roll of the dice was followed by either cheering or yelling with continuous laughter and swearing. Bill kept on asking me what they were doing and/or betting on. I just said I had no idea what those two idiots were up to.

I just talked to Spanky yesterday and he said that he thought he ended up sharing the golf cart with Bill, but he wasn't sure. That is possible since this did take place over 30 years ago.

The round was fine. We all took turns helping Bill out of sand traps. I don't think I lost more than $25 in bets. Overall, the most exciting part of the day was the dice game between Spanky and Cheesehead before we left for the course.

All my "boys" ranged in the late teens through early twenties during these years. They were all fun-loving, active males with minds to match.

Bill used to save the paper napkins he used when eating his lunch. He put them in the bottom right-hand drawer of the pro shop desk where he sat to answer phones and play starter. At that time, I had a dog named Angie that I would often bring to work with me. One afternoon, Pruggy (with Spanky and I present) took several of Bill's napkins out of the drawer, lifted Angie's tail and looked like he wiped her rear end with them. I was watching this in disbelief and saw that he didn't actually touch Angie with napkins anywhere. He then put the napkins back into the drawer. Pruggy did this for Spanky's benefit. Spanky wasn't big on things that were gross and was easily grossed out. Spanky was also quite picky about food on his plate.

For instance, if Spanky and his brother, The Mutt, both had an order of ham and eggs in front of them to eat, they would go about eating them quite differently. Spanky would eat each item separately, finishing each one before going on to eat the next. The Mutt would cut up the ham into bite size chunks and then stir up the eggs, hash browns and ham into a goulash that he would cover in ketchup.

Anyhow, Spanky was sure that Pruggy really did wipe Angie's rear end and then put the napkins back. Word passed to other employees until most thought there were Angie enhanced napkins in the drawer. It was rather interesting to watch other employees' responses if they were around and saw Bill using these napkins while he was eating.

Shortly after Bill passed away, which was a couple of years later, I started filling the drawer with mini-sized candy bars for employees to eat. Spanky happens to like candy bars as much as anyone, but to this day he still will not eat a candy bar that he even thinks was in that drawer.

That's enough Bill related stories for now. However, there are more stories from that era that should be shared.

CHAPTER 62

Prank Calls & More

When Spanky was 13 or 14, we had a gal working in the restaurant who was 21 or 22 years old. Suddenly it seemed like Spanky was hanging around the restaurant a lot when she was working. There were days when after she left work he would disappear shortly thereafter.

I never thought much about it; actually, none of us really noticed it. Until one day when I left the course at about 3:00 to go downtown to get the mail. At the top of the hill on the way out I got a glimpse of a bicycle that had been poorly hidden in the brush by the road. It was Spanky's bike.

I thought about how the gal had left, then Spanky had left, and then here is his poorly-hidden bike. *BINGO*—the light came on!

The next day when he came to the course he eventually strolled into my office. After several minutes of sharing pleasantries about this and that, I felt his guard was down, so I casually inquired, "So anyways, how many strokes did you last?"

His face went from natural to pink to red and he was about to sputter something out when I said, "Don't lie to me, Keith. You know I don't like lying."

Finally, he said, "We didn't screw!"

I said, "Oh! You just held hands I suppose."

He replied, "No, she gave me a b*** job."

To which I said, "So your first time you started with champagne instead of beer!"

Consequently, at least to President Slick Willy Clinton, Spanky did not have sex with that woman. To this day, and Keith is now 52 years old, we still give him a bad time about the day he hid his "Big Wheels" at the top of the driveway.

Moving back to Spanky's brother Mutt, one nice summer day the Mutt and I, along with my son Jeff went to play Sahalee CC. We had a good time and upon finishing we went to a nearby Shakey's Pizza. Jeff, *aka* Squirrel, was still a minor, but Mutt and I each had a couple beers to go with the pizza.

On the way home, Mutt thought it would be a good idea to go fishing at Lake Alice. The Russell brothers, who played Sno Falls every Sunday, had a cabin on the lake. We had an open invitation to use their rowboat and fish anytime we so desired.

When we dropped Jeff off at the house, I changed into fishing clothes and told Liz we were headed to Lake Alice to fish. She said fine but was studying me like she wasn't sure I should be going out on a lake.

"Don't do anything stupid," was my send off.

On the way, we stopped at the local gas station/convenience store and picked up a half rack of beer. We were having a peaceful afternoon and enjoying ourselves, even though the fish weren't biting. We weren't pounding down the beer, just sipping away.

It was after 3:00 when we started fishing, but in the middle of the summer it stayed light until almost 10:00 PM. After several hours, Wade had to pee. If we had been drinking hard instead of sipping, he would have had to pee sooner. The rowboat was not very stable. A canoe would flip easier, but not much easier.

Being young, coordinated and agile, Wade just stood up and peed out into the lake. I realized that there was no way I could pull that off without either falling out of the boat or tipping it over. Consequently, I hung on for over another hour. At that point it was either pee or head to shore, and there was still over an hour of daylight and fishing time left.

I knew I couldn't stand up and balance like Wade had done, so I tried to get turned to the side and get on my knees. Somehow in so trying, I lost my balance and grabbed the side of the boat. Immediately the boat flipped. It was like slow motion as I flew through the air before I splashed down in the lake. Out with Wade and I went our fishing poles, tackle boxes and the oars. Oh yes, the beer too and there were at least half of the 12-pack still remaining after about five hours of fishing.

Somehow during the mayhem, we saved our poles, Wade's tackle box and the oars. We also got the boat flopped back over right side up, but it was fairly full of water. Wade thought that if he climbed into the boat, he could row us to shore while I held onto the side. He climbed in and the boat sunk, so he got back out into the lake to keep the boat from sinking.

About then, Wade realized that somehow his legs had gotten wrapped up in fishing line and he couldn't kick. At that point, I had to kick long enough and hard enough to propel both of us and the boat to shore. Considering how many houses and cabins there are around the lake, I would think that someone would have noticed us, but they didn't. I guess most of the cabins were just weekend retreats with no one in them during the week.

There were two things working for us. Number one, the water wasn't cold. Number two, the lake was small. So, with Wade holding on and me kicking, we slowly inched toward the nearest shore. However it was on the opposite side of the lake from Russell's cabin. After over an hour we reached the shore. Even though Wade had saved his fishing box, he had lost his knife. Of course, he treasured that knife because it was a present from his wife, and she had purchased it for him in Italy. I had no knife from the beginning.

As a boy scout you are taught to be prepared, and I was totally prepared. I still had my teeth, so I could chew the line off his legs. Unfortunately, it wasn't a single wrap that he could have broken on his own. Somehow it was wrapped around his legs at least 10 times and it took me a considerable amount of chewing.

We emptied the water back out of the boat and climbed back in with what we had saved. Wade started rowing us back across the lake to our destination. About halfway across we heard and felt a bump. It was totally dark by now, but Wade reached over the side to try to grab it. Low and behold, there was our beer. Tell me, what are the odds of bumping into that in the middle of the lake? Since both Wade and I were Washington State Cougars, maybe it was meant to happen.

We made it to shore and drove home. By now it was 11:00 PM. I walked up the back steps to the house and took off all my wet clothes except for my shorts. Liz met me as I came in the door and was about to chew my ass out, but then took a good look at me. She just shook her head and went off to bed.

Back to the golf course for my next story. After we had the building remodeled, we added a new phone system. Prior to that we had two phone lines. Two separate phones in the pro shop, one for each number; there were no extensions or other phones to the kitchen, or the maintenance shed.

The new system had five extensions connected to the two lines and phone numbers. There was one extension in my office, two on the pro shop desk, one in the kitchen, and one in the maintenance shed. In a short time, "the boys" had gotten the hang of harassing each other with calls from one extension to another. In addition, I wasn't exempt from such calls.

One afternoon, my son Willie, *aka* Cleeto, was working with me in the pro shop. I was working and he was almost working. I was checking in customers and starting foursomes. He was supposed to at least answer phone calls and book tee times. As busy as I was, and with little help from him, I didn't notice him dialing one of the phones on the desk. The other phone on the desk started ringing and I saw he was on the other line, so I answered it with my usual, "Snoqualmie Falls Golf Course."

I then heard, "You dumb f**k!"

It was my sweet youngest son Cleeto, who dialed the other phone number right beside me and tricked me into answering. He had taken advantage of my working and not being able to see what he did.

On another day, I called the course from my house to ask about something. After several rings Island Head picked up the phone and said, "Go f**k yourself!"

He then immediately hung up without saying another word. He didn't even say Snoqualmie Falls Golf Course first. Of course, that was actually a good thing.

I think Island Head may have done this because of one of the pranks that my older son Jeff, *aka* Radar, started. Radar wanted to mess with them in retaliation for all of their phone pranking. Since they would often sneak into my office or the maintenance building to call the other line, most of them learned to look and see if one of the lines was already lit up before they answered. Then they could confidently answer with some smart reply to let the other one know they caught them. Radar figured out that he could casually go use the bathroom or go to get carts and just barely take a phone off the hook, so it looked like someone was already on one of the lines. Then when the person working with Radar answered the phone with a reply like, "Nice try, sucker" or something far worse like Island Head did to me, then they would feel stupid and have to explain their way out of their mistake with the customer. Plus it made it so they once again never knew if they were being pranked or not.

Regardless of why Island Head said it, I didn't phone back. I just planned to talk to all of them later to get the whole situation under control. I also knew that Island Head took a lot of crap from the others, especially from Spanky. Island Head was kind of the bottom of the pecking order. Plus, I remembered that I had done something quite similar to that many years earlier when I was working at Mount Si Golf Course.

Huey and I had been working together and he had taken a break to get something to eat. The restaurant at Mount Si was in a separate building that was a couple hundred feet from the pro shop. On various occasions, prank calls had been made from the restaurant to the pro shop.

Huey, the assistant pro who I talked about earlier, had been over there for about half an hour. Harry Umbinetti, the head golf pro, who leased and operated Mount Si GC was known to squeeze in extra foursomes. Mount Si was a busy golf course, and it was hard to get a starting time, especially on weekends. Consequently, we would always be behind on the starting times. On weekends being 30 to 45 minutes late was standard procedure at that time. Harry didn't care because he never worked the counter. He would arrive at 10:00 AM, check the cash register, and head to the restaurant. Golfers would call for him and get him to squeeze them in and Harry thought he made more money by doing this.

So anyways, unless one of these guys knew him well, they quite often had trouble saying Umbinetti. This brings me back to the phone call I got while Huey was in the restaurant. I answered, "Mount Si Golf Course, can I help you? "

I heard, "This is Dr. Johnson and I'd like to talk to my friend Harry Umbriago about a starting time this next Saturday."

I was absolutely sure it was Huey calling to mess with me. I barely finished saying, "Well, doctor, why don't you just go f**k yourself!" as Huey walked through the door into the pro shop.

I immediately hung up the phone. Fortunately, Dr. Johnson didn't call back or tell his friend Harry Umbriago about it.

Therefore, 30 years later I only felt bad for Island Head. When I got to the course I said, "I called the course about an hour ago and I must have dialed a wrong number. Whoever I called just picked up the phone and said, 'Go f**k yourself!' without even saying hello."

First, Island Head turned red and hardly knew what to say. Then, I explained that we had to ease off the prank calls, because it could lead to something bad happening. Last, I took Island Head aside and explained I was not mad at him, because I knew he took more crap from the rest of them. I also told him about my experience at Mount Si Golf Course years before.

CHAPTER 63

Wagers

I have been known to come up with a variety of strange bets, which is already obvious. For instance, what fly strip would catch the most flies, if Chris could eat a cinnamon roll in three bites, if Karl could drink a glass of polish sausage juice, etc.

Well, one busy Saturday afternoon at Snoqualmie Falls Golf Course I was chatting with Alan Lind and looking out the pro shop window toward the first tee and lower parking lot. Alan is the owner of The Last Frontier, which is a local watering hole in Fall City. He is also a golfer and fun-loving individual who is always willing to place a bet.

On a side note, Alan is the one who gave me the nickname Tiny Wood. It was a lovely addition to some of my other names like Punkin, Dairy Queen, Cupcake, and others to still share.

Before I move on to the bet, I should explain the events that led to my new nickname from Alan. One day I decided to be fitted for a new driver. I went to Pro Golf Discount where one of our regulars worked as a club fitter. This is the only time I ever was fitted for a club. He had me hit many drives with several different drivers. The swing monitor analyzes club head speed, position of club head at impact, backspin, launch angle, and many other things. After half an hour of this, he determined that the Nike driver with the senior flex shaft was the best one for me. I accepted his analysis, even though I've never been a fan of the Nike brand. Tiger Woods has been on their staff for years and played their clubs at this time. Although Tiger is possibly the best golfer ever, I have never been a fan of his. I also was never a fan of Mickey Mantle, even though I played at least 10 rounds of golf in Las Vegas with his brothers Ray and Roy. They were buddies with Huey, so on several trips to Vegas, they joined Huey and I for golf.

I do like Tiger more now that he has mellowed and controls his temper better. The point is that everyone at Sno Falls GC knew I did not care for Tiger or Nike. I am even pretty sure Nike was having kids overseas making clubs for them for little to no pay. None of the crew at Sno Falls GC thought I would ever own a Nike golf club. Consequently, I stunned everyone when I showed up with this Nike driver. After taking loads of crap for buying it and being a sell out, I finally said, "You can call me *Little Tiger*."

Alan Lind was standing right there, and he said, "No, you're not Little Tiger. You are Tiny Wood!" Thus, another flattering nickname was bestowed upon me.

Back to the bets. Alan and I are looking out the window and I observe two elderly ladies walking, with the aid of walkers, down the parking lot toward the lower lot. They were doing fine and did not appear to have any physical problems that could lead to injury. One of the ladies was wearing a yellow outfit and the other was dressed in purple. When they were about 50 feet from the lower parking lot, which is clearly defined by a line across the asphalt, I said, "I'll take Yellow for five bucks."

Alan looked and said, "OK, I've got Purple."

I replied, "First one to the lower lot wins."

Of course, at that point Alan and I started cheering. "Come on, Yellow!" "Go, Purple!" "Don't give up, Yellow!" "Dig in, Purple!"

It got really intense when Yellow stopped to help Purple take her sweater off. I was yelling, "Don't stop! Keep going!!!"

Alan was laughing and saying, "I've got you now! Purple, you can do it!"

These ladies were part of a group that had played a tournament that day at the course. There were about 40 who played and another 10 or so who had joined them for dinner after the golf. These two ladies had come out for the dinner after golf.

Alan and I, along with my son Jeff, were the only ones in the pro shop when the race began. During the excitement of the race, Alan and I didn't notice that anyone had walked in. Jeff later explained that the guy who came in was coming in to thank us for the golf and good food. He then looked out the window to see what Alan and I were cheering for. Once he figured out that we were betting on this race he proclaimed, "You guys are going to burn in hell!"

He must have thought we were betting on a crash or something morbid like that, but that was the last thing we wanted. We were simply caught up in a frivolous wager. By the way, Purple beat Yellow and I had to hand over an Abe Lincoln to Alan.

The only real gambling I have been involved in, besides the stock market, was with a bookie. That is because the only official gambling I like to do is sports betting. I have never liked playing cards. If I have enough beers, then playing poker with friends is all right. I flat don't like playing table games in casinos. I don't like playing pinochle or any other card game where I have a partner and need to think. Thinking and relaxing don't mix well, especially when you must keep track of cards played.

For years I wanted to get set up with a bookie, so I could do some sports betting. There was a guy, who was the sales rep for PowerBilt, who called on us regularly. Sometimes he would get to playing gin with Chris. Chris loved playing cards and rolling dice. I ended up talking with the rep about betting sports and he told me that he had a bookie that he placed bets with. After a few visits, I asked him if he could introduce me to his bookie, and he said he would talk to his bookie about it. The bookie went by the name "Doc" I guess because he was a professor at the University of Washington. Several weeks later, the rep called me and said I could tell him what I wanted, and he would then place them with Doc. He just had me get the lines out of the paper and call him with the wager.

After about a month of betting this way, I was about $700 up. Anytime I talked about getting paid, he would put me off. Supposedly, we had a $500 pay point. Either collect or pay off when $500 was reached. I was playing a pro-am at Glendale CC one day and ran into the rep in the bar after the round. By then I had pretty much figured out that the rep was keeping my bets and had never even talked to Doc about me. I was right.

At that point he did get me lined up with Doc. That was the good news. The bad news was that within a couple of weeks he skipped town. Through other golf pros and sales reps, I found out he moved to Whitefish, Montana, where he bought a restaurant.

I called city hall in Whitefish and got the name of the restaurant and got a hold of him there. He promised to pay me, but never did. That was over 35 years ago. In 2019, five of us went to The Masters in Augusta, Georgia. During the par 3 tournament on Wednesday before the official championship starts on Thursday, I ran into him in the gallery. I didn't bother to bring up the fact that he stiffed me for $700. It's a small world after all.

I became a regular customer with Doc. We had a $500 payoff point that we both made good on. I bet football, basketball and baseball with him. When it came to football, both college and pro, I pretty much broke even. I had ups and downs, but in the long run not much money changed hands.

Basketball was a different story. I did OK in college hoops, kind of like how I did betting football. When it came to the NBA it was another story. I was a loser. At one point I came up with a new system of betting. I would pick one or two games a day that I thought were good bets, then I would take the team that I thought had no chance to cover the bet. I figured that since I kept picking losers, I might as well bet against the teams that I thought would win. That system actually worked well for a couple of weeks, and then I went back down the crapper. I then decided I had enough of that, so I stopped betting basketball.

As bad as I was at basketball, I was almost that good at baseball. The first year or two of betting baseball, I came out a little ahead. Once I learned a few things I started winning much more frequently than I lost. In baseball, there are no runs given. Odds of winning are placed on the games. I formulated a system that took in factors in pitching, winning and losing streaks, home or away games, and overall feel of the teams' moods. I also would never take a big favorite and give big odds. I tended to take teams that were underdogs on the road and had lost several games in a row, but now their best pitcher was starting.

One summer when Spanky and Erin (*aka* Cheesehead) were working on the greens crew they wanted to get involved in betting. The minimum wager was $50. They couldn't afford that so I told them they could pick one game a day and I would put up $25 to match their $25. They were worried about me losing $25 on a team they chose. To ease their minds, I told them I would pay $25 to watch monkeys f**k. That became their favorite motto.

That summer they made several hundred dollars each. Then in the winter Erin went back home to Canada, but before he left, they bought me a present. It was a big clock with a pendulum, and it had a plaque that read, "Thanks from Ginuchi Incorporated." That was a combination of last names, Ginnell and Iacolucci.

After a couple of years of betting I had several guys who wanted me to get bets down for them. I ended up being a pseudo bookie since I would keep some bets and pass others along. It quickly became a huge pain in the ass. The losers weren't big on paying and the guys would get all worked up if they could not get a hold of me to place a bet.

I had a rule for myself that I tried to adhere to. If I had a hard time getting a bet down, forget it because I would probably lose it. For years Doc would take calls and personally give out the lines as well as take the wagers. Everything was done over the phone live. You would talk to Doc or his wife, or even one of his three grown daughters. I ended up being a friend of the whole family and even spent one Christmas morning at their house.

One day when I called to get the lines, I got a recording instead. The recording would give out all the point spreads and then you could record your bets. The next day I got a hold of Doc and explained that he was just asking for trouble by doing this business on recordings. I said that if a wife got mad about her husband's betting, all she would have to do is call the police and give them the number to call. He said he knew all his guys and that would never happen.

Unfortunately, he was wrong, and it did happen. The police, FBI and IRS all came down on him. Because he was in poor health, he ended up with house arrest. However, by the time everything was done, they even lost their house.

I then decided I had enough of betting and a few years later turned to playing fantasy sports. It is more fun and not nearly as expensive!

CHAPTER 64

Does He Know Anything?

My dad would be pleased to know that his training did not go to waste. He succeeded in teaching me to keep a straight face. He conditioned me to be able to do intentionally stupid things and to come through them with confidence and pride intact. You do remember my shopping trips with him? He got me to have sponge and bath salts color combinations switched multiple times. He got me to get change for a quarter three times before I got my quarter back. He even had me watch him break wooden toys, while he appeared to be mentally challenged.

One day I was on the small deck just outside of the pro shop and I was talking with Sideshow, who was practicing his putting on our putting green. At the same time, my son Jeff was conducting a ladies group evening golf lesson. He had about a dozen ladies in the weekly group. When they finished getting instruction at the driving range, they would go out to play 9 holes. Four of these ladies were ready to play and they were at the back of the first tee, not knowing what they should do next. Because they were new at golf and new to our golf course, they didn't know who I was at all. Of course, I had been the head golf pro for over 25 years and at this point I owned the facility.

I happened to hear one of the ladies ask the others, "I wonder if that guy on the porch knows anything?"

Although that question is certainly a valid one if you know me, she could have asked, "I wonder if that guy on the porch knows if we should tee off now?" Another possibility would have been, "Let's go ask that guy what we are supposed to do now", but *no!* I hear, "I wonder if that guy on the porch knows anything?"

Come on, give me a break. I *had* to respond.

From me to where the ladies were it was about 100 feet. I had to speak in a clear and somewhat loud manner so they could hear me.

Since their question implied that I was possibly mentally challenged, I chose a slightly deeper voice than my own and spoke at a slower than usual pace. I also felt the need to repeat myself as I went on for added effect.

It went something like this:

"Shawn, I do know something! I do! Shawn --- Shawn --- I know when to turn over a pancake --- I do --- I know, Shawn! --- Do you know when to flip a pancake? --- Do you? --- Shawn ------ It's when it starts to bubble on top --- That's when --- When it starts to bubble --- That's when, Shawn --- I know, because I have done it, Shawn. Really, Shawn --- I know! --- See --- I do know something, Shawn --- I do --- I do!!!!"

I do not understand why for sure, but the ladies teed off as fast as they could. Maybe it was because they finally learned when to flip a pancake, and there was nothing else they needed to know?

Along this same line, one afternoon Pruggy invited me to a BBQ at his house in Fall City. This was a few years before he got married. I went to the party and there were at least twenty guys and gals there. Hamburgers were being eaten and beer was washing them down. At some point, two young gals happened to end up standing close to me. They were in their early twenties and were casual friends of David.

These girls did nothing to prompt me to say what I did or in the challenged appearance in which I acted. Maybe the beer had an influence, but I just think it was my sick mind taking over. At the time, I was somewhere between 45 and 50 years of age.

One of the girls said Hi and introduced herself and her friend to me.

I replied in my challenged manner, *"Hi, I'm John --- I'm Dave's friend."*

One of them asked how I knew David.

That is when my little sick show really got going. I replied, *"David is my friend --- He is - I know him - David helps me --- I do carts at the golf course for David --- He lets me do them --- I wash them - I do! --- I get them clean --- David showed me how - I like David ---David is nice to me --- David picks me up and takes me there to wash the carts --- David showed me how to put gas in the carts too - He did! --- Some days he lets me do that all by myself --- David is so nice to me --- David takes me back home when I'm done - I like David!"*

Finally, they both agreed that David was indeed nice and that it was good of him to help me. They then went on to visit others. At that point, I left to go back to work and the show I was putting on was over. I also already knew almost everyone at the party.

Several weeks later, I was working in the pro shop taking green fees, running the starting sheet and answering phones. It was busy and I was doing my best to handle one customer at a time. I didn't have time to see everyone who was in the pro shop lined up at the counter waiting for service.

About that time, I look up to see one of the girls from David's party as my next customer at the counter. The look on her face as she stared at me was somewhere between bewilderment and angry. Here was this so-called challenged person handling this hectic job. The answer was obvious: I was a jerk.

Once I focused on her and remembered who she was, I said in my challenged manner, *"Hi, I'm John --- Can I help you?"*

She was far nicer to me than she should have been, but obviously not pleased. I decided it was best for me to put that act to bed before someone else acted more violently as a result.

I did have one other act that I used at my friend Tom's local Tesoro gas station. I like to blame Tom for it. It wasn't my fault that one day he had a car up on a hoist and the engine in the car was still running.

Tom no longer has this station, but when he did it was the only place that I gassed up my car. The office at the station where you paid cash for gas was very small. In the office was a desk and hardly anything else. There was room behind the desk for Tom and his landline phone. This was before everyone had a cell phone. By the way, I still do not have a cell phone. Between the desk and the customer's entry door was hardly enough room for two people. If three people managed to get in there at the same time it was packed like a sardine can. There was also a small opening from the office into the garage work area. Tom had two car hoists in the garage.

The day of my new show was upon me without my knowing I was going to do it until it happened. I went into the office to pay for the gas

I had just pumped. I have always paid cash for gas, and I still do. Of course, now that takes two trips. The first trip I pay enough to cover the cost of a fill up. The second trip, I get my cash back for whatever I didn't spend filling the tank.

When I opened the door to enter, I accidentally bumped a guy who was in there talking to Tom. At the same time, I noticed that there was a car running up on the hoist in the garage. I bumped the guy with the door because my attention was on the running car and the office was very small. Without any planning or forethought, I started talking in this voice that was somewhere between a lisp and someone with a nasal problem.

"Tom, did you know someone left a car up on your hoist with the engine running? That's dangerous, Tom. Someone needs to do something about that. If you have a ladder, Tom, I will climb up and turn the engine off. Really, Tom, something needs to be done. Where is the ladder, Tom?"

As I was carrying on, Tom had a half grin on his face and the guy in the office was trying to leave. He was doing his best to avoid looking at me, but at the same time he wanted to. He had to be thinking, who is this fat midget with a speech impediment who is saying something so utterly stupid.

I made it look like I was trying to open the door for him as I bumped him with it again. When he tried to step around me, I intentionally bumped into him, but made it appear to be accidental. All the while I was babbling about the car on the hoist and saying "I'm sorry" over and over to the guy who was trying to escape. I needed the guy so I could have a captured audience, or I mean captive audience for my show.

Once he managed to get out, Tom just looked at me and shook his head. Tom didn't realize that I would strike again on another day.

Entering the office weeks later I noticed a sign that read, "No Checks." I also saw that there was someone inside already.

Therefore, when I stepped in, I declared, "Here, Tom, I have a check for my gas."

I carried on with the act for a bit while the other guy escaped. I enjoy thinking about the discussion these people have at dinner about the weird fat midget they ran into at the gas station.

I must give Tom credit too. Tom plays golf, and on more than one occasion he played the same stunt on me at the golf course. It is tougher for him, because the pro shop is much bigger than his office, and I can keep a straight face without even trying.

CHAPTER 65

Good Times with Dale!

One of my best friends, who was a big part of my life, was Dale Sim. He entered Mount Si High in my sophomore year. Dale and family had been in Oregon where his father, Bill, was high up in the Weyerhaeuser Company. Bill Sim had been transferred to the Snoqualmie Falls Mill.

Dale and I weren't good friends in high school but being a small school, we knew each other. It wasn't that we did not get along; we just had different social lives and activities. Dale had something I didn't have. Girls were interested in him, while they did not even know I existed. Oh, the life of a teenage midget.

At that time, the most contact I had with Dale was playing basketball with him in the Hall League. High school students that didn't play on the high school team had the opportunity to play in this league at the Snoqualmie Falls YMCA. A guy named Harold Keller ran the YMCA that was located by the Weyerhaeuser Mill. Harold also provided dance classes for all 7th and 8th graders. He put on an annual marble tournament at the four grade schools. He showed movies in the auditorium there and provided roller skating on weekends. Harold was truly a Godsend to the kids of the Snoqualmie Valley and should have been more appreciated. Actually, the kids did appreciate him, which was demonstrated by relatively good behavior and no vandalism.

Anyway, back to the Hall League. There were six teams in the league. The teams coached themselves. My senior year, I was the leader of the North Bend team. The other teams were Snoqualmie, Fall City, Snoqualmie Falls, Tanner, and Evergreen. Players on each team could live in any of the towns; the town names merely identified the teams. The six leaders, as chosen by Harold, drafted their players from a list of those who signed up to play.

I was on the team named North Bend and Dale was on a different team. At the point we were to play Dale's team, they were undefeated, and Dale was the league's top scorer. The game before Dale had scored 59 points. Dale liked to shoot the ball. In fact, I don't think Dale ever saw a shot he would not take. In reality, he was a good shooter. Dale could have made the high school team if he had turned out for it.

If we were to have any chance of winning against his team, we had to shut down or at least slow down Dale. I wasn't a coach, and I had no idea that approximately 10 years later I would be coaching high school basketball. I got the idea to put our fastest player and best defensive player on Dale, while the other four played a zone defense. That way Dale would always be double or triple teamed. I chose Dave Barrett to cover him. I told Dave to, "Stay with him even if he takes a break to go to the bathroom." Dave did an excellent job, and we won. Years later I even learned there was a name for that defense. It was called a box-and-one.

My last couple of years of teaching and my first several years of working at Snoqualmie Falls Golf, Dale owned and operated the Monogram Tavern in North Bend. For a couple of those years, I played shortstop for the Monogram Tavern slow pitch team. That is when I got to know Dale.

After several years of owning the Monogram Tavern, he sold it and opened a sporting goods store. Then he later decided that the life of a small business owner wasn't his thing, so he sold the sporting goods store and went to work for a fellow classmate of ours, Dennis Fury. Dale became his right-hand man and was the heart of Fury Construction for many years to come. Soon after going to work at Fury Construction, he married Colleen Nickell. Colleen's father, John, was an avid golfer at Snoqualmie Falls Golf Course and the Men's Club President.

After marrying Colleen, Dale became a regular player at Snoqualmie Falls GC. That is when I really got to know him. He was never a really talented player, but he could get around the course, and he had fun doing it.

Over the years, Dale, an accomplished heavy equipment operator, did many jobs for me both at the course and at my home. Our house is less than a ½ mile from the course. On one occasion, he tore down an old shed at the back of my property and buried it using a Fury Construction bulldozer.

After every major flood Dale would have several pieces of equipment sent to the course to help remove sand, silt, and other debris. We
paid for the hourly fees for the bulldozers and front-end loaders, but
Dale operated them for nothing. He also got another equipment operator from Fury Construction to work free of charge. Without Dale's
assistance and Dennis Fury's cooperation, we would have had an almost impossible task to clean the course up.

When Dale's fishing partner moved away to Coquille, Oregon, Dale
went fishing for a new partner and hooked me. Dale was a true fisherman of salmon, steelhead and trout. Dale had fished for salmon both
in rivers and the ocean. He still took me on as his partner, and as a kid
I had done a lot of trout fishing. I had gone salmon fishing before, but
only on charter boats. A friend of mine had taken me steelhead fishing
a few times, but I was still basically a beginner. I had caught one steelhead and had hooked another one that I eventually lost. It wasn't like a
complete burden for Dale to take me on, but it was close. I could rig up
my own gear with either a spinning reel or a bait casting reel. I didn't
need any assistance or help with trout fishing either.

One Christmas morning, both Dale and I hooked and landed a
steelhead while fishing off the bank of the Snoqualmie River about
half a mile downstream from the falls. Sadly, we quit steelhead fishing
about a year later because netting of the rivers pretty much eliminated
any chance of success.

For about ten years we would go down to Coquille and fish for
salmon with his old fishing buddy. One of those trips I caught my 2nd
biggest salmon. The biggest fish I ever caught was a 51-pound salmon
in the Kenai River in Alaska. Lee, my superintendent at that time, and
I took a trip there one year. I caught it fishing on a charter boat. The
skipper was so good that he basically chased the fish and I reeled in
the slack.

The fish in Coquille was 26 pounds, but more than twice as hard to
land as the 51-pounder in Alaska. Fishing for chinook in the slow-running Coquille requires drifting and bouncing your line off the bottom.
In doing so, you get hung up frequently and lose a lot of gear. I got
hung up, or so I thought, and was about to break off the line so I could
tie up another. Fortunately, Dale was watching me. He had me hand

Showing off our catch from a day fishing the Coquille River. Dale is the one holding the sardine.

him my pole and just as I did the fish on the other end took off. Dale handed it back and said, "That isn't a rock!"

The Coquille is awfully slow-running and that fish actually dragged us upstream, downstream, and across the river. About the point that both the fish and I were worn out, we were close to one of the banks of the river and an overhanging branch knocked both the hat off my head and my beer off the seat. Dale got the net out and netted the fish. As he lifted it out of the water, the fish went right through the rotten netting. Dale then leaned out and grabbed the fish and wound it up in the torn net. He lifted it into the boat as we continued to drift with branches hitting us in the head. Then we also discovered that we forgot the mini bat that we used to hit the fish after we got them in the boat.

Therefore, Dale held the fish overboard and cut its gills to bleed it out. On second thought, that 26-pounder was ten times harder to catch than the 51-pounder in Alaska.

Dale also organized a couple of trout fishing trips to Canada. The first one was with Dale's brothers and included all our kids. Dale's kids, Connie and Jeff were close to the same age as Jeff and Willie. Dale had a motorhome and we had kids, bikes, and several other adults. We went to Lake Sheridan where the only fish caught in two days were by Jeff, Willie and me. In a span of about 30 minutes, Jeff caught a 4.5-pound rainbow trout, Willie caught one that was 3 pounds, and I caught two 2-pounders. Of all the other 20 people on the lake, nobody even got a bite. The last day we moved to Fawn Lake where lots of 11-inch trout were caught.

There were a number of highlights for us when we switched from Lake Sheridan to Fawn Lake. While Jeff, Willie and I had caught all the fish caught by our group, fishing the rest of the time was quite boring. It was especially boring to boys age 10 and 12 years old.

Fawn Lake provided a bit of success. Even though the fish were only 10 to 13 inches long, they did bite, and we did catch. There were several things that provided entertainment. The wind did some, the kids caused some and I created some.

While trolling one of the kids managed to get his line caught in the prop of the outboard motor. During the 15- to 20-minute period I took to get the line cleaned off, the wind blew us into tall grass that grew up at the end of the lake.

We had to paddle out of it the best we could with the one oar we had. Once out of it, I got the engine running and we commenced with fishing.

Both kids had more fun watching me struggle to get us going again than they had fishing. It was like when I was a kid when Dad would set up the projector so we could watch old movies. Without a doubt the best part was when the projector got fouled up and film ran all over the floor. Hiram and I would be the happiest little shitheads in the world.

As the day went on, the kids were getting restless with boredom. I was reading the bag of cheeseballs and noticed their description in French. Remember, we were in Canada. They were called something like "Cruisants Oh Fromage." I started throwing them at them telling them to eat these bleeping damn Fromage Cruisant things. They were dodging them and yelling back at me about the damn Fromage balls and throwing them at each other and me. Thankfully, we didn't tip the boat over.

One other benefit of Fawn Lake came by the way of the charm of one of the guys in our group. The lady who ran the resort there took a liking to him and he got to spend some time alone with her in her bedroom. He must have been up to snuff because she provided dinner for our group two nights in a row before we left! Dinner was not part of the rental agreement which only covered boats and cabins.

The next year, with just Dale and me along with our kids, we went to a lake called High Hume. The only thing that bit was the mosquitoes. We decided to leave, and we drove all night to come back and fish in Eastern Washington at Jamison Lake.

Dale and I went to Nimpo Lake in Canada twice over the years to catch trout as well. The first time Dale called and said, "Be ready tomorrow to fly into Canada to fish for four days. I will pick you up at 8:00 in the morning. All you need is clothes, fishing gear and money. Food and cabins along with fishing boats are provided."

A highly successful logging friend of Dale's was going to fly six people to Nimpo Lake and put them up in cabins where three meals a day were provided. Dale's buddy even paid for our temporary fishing licenses.

Once we got settled into our cabins, Dale and I headed out in our boat and started fishing. We had been fishing with moderate success for a couple of hours when the same exact thought struck both of us. We looked at each other and in unison said, "We forgot to bring some beer!" We had been so excited to fish that we forgot the most important thing.

Two or three years later, Dale and I drove to Nimpo Lake for a couple of days of fishing. It was at least a 12-hour drive from home. We still had a good time, but it just wasn't the same.

Oh, by the way, the lady there not only fed us 3 meals a day, but she smoked all the fish we caught so they would survive the trip home.

Dale and I, along with our wives, also went to Cabo one time. Dale and I did go marlin fishing on a charter while we were there. Fortunately for me, I did not catch or even hook a fish. After watching

Dale catch one, I was glad I didn't have any luck. It was way too much work to haul them in.

Dale and I also bowled on the same bowling team for over 20 years. It originally was Dale's team sponsored by Fury Construction. After I joined the team, I took over sponsorship and it became the Snoqualmie Falls Golf Course team.

Besides the regular league we bowled in, we participated in the King County Tournament and the State Tournament every year. When I joined the team, the league was in Snoqualmie. We then moved to Liberty Lanes in Issaquah, where we stayed until they closed. We then went back to Snoqualmie for one more year until we joined a league at Sunset Bowl in Eastgate. We stayed there until they closed about 15 years later.

The City Tournament was no big deal, just an excuse to party. Of course, that was true of our weekly evening bowling as well. The State Tournament became secondary to the golf we played on the day before the tournament started.

If you are easily disgusted, you might want to skip a couple of pages. Guys will be guys, and out of town partying guys can be disgusting.

One of the mornings while getting ready to bowl, the guy we called "Granny Franny" came out of the bathroom and said, "Hey, guys, come look at this!"

The night before we had dinner at a place with a salad bar. Anyways, floating in the toilet in plain sight was a whole cherry tomato. I didn't perform an autopsy on it, but it appeared to be smooth without any tooth marks. Somehow, I don't picture a lady at a women's bowling tournament calling everyone into the bathroom to "Take a look at this!"

My first hole-in-one I got when I was playing 9-holes with Dale one late afternoon at Snoqualmie Falls GC. It just so happened to be April Fool's Day and I got it on our 13th hole from approximately 150 yards. It came right after I double bogeyed the 12th hole.

On the next April Fool's Day, I was playing Apple Tree GC in Yakima. The 13th hole there is a par 3 of about 150 yards too. Before I swung, I said, "Watch this. Two hole in ones on consecutive April Fool's Days, both on number 13 and both with a 7 iron."

The shot covered the pin, took one hop, and then hit the pin. This one didn't drop in the hole, it stayed one inch away.

Back to disgusting, I must share this because Dale would be proud. One hot and sultry day at Snoqualmie Falls Golf Course there were easily 25 guys in the clubhouse drinking beer and watching the British Open on TV. This was before the remodel of the clubhouse when we finally put in air conditioning. The building back then held heat in and had very little circulation of air. In fact, the building would hold the heat overnight. Suddenly an awful stench sent all but two people out the sliding door headed for the fresh air on the porch. Dale was fighting his way out even though he was the cause of the putrid gas warfare. If the walls had been painted the paint would have melted right off them. Once everyone was out on the deck gasping for air, Dale said proudly, "That was a good one—wasn't it!"

I have always contended that the 8th wonder of the world is that people can stand their own farts. In this case, Dale proved me wrong.

Oh yes, that day I learned who the two toughest men in the world were. The brothers Ron and Frank Neeves were the two who didn't leave the building. They sat at the counter not two feet from where the bomb went off, drinking their beers and watching the Open Championship. The Neeves brothers were born and raised in London. Frank's son David Neeves is one of my best friends and he and his beautiful wife Kathy still play regularly at Snoqualmie Falls.

When Dale retired from Fury Construction, he and Colleen moved to Wenatchee, WA. I visited them a few times for golf and fishing.

Several years ago, Dale was taken by a stroke. He had been over visiting with my old partner Chris at his course in Quincy, WA when it happened. Colleen asked me to perform the services for him in Wenatchee, which I gladly did. Dale was a good and loyal friend.

CHAPTER 66

Being a Club Pro

Once I started at Snoqualmie Falls GC, I had no time to work on my golf game and practice. I played the occasional 9-holes at Snoqualmie Falls, but other than that I would play in a one-day PGA branch pro-am every couple of weeks.

Occasionally local pros put on special pro-ams at their courses and invite fellow club pros from the area. These aren't sponsored by our PGA branch. One such pro-am was held at Tam O'Shanter GC in Bellevue, WA. I had attended PGA Business School #1 with Jack Frei, the head pro at Tam O'Shanter GC. All the amateurs were members of Tam O'Shanter, so we as golf pros didn't bring members from our own clubs like we do at chapter pro-ams. After the pro-am, there was a dinner where each of the pros was to give a five- to ten-minute lesson on some particular part of the game.

At this point, I had been at Snoqualmie Falls for two years. There was a dozen of us invited, which made 13 pros total counting Jack. All the other pros, except for Jack and I, had been club pros in the section for over 10 years. They all knew each other and several of them were from fancy country clubs. I was the nobody from nowhere who worked at the public course that was hardly on the map yet.

Before teeing off, we drew topics out of the hat to see what we were going to teach that evening. I drew sand play, which was the one topic I didn't want. I have always been a terrible sand player. I tried to trade topics with everyone, and no one would do it. I begged Jack to give me something else and he refused. All through the round I dreaded speaking on sand play that night. I wasn't afraid to speak, I just wanted to have it be something I knew something about.

After dinner was over the 13 pros moved up to a stage where there was a podium with 13 chairs several feet behind it. We were called up one by one to give our speeches. The host pro, Jack, acted as the MC

I have my tees monogrammed so when others find them they wonder what weirdo used this. I put the puppy paw on my golf balls for easy identification and I love puppy dogs.

The Captain G Spot tee is hard to read due to the colors and lack of contrast. I should have had tees made with "Fluffy Stumpf**ker" on them… maybe I still will.

The caddies in Scotland loved the Wee Poison Dwarf tees – one of them looked at me and said, "Aye, I see, Laddie."

Note that the second batch of Wee Poison Dwarf tees came with the mis-spelling DRAWF. Definitely destined to be a collector's item someday!

but he didn't give a mini lesson. There were 11 established golf pros and one newbie—Me!

I was called up about midway through the presentations. I stepped up to the microphone and introduced myself. Still speaking into the mike, I told the pros seated behind me that any movement of their heads during my talk was to be up and down in agreement. That I would not accept any shaking of heads in disagreement or in a non-accepting manner.

I then turned back to the audience of around 50 to teach sand play. I explained that my course only had sand on the riverbank that surrounded it on two sides. Also, we did have sand left on the course after major floods.

Next, I explained that when I practiced, I had to be careful of freshwater clams and river rocks. I added how I traded in my childhood bucket and shovel for my current sand wedge.

I finally moved on to some real teaching. Most of them already knew the quick foot move in case you had a buried lie in the sand. First, yell, *"Look at that plane,"* and point up in the air. As your playing partners look up, bump the ball into a better lie with your foot.

I also got technical and explained "fried egg" lies. I explained the difference between playing the varieties of such lies like over easy, sunny side up, and hard. Periodically during my talk, I would turn to make sure the other pros were nodding in agreement and remind them to continue to do so.

When I was through, I had the pros and the audience all laughing. One of the pros there was the executive secretary of our PGA branch, Ron Coleman. After that night, Ron gave me a new name: "Sand Man". He and several others still call me that, and that was in 1975.

After four years of playing in a Washington, Oregon or Northwest Open I realized I could not be competitive anymore. Fellow golf pros, who I had competed with in amateur events before turning pro, would come up to me and ask, "What happened to your golf game? You used to be good!"

All work and no play made Johnny a crappy golfer. I did continue to play in one day pro-ams, so I could take our members to play private clubs that they wouldn't be able to play otherwise. I finished in the money fairly often and didn't embarrass myself too badly.

Once I started playing in the senior pro-ams I won money more often than not. Twice I was selected to play in the Hagen Cup. The ten top senior club pros from the Western Washington Branch of the PGA played matches against the top ten from the state of Oregon. I did alright in those events by winning about half of my matches. My golf game also had made a bit of a comeback because I didn't have to work nearly as much.

After I had been at Snoqualmie Falls for about 10 years, there were two pro-am events that I played in annually for nearly 30 years. There were also two non-tournament fun trips that I took annually.

The other part of being a golf pro involves working with the people to make sure they enjoy the experience and want to continue playing at your facility. This involves having good course conditions, good staff, good environment, and too many other things to list. We have always treated Snoqualmie Falls Golf Course as a small family-run operation with a friendly small town family atmosphere. This has made us successful, but more importantly it has made us a lot of friends and I truly feel like it is one big Sno Falls family. I see this anytime we have trouble and so many friends come out to help us .

CHAPTER 67

Bucket List Pebble Beach

M any years ago, I decided that there were three golf courses that I would have to play before I bought the farm. They were Pebble Beach, St. Andrews, and Augusta National.

In 1985, four of my golfer friends who played at Snoqualmie Falls GC invited me to go to the Monterey Peninsula with them to play golf. The five of us headed south in a motorhome they borrowed from a buddy who owned the Gaslamp Tavern in Issaquah. As you all know, foursomes are preferred in golf. Fivesomes are frowned upon and forbidden in some cases. Fortunately, most rounds we were allowed to play as a fivesome, because we had a PGA pro (me) in the group.

One round at Silverado we had to split into a twosome and a threesome. Gene Armstrong and I were the twosome. We could have easily kept up as a fivesome and the way it was we had to wait before almost every shot. I was getting more irritated with the slow play and waiting as the round progressed. I had teed my ball up on the 15th tee and was standing there fuming away as I waited to be able to hit. Gene saw I was irritated and asked what was wrong.

I replied, "Never mind. Piss on it!"

Gene proceeded to pull out his anaconda and do just that.

I was shocked that the waterfall didn't knock the ball off the tee, but somehow it didn't. So, there my ball was, teed up in a puddle of pee foam. I didn't want to pick it up for obvious reasons. I should have left it and teed up another ball, but instead I went ahead and hit it. Fortunately, I picked the ball off perfectly without splattering pee all over myself or Gene. It may have been the best drive of the day, and the tension was broken between Gene and me.

About 20 years later, Gene showed off another trick using his favorite toy. Gene was playing with me in the pro-am portion of the tournament in Sequim. When we were on the second tee Gene strolled over by a wooded area to pee. As he was relieving himself, he commented that there were nettles there.

"Hey guys, look at this!" he said as he grabbed a hand full of nettles and wiped them across his sizable unit. "That feels good," he said as he tucked himself away.

A practical soul might feel it would have been wiser to use the hand that had a golf glove on it. Upon further thought, since the nettles hit the private parts I guess the comfort of the hands was a secondary concern. Speaking of hands, let's get back to the story at hand.

Our highlight of the trip was, of course, to play Pebble Beach. One of the assistant pros at Pebble, Bob Hickam, had grown up playing Snoqualmie Falls with his parents. Jack and Margaret, his parents, still played there.

Pebble Beach is a public golf course, but it is very expensive and hard to get on. Today (2022), it costs one person $620 with a cart rental and $575 without a cart to play there. At the time of our visit, the fee was $150 to play without a cart. Bob Hickam arranged a fee of $15 including a cart for each of us to play Pebble Beach that day. On top of that we were the first group to tee off after the morning shotgun tournament they had that day. This all meant that we were teeing off at noon on Pebble Beach with an empty golf course in front of us for only $15 with carts included.

Since this was one of the three courses of my dreams to play, I really wanted to play well. As I teed up on #12, I stood at one under par. I had made it through the toughest holes on the course playing numbers 8, 9 and 10 in par, par, birdie. My usual three-putt gag move checked in and by the time I walked off the 18th green I had shot 75.

The next day we played Spyglass Hill and then we headed for Reno, where we were going to play Lakeridge Golf Course, which had an island green on #15. The other three guys on the trip besides Gene and I were Chuck Doty, Steve Anderson and Bill Morse. I had known them from when I worked at Mount Si Golf Course, and they'd always tried to sneak on without paying. Chuck Doty is the father of David Doty, *aka* Pruggy.

The day we played Lakeridge Golf Course the wind was blowing, and it was sunny while we warmed up on the driving range. It wasn't really warm, but it certainly wasn't cold either. Shortly after we made the turn and started the back nine, the sky turned dark, and the wind quit blowing. Along about the 15th hole, snow started falling. By the time we finished the round, we couldn't putt through all the white stuff that had accumulated on the ground.

We headed into Reno and parked the motorhome, so we could walk around, gamble a bit, get some food, and find a couple of cheap hotel rooms for the night. Each night we would get two rooms and Bill would stay in the motorhome. He did volunteer for this duty, so he could claim that bed to sleep on when we were in travel mode.

I volunteered to go get the motorhome and bring it to the hotel. At this time, I hadn't learned yet that I could get lost in a phone booth. This turned out to be my first eye opening experience in that matter.

Through 3 to 6 inches of snow I walked hour after hour. About every half hour I would end up back at the same location. Finally, after about two hours, I gave up and went into a casino. I played blackjack for about half an hour and then set off again in search. Heck, I wasn't even drinking at this time, and I hadn't been drinking at all for over a year. Anyway, I stumbled onto the motorhome by accident at last. The next miracle was that I was able to drive it back to the hotel without getting lost again. Bill didn't like to sleep in the cold motorhome that night, but he did keep his rights to the traveling soft mattress.

Pebble Beach was the highlight of the trip for four of us. Bill was torn between Pebble Beach and the five hamburgers for a dollar we stumbled on at an Arctic Circle one night. I'm not inferring that Bill was cheap, because he did offer to buy dinner for all of us that night. When I ordered the bacon cheeseburger for $2.50 instead of having the five burgers for a buck it was a good thing he didn't have dentures, or they would have fallen out.

All and all it was a good trip and when we finished we were all still friends. Plus, I was able to check Pebble off of my list. Since then, I have played it three more times. Twice with my son Jeff and once with my other son Willie. I didn't break 80 on any of those rounds though.

CHAPTER 68

Bucket List St. Andrews

In order to check off St. Andrews, I realized I would have to go to Scotland. In 1988 I was invited by my childhood buddy and fellow golf pro, Gary Barter, to go to England to watch the British Open. It was being held at Royal Lytham & St. Annes. The following week we were going to Scotland to play The Old Course at St. Andrews along with a few other courses.

I was invited to replace Laurie Evans who had dropped out of going, so the group was Roy Eckersley, Richard Rutledge, Gary and myself. Roy was the pro at the time at Ocean Shores GC. Ocean Shores is where I am sitting right now in my house writing on double-lined paper hoping this someday becomes a book for others to enjoy. Richard was the one to build and operate Twin Rivers GC several years later. Twin Rivers sits directly across the river from Snoqualmie Falls GC. Gary and his family are currently the owners of Mount Si Golf Course.

In order to go on this trip, I had to miss my 25th high school reunion. I had been the emcee for the 20th and was scheduled to do the same for the 25th, but I had to bail out if I was to play The Old Course at St Andrews. Later I was forgiven, and I did emcee both the 50th and 55th class reunions. These happened to be the only other ones we have had.

Roy was born in Manchester, England and he had grown up there. Knowing all things English and Scottish, Roy organized the entire trip. The first two nights we stayed with his mother in the house he grew up in. It was called a terraced house, because it is attached to others in a row. The house couldn't have been more than 20 feet wide, with a hallway taking up about 4 feet of that. The small bedrooms were all upstairs. Roy grew up there with his mom, dad and three siblings. It is hard to imagine them all fitting and living together in that small home.

Anyways, after flying all night we landed, and Roy's brother-in-law took us to the house. We then went to a pub for a pint or two and some lunch. After that, we went to play at a public golf course in town. We had a fivesome since his brother-in-law joined us for golf. The brother-in-law's son caddied for him as well, so we had five players plus one more person carrying clubs and walking along.

On the back nine I was walking down the far-right side of a fairway, because my drive was the farthest right of the five of us on the hole. The fairways were separated by long grass that was approximately 2 feet tall. Fortunately, the tall grass was very thin, so a ball could be found and played out of it. Another hole ran the opposite direction of the one we were playing and was separated from our hole by about 40 yards of this long grass.

Suddenly I heard someone yelling and I looked up to see this guy headed my way waving a club in the air as he was yelling. I tuned in and heard him yell in his cockney accent, "What's this with a 6 ball? You can't play a 6 ball. You better sort this out!"

On and on he shouted as he approached me all the time waving his club in the air. I didn't know what to do and I was the only one close to him. The other five guys were all on the left side of our hole. What I did know was that generally the English don't much like us "Yankee Blokes". I didn't want to speak and end up with a club broken over my head.

As he charged and got within ten feet of me, I gave him a bewildered look and pointed first to my mouth and then to my ear. I did this back and forth many times, while I shrugged my shoulders. I had never pantomimed a deaf mute before, but I guess I pulled it off when it really counted. He came to a dead halt, dropped the arm with the club, turned around and walked away. That was and still has to be the quickest thinking I have ever done.

The next day we went to a bed and breakfast that was located within walking distance of the entrance to Royal Lytham & St. Annes. The facility was nice, and every day breakfast was served. Almost all the people staying there were "Damn Yankees". The breakfast food reflected that. There was ham, bacon, sausage and hash browns with scrambled eggs.

After two mornings of that food, I asked the gal, "What do you guys eat here in England?"

St. Andrews in 1988. Pictured left to right: Richard Rutledge, Roy Eckersley, John Groshell and Gary Barter.

The gal was thrilled that a Yankee actually cared about something other than ham and eggs. She asked, "Would you like to try kippers?"

I said, "Sure!"

The next morning, she proudly presented me with a plate of kippers. I ate them with some scrambled eggs and it was delicious. When she came for my empty plate, she asked how I liked the kippers. I responded favorably and she asked if I would like to try Finnan Haddie the next day?

I said, "Sure! Why not?"

The next morning, I liked the Finnan and Haddie just fine, so she asked if I would like to try Black Pudding the next day? I had no idea what that was and all I could picture was chocolate pudding. I knew I liked chocolate pudding, but for breakfast I thought it could be something different.

The next morning, she came with this thing on a plate that looked like it could be one of Mike Tyson's body parts. It sure as hell didn't look like pudding to me. The skin on the black colored sausage was hard to poke through with a fork. Then when I took a bite of it, I found out it was mushy in the middle. I don't remember what it tasted like, but I managed to eat about half of it by mixing it with bites of eggs. I rolled up the rest of it in a napkin and put it in my pocket.

When the nice lady came back and asked me if I liked it, I said, "Tomorrow let's go back to kippers."

Also, I should mention that when I found out that black pudding was actually blood sausage, I nearly threw it up.

Being a short walk to the course entrance was very nice. Fortunately, there were grandstands set up behind and alongside many of the greens. There were really only a couple of ways to watch the tournament. A person could either walk around and stand in the gallery or find a good spot in a grandstand and watch from there for a while.

There are many things in life that don't favor short people, besides the difficulty of getting a date. Apparently, there is an unwritten law that tall people must stand in the front of golf galleries and short people stand in the back. I have been in golf galleries in Scotland and the United States and for an unwritten rule, it certainly is adhered to. At a towering height of 5'5" I found it necessary to find seating in a grandstand in order to see any of the action.

We chose to sit in the stands behind the first green on the last day of the tournament. The first hole was a lengthy par 3 so we could watch the entire hole be played. Once we had watched every group play the first hole, we walked over and found good seats in the grandstand beside the 18th green. At that point only five groups had finished their rounds. We stayed for the remainder of the groups to finish and watched Seve Ballesteros putt out to win the Open Championship of 1988. Watching everyone play number one and nearly everyone play number 18 was a really great way to experience a big tournament.

The next day we drove to Scotland for a weeklong of golf. Personally, I would have enjoyed more sightseeing and less golf, but I was in the minority. We had two cars for the trip. There was nothing available that could hold all four of us, our suitcases and golf clubs. One car was big enough for 4 people and 4 sets of clubs. I drove that vehicle. I got a kick out of driving from the right side of the car and traveling in the left lane. The other car was smaller and only used when we traveled to a new location to stay.

We stayed one night at Roy's old house and five nights next to Royal Lytham & St. Annes. When we went to Scotland we stayed one night by St. Andrews, another in the middle of Scotland somewhere, and the rest in Ayr, Scotland.

Besides walking around Ayr for a few hours, the only sightseeing came when the smaller car broke down. While it was getting fixed, we spent several hours in a little town that was quaint and beautiful.

As I have already made obvious, golf was the main focus of the trip. Therefore, it is no surprise to golfers everywhere that St. Andrews was the course we all had to play. For me, it was step two in my goal to play the big 3 courses in golf. When we checked in to play St. Andrews, I wanted to get a caddie. Not because I was lazy, but so I could have someone who knew the golf course tell me where to hit the ball and help me read my putts. I went to the caddie tent and all of the old timers were already on the course. Only young, less experienced guys were available, so I skipped getting a caddie. That was a big mistake!

There are a lot of tee shots at St. Andrews where you need to know where to go. Standing on the tee, you can't see a lot of the pot bunkers or long grass hiding in the undulations of the golf course fairways. On a few holes where we couldn't tell where to go at all, we would pick different spots to aim at and hope it would work out. I always picked wrong. If I picked a target on the left side, I should have picked right, and vice versa. I don't remember how many pot bunkers or areas of long grass I hit into because I hit my shot to the target I had picked, only to find out it was wrong again.

After a while, I got frustrated and ended up shooting a very disappointing 82. The course was spectacular, nonetheless. Also, something rather funny happened to a miss-hit shot of mine. It ended up right next to the hole on the wrong hole. St. Andrews has many shared greens and that meant I had one of the longest putts ever to get to the cup on the hole I was currently playing.

Another day we drove into Troon and asked if we could play. There was hardly a person on the course. Unfortunately, the starter turned us away because they only allowed one non-member group per day to play, and that group was already out on the golf course. I think that was the only day that Roy hadn't lined up a course ahead of time for us to play.

We played Royal Prestwick and that was really cool. It was not a long golf course, but it was quite tricky. We went without caddies there as well, so on many occasions we had no idea where to attempt to hit our shots. That day I didn't let it bother me, however, because Prestwick wasn't one of the three courses I had to play in my lifetime.

The most fun round I played was at a private course somewhere in the middle of Scotland. Somehow Roy had gotten us permission to play this rather enjoyable, private club, and I was glad he did. I just wish I could remember the name of the course. Anyway, it was a windy day, and I mean even for Scotland where they don't even realize the wind is blowing if it isn't over 20 knots. Fortunately, I have always been a good wind player thanks to developing that skill in college playing at Clarkston CC. That was our home course at WSU and it sits right by the Clarkston River. The wind howls up that gorge daily and you must learn how to hit it solid and keep your trajectory nice and low.

Anyways, playing in that strong wind that day, on a fairly tough golf course, I shot a 72. After the round we went into the bar at the clubhouse for a cold one. There were a few guys in there who had been watching us play our round. The golf course actually played around the clubhouse, which sat in the center of the property. In fact, they had a telescope set up in the bar so they could watch the golfers out playing on the course. Knowing that three of us were PGA pros, they had been following us and betting on what we would do. By far I had the best round, and I had won a few bets for some of them. Of course, for every bet I won for them someone else lost for betting against me that day. Whatever the case, we had a relaxing afternoon. I mentioned to them that I had noticed the people in Scotland were much nicer to us Yanks than the people in England had been. Therefore, as we were leaving, one of them jokingly yelled to us, "Go home, Yankees!"

We stayed in Ayr and one day there I had time to walk around and shop. I spent more money buying stuff for people back home that day than I did on anything else the whole trip. I ended up shipping back two big boxes of shirts, sweaters, golf hats and various trinkets.

When I finally finished shopping, I was walking around with my camera hanging around my neck, carrying packages in my arms, and heading back to our hotel. Well, I was trying to head back to our hotel. After walking around for 30 to 45 minutes I recognized that I was back at the same place I had been when I started heading to the hotel. This happened again about 45 minutes later. I was repeating my experience in Reno, but at least it wasn't snowing this time. After finishing three of these 45-minute loops, I decided to go in a bar and have a drink to refresh and hope to figure out a way to find my way back to the hotel.

There I was: Mr. Joe Tourist Yankee with bags of presents and a camera. I sat down next to an elderly gentleman who was wearing a suit coat and he had a fedora on his head. I ordered a gin and tonic and the bartender brought a glass with one ice cube in it. The shot of gin he put in the glass melted the ice cube before the tonic water hit the glass. That was fine though, since it still tasted good at room temperature. I learned on that trip that ice is more valuable than diamonds in England and Scotland.

After a while, I asked the bartender for directions to the hotel where we were staying. He quickly fired through the directions in his Scottish brogue, which managed to lose me about two words into it.

When he walked away the gentleman to my right said, "You didn't understand a word he said, did you, laddie?"

I replied that I hadn't understood at all. He said he would show me the way when I was ready to go. I bought each of us a couple more drinks and we had a nice visit.

Eventually, we got up and ventured out to return me to my hotel. We had gone about three blocks when we came to a statue of a Scottish war hero. From there my new drinking buddy and guide pointed down the street to a building that was about two blocks away.

He said, "Can you find your way to that building, laddie?"

I said, "Yes, but not before I get your picture in front of this monument."

Earlier he had mentioned that he had been in WWII. He seemed completely thrilled to have me take his picture in front of this Scottish war hero. I then thanked him for his help, and we parted ways. That was the best job of getting lost that I had ever done, because it at least became fun and I made friends with an awesome Scotsman.

After two weeks in England and Scotland it was time to pack up and go home. We had watched the "Open Championship," played 9 rounds of golf on different golf courses, and enjoyed many other great experiences along the way.

For the trip back, I dressed up in red and green plaid knickers with a matching fedora. Between the knickers and the hat, I wore a red shirt. Long socks finished off the ensemble. I knew we had a two-hour layover at O'Hare airport in Chicago and I didn't care how I looked. The other three guys didn't want to be seen with me though.

CHAPTER 69

Golfing Buddies

There were three other club pros that I played non-tournament golf with. These were my best buddies in the golf business. All three of them were PGA professionals, but one of them got his amateur status back and became a sales rep for various golf products. His name is Bill Jackson and fortunately he is still alive today. I will talk more about Billy after I give you a look at Dave and Tony.

I met Dave Leon when we were paired together in the Northwest Open at Illahee Hills in Salem, Oregon. That was the first time I took the playing ability test, which I already talked about earlier. I then got paired with Dave again a couple of years later when we were trying to qualify for the National PGA Championship. This was in 1976. Other than being paired together at Illahee Hills, Dave and I didn't really know each other well. As we were walking down the first fairway after hitting our tee shots, Jim Dignam, the Wilson Sporting Goods rep and my friend yelled, "Look at that pairing! A fat Mexican and a fat midget!"

That broke the ice as Dave and I relaxed, so that it was an enjoyable day in spite of the tournament nerves.

There were two notable things about that day. The first notable thing was that the playing conditions were exceptionally difficult. The wind was blowing very hard, and the course was set up tough. Back tees were used to make it long and the pins were tucked in challenging locations on the greens. In those very tough conditions, I shot a 76. Most of the club pros shot between 85 and 90 that day. In fact, that 76 may have been the best round of golf I have ever played, even though it was a much higher score than many rounds I have played before or since.

The other notable thing was that the other guy in our group lasted five holes and then quit. He seemed OK when we teed off, but as we played along, he kept drinking some pink colored beverages from plastic bottles. After we teed off on number six, he pardoned himself and stumbled off toward the clubhouse. Several hours later, when we finished our round, we saw him passed out in the bar.

Dave was from Tucson, Arizona and had been possibly the best junior golfer in Arizona as a kid. He had won many junior tournaments. Unfortunately, he was another victim of the all-work-and-no-play scenario. Being a golf professional at a busy municipal golf course, he had very little time to play or practice. This doesn't happen to every club pro, and especially not at clubs where playing with the members is part of the job. Dave was still talented, but you can't compete with others who practice and play tournaments regularly, because they get in the repetition to repeat their swing more often as well as handle the nerves of tournament golf. Dave and I used to call them EDPs, which stood for everyday players.

Dave liked Mexican food and especially with extra hot salsa. There was a Mexican restaurant close to Linden CC, where Dave was the head pro. We would usually go there to eat after playing at his golf club. They made a special salsa just for Dave that would actually make him sweat. He managed to get my son Jeff to try it once and it burned Jeff's tongue so bad that his tongue had a spot that was numb and unable to taste for a couple days.

One year the four of us (Billy, Tony, Dave and I) went to Tucson for a week of golf. Every day one of Dave's golf pro buddies would set up a golf game for us. Dave was still remembered in the Tucson area for all of his past golf accomplishments.

Before going any further, I think I should share Dave's favorite joke. He would say, "Do you know when a Mexican becomes a Spaniard? When he marries your daughter."

For at least 25 years, Dave, Tony, Billy and I played in two different tournaments. Tony and I were partners at Dungeness GC in Sequim, WA. Billy and I were partners at the Grays Harbor pro-am. Dave had other partners, but the four of us stayed together and ate together when we attended these events.

Dave was the second friend of mine to get Lou Gehrig's disease. He had been having back problems for months and had been seeing several doctors for help. It was like they had to eliminate all other possibilities before they came up with the prognosis. He was told that

Dave Leon and me in front of his pro shop at Linden C.C. in Puyallup, WA.

there was a fast-moving type and a slow-moving type, and he had the slower-moving type. If that was true, I would hate to see the fast-moving version of the disease, because his condition declined very quickly.

Billy and I went to his house a few times to visit, while he was declining. Of course, I went by myself on several occasions as well. Never once did Dave act down or distressed. Never once did he complain or say, "Why me?" Dave always asked about me, my wife and my kids. The disease didn't take his grace, pride or caring spirit away.

Tony Fatica worked as Dave's assistant pro at Linden CC. At the point that I started working at Snoqualmie Falls GC in 1972, Dave and Tony were already at Linden CC. In 1973, I was putting on the practice green at Broadmoor CC before teeing off in my first pro-am as a pro at Snoqualmie Falls GC. I had played in pro-ams when I was at the Yakima Elks GC, which was in the Inland Empire Chapter. This however was an event in the Western Washington Chapter of the PGA. Anyway, this guy approached me on the practice green and said as he reached out to shake my hand, "Hi John, I'm Tony Fatica. Welcome to the Western Washington Chapter. I hope to play with you in the future."

I don't know how he knew my name or that I was new to the Chapter, but he just wanted to make me feel welcome.

Tony and I became partners in the pro-pro best ball at Dungeness GC in Sequim, WA. Tony was 20 years older than me, which made us the oldest team in the event the final 10 years that we participated. We did win several lap prizes by scoring the best 9 holes of non-winners, but the going was rough. We were the oldest and part of the non-tournament players group as well. Tony did get a hole-in-one though.

Tony was born in 1924 and his first assistant pro job was at Milwaukie CC when he was 15. He worked for a guy named Taters Perola. One of his jobs was to drive Taters around, while Taters fooled around in the backseat with the wife of one of the club's members. He was given strict orders to look forward and keep his mouth shut.

Like many of the old-time club pros, Tony could fix golf clubs. In fact, besides being great at fixing them, he could also make them. I still have a putter he made me out of an old MacGregor oil-hardened driver's head. He built it with a custom long shaft and set it up so I could use it to putt side-saddle. I used that putter for years and still cherish it to this day.

Tony was a golf professional for over 70 years, but he was also an airplane pilot. He loved to fly and golf, but more than that he was a top-notch quality guy. He even played in a pro-pro event with my son Jeff once Jeff became a PGA member. In fact, he taught Jeff the club repairing basics to help him pass that portion of the PGA training to become a PGA member professional. Tony graced this earth for over 90 years and all of us that knew him feel fortunate.

My third golf pro playing buddy, Billy Jackson, is the one still standing. Billy did reclaim his amateur status over 30 years ago, but when I met him, he was a golf pro. We were paired together at Broadmoor CC where we were both trying to qualify for the Washington State PGA Match Play Championship in 1976. Neither of us was successful. My

Bill Jackson aka "Billy Jack" must have caught Tony Fatica cheating
at solitaire.

day was psychologically over when I four-putted the first hole from
three feet away. Between nerves and super-fast greens, the fourth putt
was longer than the first putt had been. In spite of our struggles, Billy
and I hit it off quite well. After that we had little contact until the early
'80s when we hooked up to play in the pro-pro tournament in Sequim.
It was then that Billy informed me that I had screwed him out of the
golf pro job in Yakima.

When I had applied for the job at the Yakima Elks in 1972 it clearly stated on the employment bulletin that *"All applications are to be in
writing only. NO phone calls!"* I had looked up the phone number and

called the new head pro immediately. This was a slight challenge too, because I had to find a phone number for Don Williams at Helena CC. He was becoming the head pro at Yakima Elks, and he was doing the hiring of the assistant professional position.

When I got in touch with him, he replied that, "All applications were to be in writing. No phone calls!"

I responded by saying, "I know, but I just wanted to make sure you would know that I want this job!"

That was it—the job was mine!

Billy had, of course, applied for the job the right way without violating one of the only rules by calling like I had done. He was a smart guy of course and figured out that I was the winner of the job, and I was nice enough later to tell him that I got the job by not following the rules on the employment bulletin. I'm sure he was really happy for me.

I mentioned this tournament earlier but didn't discuss the calcutta that went with it. The two-day tournament was played on Monday and Tuesday with the calcutta bidding done on Sunday night before the tournament started. All the two-man teams were bid on, starting at $50 a team with minimum bid increments of $50. Billy couldn't make it there in time for the bidding, so it was left up to me, and I had never been involved in one of these before.

When the Groshell/Jackson team came on the block I made the opening bid of $50. A couple of teams had already gone for over $1,000, but several teams had gone for the $50 minimum. I knew we weren't a hot commodity, so I was sure I could get us for $200 max. The auctioneer had gone going once, going twice, when someone piped up $100. I didn't realize that every team had the option of buying back half of their team from whoever won the bidding. Also, I had told Billy that I would buy our team, so I responded with a bid of $150. The auctioneer, Jim "Digger" Dignam, went on with going once, going twice, and sold for $150. Digger was the Wilson rep who had yelled to Dave Leon and me about the pairing of a fat Mexican and a fat midget. I glanced over at the guy who had bid me up and he was chuckling at me, because he was happy, he had cost me an extra "C" note.

After the calcutta was over I asked Digger who the guy was who bid me up and he said it was Jerry Mowlds. Jerry was the president of our section of the PGA and he had been a big part of our section for years. Jerry was a well-liked guy, but I didn't know him, and it pissed me off that he had cost me an extra $100 and then laughed at me.

One year later, I scraped together $3,000 to prepare myself for re-taliation at the calcutta. I didn't want to buy teams; I only wanted to bid him up and then drop the teams on him at a higher price. The $3,000 was in case I got stuck. As the bidding started, I didn't see Jerry anywhere, but there was a guy bidding who occasionally looked to the back of the room between bids. I moved up towards the front of the room and looked toward the back. There, hidden in an alcove, was Jerry Mowlds. He was signaling his buddy to make bids for him. He signaled with a horizontal hand to make a $50 bid increase and with a vertical hand to make a $100 increase. Each time they were bidding on a team I would wait until Digger said going once, going twice and then I would up it by $50. Every time I would push it and up them at least three times, thus costing Jerry at least $300 per team. Fortunately, I never once got stuck; I quit bidding before them every time. I kept track of what teams I did this on and how much it cost him on every one of them. I ended up doing it on four different teams and it cost Jerry over $1,000 total. That made up for the Ben Franklin that betting cost me the year before, but more than that it took the grin off his face. The next day Digger came to me to let me know that Jerry had asked who I was.

Oh yes, Billy and I won nothing in the tournament that first year, but we did make new friends at dinner that Monday night. Sequim is very busy during that tournament weekend, so it is tough to get a table or even a seat for dinner. We had stopped by a couple of the most pop-ular restaurants with no luck. The third place we tried was full in the dining area, but they had a few seats available in the bar area up at the bar. We sat beside two other pros that we knew, but not well. They were the two pros from Port Ludlow named Lyndon Blackwell and Brian Davis. I sat by Brian, who then got up to go to the bathroom. As soon as he left the waitress brought his dinner salad and set it down. Lyndon told the waitress Brian was coming right back. I proceeded to slide the salad over and eat it. I finished the salad before Brian got back and I pushed the empty plate back over to his spot. When he returned to an empty plate, he was a bit shocked. He was looking around wondering what the deal was and finally I said, "I ate it, thanks. It was good."

He looked to Lyndon, who confirmed what I said. I then gave him my dinner salad, which I got them to bring right away.

I have gotten to know Brian quite well over the years and we still laugh about the salad bandit. Brian is now the head pro at Grays Harbor Country Club where Billy and I played in what is now "his" pro-am last year. Once Billy got his amateur status back, he started playing with me in pro-ams. Without a doubt, Billy has played in more events with me than anyone else has. Besides the one-day pro-ams, Billy and I have played every year in the Grays Harbor pro-am for about 25 years. In that event a pro brings one amateur and the foursome is then filled out by two members from Grays Harbor Country Club. For at least 15 of those years, Billy and I along with Dave Leon and his amateur partner would stay at my house in Ocean Shores.

Although we certainly haven't dominated the winning part of the tournament, we have had more fun than most teams. Most of the fun has come through bad shots, poor scores, and stupid things I have done. Having two players from Grays Harbor can be interesting. Most of the time they want to enjoy themselves, but on occasion they get far too serious. Over the years, Billy and I have gotten to know most of them, and they have learned that while we want to win as much as they do, we also want to enjoy ourselves.

The pace of play is usually slow in this tournament, and the 4th tee always has a backup. It isn't unusual to have two groups there waiting to hit. Also, the fourth tee is right by the clubhouse, so there often are spectators hanging around. This tournament is a big deal to golfers in the Grays Harbor area. Watching club pros play isn't exactly a big deal, but a lot of people there think it is, plus there are no entry fees or gallery fees to watch. The horse race that is held on Friday afternoon used to draw a couple hundred spectators and I even won it one year.

Anyways, when we came to the 4th tee one day, we had to wait over 10 minutes before we could hit. There were two ladies sitting on the bench watching the players. They were probably about 70 years old, and I was about 55 at the time. I was chatting with them a bit when one of them asked, "Who is the pro in your group?"

I replied, "We don't have one."

They asked, "why not?"

And I said, "They couldn't find one that would play with me."

Billy was up at the front of the tee talking with our other two players. They were standing over 50 feet away from us at the time. For no particular reason, I then said, "You see that guy up there?"

They said that they did.

I then said, "He really isn't very bright, in fact he is really kind of stupid."

Sometimes I do things to see how people will react, and in this case, I knew they wouldn't like me.

Well, they both said, "That is awful. How can you say something like that?"

I replied, "Well, if you don't believe me, I'll get him to come over and talk to you. Then you will see!"

I then yelled, "Hey Billy, come over here and talk to these ladies. They want to talk to you."

As he approached, they both told me I was the worst person they had ever met, and I should be ashamed of myself. Billy walked up and the four of us exchanged a few pleasantries. When the green was open and we could hit, I turned to the gals and said, "See what I was telling you?"

They didn't stay to answer or watch us hit our shots, instead they just walked away.

A few holes later, Billy and I noticed them one fairway over talking to several other ladies. They were pointing toward us and I am sure they were telling their friends that I was the worst person on Earth. I might have a tough time getting elected to the County Council in Grays Harbor County.

The 8th hole at Grays Harbor Country Club is tough. It isn't long, but it is tight and the green is narrow and mounded. Even if you get on the green in regulation, putting is very tough. Since the course is only 9 holes, you play it twice each day. Day one the first time around I made a triple bogey 7 on the par four. Our team still made a par, but Billy was flipping me crap about my triple bogey 7. The second time around, Billy managed to outdo me and ended up making a 9. I did happen to make a couple comments about that back to him.

The next day of the tournament, I really went all out on the hole and made a 10 by hitting two shots out of bounds amongst other problems. This seemed to bring a lot of joy to my good friend Billy. The final time through the hole, Billy racked up a smooth 13 on it. After the round, while all of the golfers were gathered around the scoreboard, I made sure that everyone knew Billy had gotten a 13. I figured that is what good friends do.

Another year there, Billy had won a driver by getting the closest to the hole on #9 the first day. The next day he had this new driver in his bag, but he wasn't using it. He also wasn't hitting his old driver very well. After about a dozen holes, one of our Grays Harbor members asked Billy, "Why don't you hit the driver you won? There is no way you can do any worse with it!"

One last lowlight: one year Billy was in the bunker on the front right side of the 9th green. The green was at least 100 feet long and it was at least another 150 feet more to the pro shop. The pro shop is a two-storey building that is about 50 feet wide, and on the other side of the building is the pool. Billy caught the sand shot thin and launched that puppy all the way into the swimming pool at least 100 yards away. To be fair, I think it did take one bounce off the pro shop roof. There should be a plaque set up there to commemorate the shot.

Every year Billy would, free of charge, run their horse race on Friday afternoon. One year when I was eliminated with a hole to go, I went over to the pro shop to get a beer and find a place to sit down. The final hole was the 4th hole, which is by the clubhouse. As you may remember, that is where I impressed those ladies.

The horse race had ended, and the mob was headed back toward the pro shop and then a commotion broke out. People were gathered around the cart path by the 4th green, but most were coming back to the pro shop. I asked what was going on and people said someone had been hit with a golf ball. After talking to a number of people, I determined that it was Billy who had been hit. The ball had been thrown by the pro that lost the last hole to finish second. Apparently, they were walking back toward the pro shop when he decided to throw his golf ball into the woods out of anger. The problem was that Billy's head got in the way. He was only about 6 feet from Billy and hit him squarely in the head. To add to it, the guy was young, big and strong.

Someone had already called an aid car as I waddled out to see him. Billy was semi-conscious, and his head was bleeding hard enough to form a trickle of blood running down the cart path. The aid car arrived and took him to the Aberdeen Hospital. I followed in his car and stayed at the urgent care waiting for him. It took them until 1:00 AM to get the bleeding to stop. I don't know how many stitches it took as three different doctors took turns sewing. In fact, I managed to accidentally piss off the third doctor when I asked if she had the bleeding stopped yet. Finally, once they got the bleeding stopped and they determined that Billy didn't have a concussion he was released.

We still managed to play the next two days. The pro that beaned him didn't think he should be responsible for it. I harassed him when I saw him both days. I also contacted PGA board members pushing for some kind of action against him. Meanwhile, Billy couldn't even be mad at the jerk who hurt him. He is an amazing and awesome person. Billy has been a wonderful friend for many, many years.

Raising My Family on the Golf Course!

While I have mentioned things about my family, I haven't given it the attention I should. Jeff was born the day after I signed the papers to own 20% of Snoqualmie Falls Golf. That being the case, our family's life has been closely tied to and strongly affected by the golf course. Jeff has gone from baby in a crib in the clubhouse to the guy running everything there with the help of David "Pruggy" Doty. The name Groshell and Snoqualmie Falls Golf Course have been tied together for 50 years and counting.

Once Jeff and Willie got to walking around and being able to hang out with Dad at the course, I got the idea to take them golf ball hunting. At the time, they would have been three to five years old. I would hide six or eight balls in my pockets and take the kids out to the woods to the right of the 4th fairway. As they scurried about looking for balls, I would drop balls here and there without them knowing it. They weren't the best golf ball hunters yet. I would drop balls in the open where I thought they could never miss them and they still would rarely spot and find them. There is no doubt that a blind chimp would have been better at finding golf balls.

When I first started playing golf, I hunted for golf balls to sell to the pro shop so I could play golf. I always got excited when I would find a ball. For many years, I even had dreams about finding golf balls. I'd be crawling through brush and find one, then another, then more and more in bunches until I couldn't pick them all up. But I'm OK, really I'm OK - OK - OK - OK. Really, I swear I'm OK!

Jeff and Willie would hang out with me whether I was cooking in the restaurant or working in the pro shop. Boys being boys, often they would end up pushing each other around or even wrestling. They didn't do this in the kitchen, only in the pro shop.

Over and over I would tell them, "Knock it off!" or "Stop wrestling!" or "If you don't stop it you might break something."

Look at the Happy Family – all dressed up and behaving well – even me!

At that time, we had lifesavers, gum and candy bars for sale in the pro shop. We also still ran the regular food concession then and for the first 17 years I was there. I had built the wooden shelves that held the stuff in the pro shop. Anyway, one day when they were wrestling, I decided to make a lasting impression on them. I wasn't mad, but I did want them to stop goofing around, and I had asked them to stop many times that day already. I finally yelled, "If you don't knock it off, something like this might happen!"

I then spun around and intentionally sent two shelves flying that had the boxes of lifesavers and gum on them. Their jaws dropped and their eyes got as big as sewer lids. Packages of gum and lifesavers were spread all over the pro shop. One of the shelves was even slightly damaged.

What was interesting to me was the difference of their reactions.

Jeff, the older and more serious one, looked petrified as he took in the mess and situation I had created. Willie, the screwball, looked surprised but he still almost had a smirk on his face. Once they recovered from the shock, they did pick up all the stuff while I put the shelves back in place on the rack. After that, they would stop wrestling around quickly if I asked them to stop. Although that happened over 40 years ago, they both remember it well and we still laugh about it.

I never pushed Jeff and Willie to play golf, but I encouraged them when they got interested. Liz's parents played a lot of golf at Snoqualmic Falls and occasionally Jeff and Willie would join them. Of course, I didn't let either of them just start out playing. For over a year I helped them prepare to get around a golf course. There were lessons on grip, swing and short game. We also got into etiquette and safety. During this time, I would play a hole or two at a time with them as well.

Willie played left-handed, so I shortened the only left-handed set we had to get him started. We had a right-handed junior set for Jeff to use. When they first started playing it was only with family for the entire first year and they weren't allowed to play by themselves for over two years. Fortunately, we had a few regular members that were happy to have them play with them as well. By the time they were old enough to play in junior golf tournaments, they were both ready and able to do it.

I was always involved in playing sports growing up and all through school. Since I had experience as a high school baseball coach, I stepped up and coached little league for five of the years that Jeff and Willie played little league baseball. Although I tried not to be, I was probably harder on them than I was on the rest of the kids on the teams.

Jeff was always serious and tried to do the best he could. Willie was not as serious, and his concentration could drift to throwing rocks or picking dandelions in the outfield. One day, while trying to get Willie to pay attention, I ended up making him cry. That taught me to ease off him and let him have fun.

I always had a short talk with all my players to start practice. During one of these talks one of my players raised his hand and I said, "Yes, Billy, what is it?"

He responded, "My mom said you were her teacher in eighth grade."

That was the first time I actually had to face the fact I was getting older.

All of my teams did fairly well, because I tried to coach fundamentals, not just winning. I tried to correct mental errors like throwing to the wrong base, missing the cut off man, or getting picked off. A bad throw or a missed catch were unfortunate, but I didn't get upset with players when it happened.

Jeff was an excellent defensive player, but he had a weak arm and holes in his bat. Willie could hit and field fairly well, but never hustled his way to stardom. They both played soccer, but I never played it. I could tell the difference between a soccer ball and a hockey puck, but I couldn't skate well, and it gave me shin splints. Hockey did enter our lives not much later though.

Toward the end of their little league years is when they were old enough for junior golf tournaments. Washington State Junior Golf Association provides most of the tournament play for junior golfers in the state. It was started in 1977 by Joan Teats. It is still the main source for tournament play in Washington. It is a showcase for the best junior golfers to compete. It does not develop or teach juniors how to golf. If you can't play decently, you are not allowed to enter events.

There are six districts in the state. Each district puts on four sub-district tournaments, one district tournament, and then they all come together for the final state tournament. There are a lot of rules for players and parents to follow. One of them is that once play begins, parents, relatives and friends may follow any competitor, but they can't talk to them until they finish their round.

Jeff qualified to play in the District Championship for the 11-year-old and younger group. I took him to Auburn Golf Course where it was being held. I watched him warm up on the range and practice putting on the practice putting green. I also helped him check in for the event.

When he was called to the first tee, we headed that way. As he was getting away from me and closer to the first tee I said, "Hey Jeff, come here."

He turned toward me and said, "You can't talk to me now!"

Willie and me – I'd just received a Nellie Fox autographed ball for my birthday!

I said, "Just get over here!"

He walked back toward me, all the time looking to see if someone was going to see him talk to his dad. When he got to me, I said, "If I tug on my right ear, hit a 5 iron—my left ear a 7 iron. If I fart, hit a 9 iron."

After all, as his baseball coach he was used to getting signals from me. Being my serious son, he looked somewhere between scared and astonished. He got a sheepish look on his face and said, "Dad, you are unbelievable!" He then stepped up to the tee and was a bit more relaxed.

For two years I was appointed the director position for District Two. My job was to line up the courses for the sub-district and district tournaments. I also had to be the rules chairman and the on-the-course marshall during the tournament rounds. At that time, in the '80s, most of the junior golfers were from country clubs. Thanks to many new junior programs and clinics, there are just as many new junior golfers from public courses today.

It was a challenge to get public courses to host a sub-district event, since no fees were charged back then, and the course would lose all that revenue. When we hosted them, which we do quite often still today, it used to cost us about $4,000 in revenue for the day. Today it is similar even though green fees are higher, but that is because they actually pay a small amount to the course now. Private courses suffered no loss of revenue since their revenue was through dues paid by members. I'm sure that the private clubs did have a few members complain about not getting to play though on the given day that their course hosted an event.

The other drawback for public courses was that some of the juniors from private clubs thought it was below them to play "these courses." More than a few times while giving up thousands of dollars so they could play Snoqualmie Falls GC, I heard things like, "Why do we have to play *here*?"

The second year that I was the District Two director, the state final tournament was held in our district. I didn't have to line the courses up for that tournament, but we got to use Sahalee CC and Bear Creek CC. Sahalee is somewhat famous for hosting a few tour events including the PGA Championship in 1998.

There is a banquet held the night before the first round of the state tournament. The dinner was semi-formal and was for the six directors from all over the state. Joan Teats was there as well as another dozen administrators and supporters.

Part of the activities were for each of the people seated around this big table to make a few comments. Shortly before the individual talks were started, I was called out of the room to take a phone call from my son Jeff. He reported that Willie had shot himself in the toe with his BB gun. It wasn't too serious, but he thought I should know. The next day we did have to take Willie to the doctor to get the BB removed, and it did take a lot of effort and time to get the round BB out of his toe where it had lodged. Nonetheless, the news might have dampened my enthusiasm.

The first five speakers all went on and on about how wonderful the WSJGA and its tournaments were. They talked about how they developed and encouraged junior golfers. Of course, none of these geniuses owned public golf courses or ever ran junior tournaments.

Once it was my turn, I couldn't keep my Mr. Hyde down. He stood to talk while Dr. Jekyll sat. I explained that the WSJGA needed to give some thought on how to keep public courses motivated to hold events if it was going to succeed in the future. I went on about the fact that public courses lost thousands of dollars just to have juniors tear the courses up and complain about having to play there. I also explained that if a fee weren't paid to public courses there would come a day when public courses would no longer be made available.

The next three gentlemen proceeded to tear me a new you know what. That I shouldn't be allowed to stay in the room, etc. etc. Next up was Rick Acton, who at that time was the head pro at Sahalee CC. He had played on the PGA tour as well, and he was highly respected in professional golf throughout the entire Northwest. Rick stood and said, "You should all pay attention to what John Groshell said. He knows what he is saying, and he is right. You owe him an apology for what you said about him!"

I never did get an apology, and the next year they got a new District Two director. In fact, I may have been the only director to ever be fired. I did however appreciate Rick standing up for me that night, and the WSJGA now pays public courses a small fee per player, and they give a thank you sign to the course that is signed by the juniors playing in the event.

CHAPTER 71

Family Travel

As a family, the four of us did things and went places together. Liz could play golf. In fact, I met her because she, her sister and her parents played golf at Mount Si Golf Course. That helped us do more together, because all of us could golf together.

The first week or longer trip took place in 1981 when we went to San Diego for the Holiday Bowl. The All Cougar Bowl game pitted the Washington State Cougars against the Brigham Young Cougars. Jeff was nine and Willie was seven at the time. We took them out of school about a week before their Christmas vacation so that we could visit Disneyland, Knotts Berry Farm and Sea World before those attractions got busy with everyone else out on vacation. That was one of our better moves, because we avoided long lines at the parks. Our WSU Cougars lost 38–36 to the BYU Cougars, but it was a good game. We were then able to get back home for Christmas.

We made another California trip about five years later when Jeff was 14 and Willie was 13. This time we drove down and brought three sets of golf clubs with us, leaving Liz's clubs at home. The trip plan was to do all the parks again and some other sightseeing with the three guys to play a couple of rounds of golf.

Southern California was way too hot for the older plump guy. Of course, I never liked heat when I was young and in shape. Overall, it was OK because we spent most of the time in San Diego where it wasn't so hot.

I guess Jeff and Willie liked to watch the old man sweat. They wanted to go to Palm Desert one day and play the Stadium Course, a tough course used for tour events. One day, the three of us left the comfort of San Diego to go to the furnace in Palm Desert. By the time we teed off at 10:30 it was over 100 degrees. We were the only group playing as far as I could see. Their mid-summer rate of $25 including a cart was nice but didn't make it less miserable.

A day's catch after fishing at Flathead Lake in Montana. Left to Right: Willie, Jeff, Me and Liz.

This was the first time I ever saw giant fans blowing air on golf greens. I guess the air circulation prevents them from turning brown.

We did finish the round and by then it was pushing 120 degrees. When I opened the four-wheeled oven we called a car, the heat almost knocked me over. My one oversight of the day was that I hadn't brought a turkey with me. I guarantee it would have been thoroughly cooked in that car.

The next day I had to fly back home and go to work. Liz got to drive back after a couple more days in San Diego. The two-week trip was planned as two weeks for them and eight days for me.

The highlight of their return was a stop at Pea Soup Anderson's. Willie especially liked the characters of "Pea Wee" and "Split Pea".

A number of the family trips I went on revolved around football games. For years I bragged that I had attended every WSU bowl game since 1931. That was quite a feat, since I was born in 1945. The key word in that statement was "since". WSU played Alabama in the Rose Bowl in 1931. Their next bowl game was the Holiday Bowl in 1981 that the four of us attended. I did manage to attend all of their bowl games through the New Mexico bowl in 2013. They won 5 of them and lost 4.

After that first bowl game there was only one more that all four of us attended. That was the Rose Bowl in 1998. Keith, *aka* Spanky, and I attended the Aloha Bowl in 1988 and the Copper Bowl in 1992. Willie made us a threesome at the Copper Bowl. Willie and I did the Sun Bowl in 2001. Liz, Willie and I did the Rose Bowl in January 2003 as well as the Holiday Bowl in December 2004.

The New Mexico Bowl in 2013 was my last bowl game and son Jeff went with me for that trip. The Cougs managed to lose that game with a 15-point lead as well as possession of the ball with only three minutes to go in the game. The coach, Mike Leach, had them passing and hiking the ball with over 20 seconds left on the play clock. They could have won by taking a knee each down and letting the clock run out.

That trip was also a disaster on another level. We had a two-hour boarding delay at SeaTac to catch our flight out. They then loaded us on the plane where we cooked for an hour and a half, before they decided we couldn't safely use that plane. We then changed planes and finally got on our way. Unfortunately, we had a connecting flight in Phoenix that left for New Mexico before our first flight had left SeaTac.

We then became the only passengers they forgot about, so they didn't book a hotel room and a ride to the hotel for us. By the time this was all squared away we got about three hours sleep and were back at the airport to catch an 8:30 AM flight to New Mexico. Jeff and I lost a full day of our trip, we were not reimbursed for the hotel, and we got a flight voucher that was completely worthless as it turned out, due to strange stipulations on its use.

The only other bowl game I attended was the Super Bowl in 2015 when Pete Carrol gave the game away. Spanky went with me, and we had lousy seats that cost me $9,200. It was second down with one yard to go and two timeouts available. Marshawn Lynch had just gone 4 yards on the first down play. We could hand off to Marshawn and call timeout if he was stopped. We had three plays for the strongest runner in the league to go one yard.

Our seats were so high up, the speakers hanging down blocked our view of the scoreboard. We were surrounded by New England fans. I had paid a ridiculous $9,200 to a broker because I didn't get drawn in the Seahawk Season Ticket Holder Lottery, even though I have had season tickets since day one in 1976. By the way, I was not drawn in either of the other two Seahawk Super Bowls either. Most season ticket holders will sell their tickets for a huge mark up if they are drawn in the lottery. If they changed their policy and only allowed them to pick up the tickets at the site by showing ID, then this would end. Then only season ticket holders that actually wanted to attend the game would register for the lottery and they would have a much better chance of getting the tickets.

Anyway, back to my last game as a Seahawks fan, at least until Pete Carrol is gone. On the 2nd down with 26 seconds left, I was told (I couldn't hardly see the play from our seats) that Russell dropped back to pass. He intended to throw to a receiver who had only caught seven passes all year long. The pass was thrown into the middle where it was intercepted. Without a doubt, it was the worst play call in the history of football. Ten-year-olds playing in a field drawing up plays in the mud with sticks, wouldn't be that stupid.

Spanky and I got to walk three miles back to the makeshift parking lot that cost me $50, shaking our heads in disbelief the entire way.

Back to family fun; let's forget about football heartbreak. One summer we rented a motorhome and went to Yellowstone Park. Even though we saw very few bears we had a great time there and got in a couple of rounds of golf on the way there and back. We did see a rare adult male moose drinking out of a river in Yellowstone. We pulled off to look at it and I unfortunately showed my lack of knowledge about wildlife. I decided to get out of the car and let Jeff and Willie come with me down closer to the moose to get some good pictures. I was snapping away like a good tourist enjoying this wildlife encounter when I realized I may have made a big mistake. The moose apparently wasn't fond of being the model for my photo shoot. He quit drinking, turned to pose for a couple more quick pictures, and then snorted while pawing the ground like he was going to charge.

That's when the light finally clicked on in my head. I told Jeff and Willie to back away while being ready to jump behind a tree if the

Son Willie plays golf too! He is a single digit handicap. Here he prepares to tee off at Victoria Country Club.

moose charged us. I quit taking pictures and slowly backed away as well, trying to stay between the moose and my kids. Fortunately, the bull moose allowed us to retreat without charging and I learned not to do that sort of thing again.

A few years later, we bought a small motorhome and did a Montana trip to the Flathead Lake area. That trip we went to Glacier National Park where I barely navigated the motorhome up the Road to the Sun and back. That was one of the most stressful and scary driving experiences of my life. The road was too narrow for anything like a motorhome, and one side dropped off a cliff. The other side was against the shear rock of the mountains and on that side, I did hit the rocks a couple times with the rearview mirror of the motorhome. That trip also involved some great fishing on Flathead Lake and quite a few rounds of golf in the area.

During our rounds, there was always a lot of needling between the three guys. We seldom gave Liz any grief and we usually tried to be encouraging but she normally played just fine. Quite often she would inquire about what club to hit. Usually, Willie would step right up to help, and quite often she even asked Willie for his advice. It would go something like this:

Liz: "How far is it to the pin?"

Willie: "About a buck twenty (which meant 120 yards)."

Liz: "What club should I hit?"

Willie: "Hit a five iron."

Liz: "Really? Are you sure I need that much club?"

Willie: "Hit a six iron then!"

Liz: "Really?"

Willie: "Hit a seven iron then. Hell, it doesn't matter anyway, you hit them all the same distance anyway."

Willie was always a really helpful little guy. Anything to help his mother seemed to make him happy. Liz must have liked his wonderful help though, because no matter how much he gave her a hard time or bad advice she didn't seem to ever think twice before asking for more.

We had quite a few rounds of golf as a family, but the beginning of one of those rounds stands out. Willie was actually going to Linfield College in McMinnville, Oregon. We decided to line up a round for the four of us near where Willie was going to school at a course called Pumpkin Ridge.

As we drove into the parking lot I said, "I think I will get a cart today. I'm sick of having my feet hurt."

I could walk 18 holes without a lot of pain, but after I finished and sat down for a few minutes standing back up was very painful in my heels. Later I learned it was called plantar fasciitis. I was lucky enough to have it in both feet at the same time.

Anyways, Liz said, "You can walk. You don't need a cart. Yick–Yick–Yick! Get me a hand cart though."

Well, yes, it did piss me off, so just to show her, I walked! As we were walking off the first tee and heading up the fairway we passed a sign that said, "KEEP CARTS ON PATH." As Liz was walking along in the start of the fairway of this long par five I said, "Didn't you see that sign back there?"

She replied, "You mean the one that said keep carts on path?"

I said, "Yes."

She said, "But that is for power carts."

"Did it say power carts?" I responded.

"No," she said.

"Well, over to the path then," said I, knowing I was going to pay in the long run.

What I found interesting was the responses of Jeff and Willie. Jeff was saying to me, "Come on, Dad, don't do this. Please."

Willie was chirping away, "Way to go, Dad. This is great!"

Watching Liz play the hole was like watching the video game Frogger. Up the path, stop, 90° turn and out to the golf ball, back to the path, up the path to across from the golf ball, 90° turn and back out to the golf ball, on and on at about 100 yards per cycle until she reached the green. She ended up walking over 1000 yards to play a 500-yard hole.

Realizing that the round was going to take about seven hours at that rate I said, "Just go ahead and walk in the fairway. After nine holes I will check in the pro shop to make sure that is alright."

And YES! My heels hurt all night after that round!

CHAPTER 72

Hockey Life!

When the kids were barely teenagers, we went to a Seattle Breakers hockey game one night. The kids loved the fast action and Liz liked to watch the players fight. We liked it so much we went again a few weeks later. There was an announcement asking if anyone would like to be a billet, to house and feed a player or two.

Liz knew all these guys were obviously fighting over her, so we volunteered. Over a six-year period we had 26 different players. Some would only be with us for a couple of weeks before they were traded. Sometimes we would have two at a time with us. Players in the league ranged from 17 to 19 years of age. As we gained seniority, we got players who stayed with us through the full season. Of the 26 players we had, only one wasn't Canadian. He was from Los Angeles, and he was the only jerk of the group.

So, we provided a car, room and board and in return we got season tickets. We also had the fun of having them around. They were all good with Jeff and Willie and I'm sure they speeded up their education in social matters. Also, we all got damn good at ping pong. Plus, Jeff and Willie got lots of rides to school. Having the hockey players around was good for the kids growing up.

Not only did we attend every home game, but Liz and I went on two long road trips with the Hockey Booster Club. We watched games in Kelowna, Medicine Hat, Swift Current, Lethbridge, Brandon, Kamloops and New Westminster.

One night in Kelowna my ticket was drawn to do the puck shoot between periods. They walked me out to center ice to take the shot for some sort of prize. In Seattle there was a rubber mat for the contestant to stand on to reduce the chance of slipping. In Kelowna, there was no such luxury. When I tried to shoot my feet went flying and I fell flat on my butt. I got up to my knees and gave the crowd the good old baseball safe sign.

Erin Ginnell. He played hockey and worked at the golf course and took me on his honeymoon!

One morning as we were loading the tour bus, there was a cat hanging around. Several of us were petting it before we took off. After about four hours of driving we stopped for gas. When the driver opened the hood to check the oil, the cat came flying out from under the hood and took off running down the street.

On another road trip, there were more fans and thus a bigger bus. Amongst the group we had a number of younger fans in their early twenties. One of them was very boisterous and a real pain. One day, he was drunk by the time we loaded the bus. After an hour or so, he passed out. A couple of the younger guys and gals then put lipstick and make-up on him, including mascara and rouge. Later at a stop to eat he woke up and went in to eat with everyone. He didn't realize how he looked, but he did notice people looking at him. When he finally went to the bathroom, he found out why.

The two players we housed the last couple of years were Ken McIntyre and Erin Ginnell. We had both of them at the same time for a while, and they were both great with the kids. Erin was also a good golfer and ended up coming back to live with us when he was done playing hockey.

At the point that Erin and Ken left the Seattle team, which had changed names from the Breakers to the Thunderbirds, they went to play for the Minot Americans in Minot, North Dakota. Erin had a relative who coached them. That year, the four of us flew to Regina, Saskatchewan where Kenny's family lived. First, we spent several days with them, and we saw what really cold weather was like. It was January and during the day temperatures were about 25 degrees below zero. At night it got down to 40 below zero. There is a difference between those two temperatures too. It is hard to even breathe the air at 40 below. They also plug in their cars, because if they don't the car probably won't start.

One day we went to a festival on the lake in Regina. It was 25 below zero on that bright sunny day. In fact, a few hours before we went to the festival, we went skating at an outdoor ice rink. Anyways, at the festival there was a hole cut out of the 3-foot-thick ice on the lake. People could get tee shirts as a reward if they jumped in the hole into the lake. After climbing out there was a tent with heaters for them to go into and warm back up. If I had been a few years younger, I would have done it.

That night we went to a hockey game in Moose Jaw. It was difficult breathing at 45 degrees below zero as we walked from our car into the arena. The roof was bowed in the middle, so if you were seated half way up in the stands you couldn't see at least half of the people on the other side.

After that, we rented a car and drove to Minot, North Dakota to watch Kenny and Erin play hockey. The four-hour drive down on a nice sunny day was fine. The day after the game we had to get back to Regina to fly back home. For some reason, we didn't leave Minot until it was almost dark. It didn't occur to me that the four-hour drive back in 45° below temperatures on an empty road, might not be a good idea. As I drove with the heater on full and the defrost blowing hard, I had Jeff or Willie scraping ice off the inside of the windshield.

There were no other cars on the road. People there weren't as dumb as I. If the car had stopped running, we all would have frozen to death.

The four of us did a summer trip once into Canada, and on the way to Calgary we stopped in Revelstoke to visit the Sicia family. Their son Lawrence had been with us all of two weeks before he was traded. You would have thought we had taken care of him for 10 years by the way they treated us. Each day when we tried to leave, they wouldn't let us. We actually had to meet Kenny in Calgary to bring him back to Washington.

They said, "You can't go. Uncle Bob and Aunt Judy are coming to dinner tonight to meet you." Each day there was some reason we couldn't leave yet. Finally, we did escape. The Canadian people are fantastically gracious and nice.

As I mentioned earlier, Erin did come back to live with us and work at Snoqualmie Falls Golf Course. He was interested in trying to get US citizenship and/or a work permit or green card. I went with him to the Department of Naturalization in Seattle to see what he would have to do. Although 90% of the people working at the Department of Naturalization were Asian and many of them hardly spoke English, they informed us that there was only one way. As a Canadian, he would have to marry a citizen of the United States to become a US citizen. If he wanted a green card to stay here and work, then his employer (me) would have to prove that there was no citizen in the United States that could do the job that he would be doing. It seemed like an easy and totally fair process to me. Not!

Erin ended up leaving us and he went back to Canada to finish school. Several years later he got married in a small town that was a 3-hour drive from Winnipeg. Liz, Willie and I went to the wedding. We flew to Winnipeg and then drove to the little town where the wedding was taking place. After the wedding, I went on the honeymoon with them. Erin, along with his wife Jay, had rented a motorhome. The three ushers and I joined them for the five-hour drive north to Flin Flon. We went to the resort his parents ran at Denare Beach. After three days of fishing, drinking and lounging around I caught a flight from Flin Flon to Winnipeg. I then flew to Vancouver, BC where I caught a connecting flight to Seattle. By the time I landed at SeaTac I had almost dried out.

Erin ended up getting into scouting for NHL teams. He first was a scout for the Columbus Blue Jackets when their franchise first started. He then worked for the Florida Panthers. Presently he is the western Canadian amateur scout for the Las Vegas Golden Knights.

CHAPTER 73

A few more trips!

The last time Liz stepped on an airplane was when she and I did a Jay Buckley baseball tour. For that tour we had to fly to Chicago and then back to Seattle after the tour was over. That was in 2009. Consequently, we haven't done any trips that involved the four of us since then.

Liz and I went on Buckley tours five different years. For those tours you get yourself to the starting point by whatever form of travel you wish. Since the starting points were either Chicago or Newark, NJ we always chose to fly there.

Once the tour bus is loaded, all travel, lodging and game tickets are part of the package. The trips out of Chicago included games in St. Louis, Detroit, Cleveland and both Chicago teams. Being born in Chicago, I am a White Sox fan for two reasons. First, my childhood hero was Nellie Fox. I identified with him because he was short and scrappy and damn good. I was and still am short. In sports, I never gave up and sometimes I was almost good. The second reason I was a White Sox fan was because my brother Hiram liked the Cubs.

The trips that started in Newark included both New York teams, Philadelphia, Boston, Baltimore, and a day at the Hall of Fame. Also included was a tour through the Hillerich and Bradsby Louisville Slugger Factory. We also took in the Yogi Berra Museum and Learning Center.

Some older people, like myself, who follow baseball, know Yogi was known for Yogi-isms. The well-known ones are, "If you come to a fork in the road, take it." Another one, in reference to a restaurant that was always busy, "That place is so busy no one goes there anymore." My personal favorite, although not as famous, came when Yogi was attending some big function in New York and the Mayor's wife said to Yogi, "You look pretty cool in that summer suit you're wearing."

Yogi, without missing a beat replied, "Thanks, you don't look so hot yourself."

Anyways, those tours are a lot of fun. Extra time is given to sight-seeing and shopping if desired. Time on the bus is filled with informative movies about the cities we were visiting or about ball players of both old and new from the ball clubs we were going to watch. For the price, you couldn't begin to do a similar tour on your own.

Once Liz had her wings clipped, most of my trips have been with Jeff. What finished off Liz was that she didn't want to deal with the security checks and hours spent in airports. My last flight took place in December of 2019. Jeff, along with his son and my grandson Trevor, and I were going through security in Charleston, SC. First, one TSA guy pulled my wallet out of my shoe and dumped everything in it all around the bin I had put my shoes into.

The next guy stepped up the assault. I use a money clip for currency, and I had put the clip in the bin and kept the paper money in my buttoned back pocket. This is how I have always gone through security so my money wouldn't be loose for anyone to take. The x-ray machine picked up the paper money in my pocket. It didn't beep or light up, but the security guy could see it on his screen. While he berated me for not emptying my pockets, he demanded that I remove the money and hold it over my head as I went back through the x-ray machine.

He then gave me a thorough up and down and between the legs scan with his hand. Thankfully he was wearing rubber gloves, because he then reached inside my pants in both front and back and roughly performed a search. He did all of this with other people passing through right beside us. I will admit that I was quite shaken. He then made me stand there for several minutes before he let me go. I wanted to raise hell for how I was treated, but I also wanted to catch my flight and get the hell out of there.

So that was my last flight, but as I mentioned most of my trips before that and after Liz quit flying were with Jeff, and most of those trips at least involved playing golf.

One of those trips took us to Northern California where we played Pebble Beach, Spyglass Hill and Cypress Point. Yes, I said Cypress Point. Cypress might be the second most exclusive club in the country, with Augusta National being the first. A couple of years before I had

Willie standing outside Comiskey Park before the final game ever played there. As the final game wound up, fans began hunting for souvenirs.

Notice all the police on the field – there were many more in the stands. It was the very last game and security was high to keep people from tearing down the stadium after the game. I think the reader board says it all: "Thanks for the memories – 1910-1990" – 80 years at Comiskey Park.

tried to get us on there, but I had been unsuccessful. They allowed one PGA professional a week to play there. My son Jeff managed to surprise me and get us on by calling months before our trip and getting us on their little black appointment book months later. He then planned the rest of a golf trip in the Monterey area around the surprise round he booked at Cypress Point.

On that trip, we also played Tehema Golf Club. Tehema was built and owned by Clint Eastwood, who had it for his friends to play and for his own use. Bob Hickam, the pro who grew up playing Snoqualmie Falls GC and had gotten me and my friends on Pebble Beach years before, was at this point the club professional for Tehema.

This reminded me of another golf trip I took years ago with Jeff when he was a freshman in college at Dominican College in San Rafael, CA. I flew down to visit him at school and go golfing at various places in the area. One of those rounds we went to play Silverado GC. I had played it years before with my buddies, but Jeff had never played it before. As it turned out, Jeff and I were rewarded with a special treat that day at Silverado.

When we went to the practice green to hit a few putts before the first of our two rounds that day, we noticed a rather familiar looking tall gentleman practicing his putting at the same time. Jeff started talking to him and we both realized it was Michael Jordan.

Shortly, we headed over to tee off on #1. We were looking forward to a pleasant day of golf, as the weather was good, and we were going to play all 36 holes at Silverado GC. As we walked onto the first green to putt, up drove two golf carts with two Michael Jordan escorts in each cart. They made it difficult to read our putts or even putt as they were roaming the green fixing spike and ball marks for their highness Mr. Jordan. They would remove any debris, rake the bunkers, and fix any imperfection to get the playing area as perfect as possible for Michael Jordan and his group. They bothered us on every green for all 18 holes, even though we stayed two holes ahead of Michael Jordan's group for the entire round.

After we walked off the 18th green, I asked Jeff if he would like to get his majesty's autograph. He was hesitant but did say yes. I suggested that he wait until Mr. Jordan finished and walked off the green. Then once his round was over he could go up and ask him to sign his scorecard.

Jeff waited for them to finally reach and finish the 18th hole. After Jordan walked off the green, Jeff slowly walked up and meekly asked, "Mr. Jordan, would you please sign my scorecard?"

What Jeff got back was, "I don't sign autographs on vacation!"

At that time, Michael had retired from basketball, and he was trying to get into Major League Baseball. There was also no chance that Jeff was going to start a rush of autograph seekers, as we were at least 100 yards away from the clubhouse completely out of sight from everyone except for our groups. Jeff was also just a new college kid hoping for an autograph on his scorecard. He wasn't looking for an autograph to turn around and sell it. In my opinion, Jordan owed us at least an autograph, because we had gone through 18 holes of harassment from his entourage preparing every hole for him with no regard to how it affected our round.

As we headed for the clubhouse for lunch, one of Jordan's pals

Jeff and me on the 18th tee at Pebble Beach. Please note the water level is higher than usual from all the balls Jeff hit in the ocean on #8.

came up and said he was sorry about Jeff not getting an autograph. He also claimed that Jordan wouldn't sign anything for his kids.

After we had lunch in the clubhouse with his group taking up a couple of the tables next to ours, we went out to play the other 18 holes. I was thinking the second round would be more pleasant, because we would at least have the chance to putt without interruption and distraction. Unfortunately, I was wrong, because the carts rolled up again and the green cleaners attacked for another 18 holes.

Jeff and I have had a few other trips to play golf. Usually we are a twosome, and quite often the course will put a single or another twosome with us for the round. One of these trips we were a threesome with Jeff's college friend Tex, who is also a golf pro, as our third. We were playing at Pasatiempo GC in California and the starter sent a single out to join us as we took the first tee. The single was an attorney from New Jersey, and he wasn't afraid to render his opinion.

On the first hole, Jeff was waiting for the green to clear so he could hit his second shot on the green of this medium length par 5. The

Son Jeff and me at Cypress Point CC on the Monterey Peninsula.

single couldn't understand what was happening. He asked, "Are you going to hit?"

Jeff replied, "I will hit once they leave the green and it is safe to hit." Jeff was sitting about 220 yards away from the green after a 300-yard drive waiting to hit his 3 iron onto the green.

The attorney then said, "It is only your second shot, and I have never seen anyone knock it on the green in two shots." He then walked up the fairway towards his ball and continued to glare back at Jeff, who was still waiting for the group in front of us to safely exit the green.

Once Jeff could hit, he proceeded to hit a beautiful 3-iron shot onto the green leaving himself a nice chance for an eagle.

Seeing Jeff accomplish this feat did nothing to slow down our single. He still regularly encouraged all of us to hit shots when we would hit into the group in front of us. He also regularly tried to ride in the cart with me, whenever Tex didn't get in to ride.

Jeff was walking, and I was using a two-person power cart. Jeff let Tex put his clubs on the cart with me and on rare occasions Tex would ride with me instead of walking with Jeff. However, I asked Tex to ride with me more and more as the round went on, because I was not enjoying the company of our clueless and obnoxious single. This ended up leading to the greatest part of the round....

On about the 16th hole, which was a steep uphill par 4, Tex jumped in the cart just before our single friend could get in. This forced the single to walk up this steep fairway to his ball. When he finally reached his ball, he said to Tex, "I thought they taught better manners in Texas, and you would let your elder ride in the cart."

Without any hesitation, Tex replied, "I don't know about manners, but they did teach us to pay for our own cart."

It was all I could do to keep a straight face when the single turned to me in hopes that I would correct Tex. I didn't try to correct Tex, but I was really proud of his quick-witted reply.

Since I mentioned that being paired with other people is quite often part of our golf rounds when I take golf trips with Jeff, there are a couple more things I should share. As I have aged, my golf game has dropped off from what it used to be. I used to reach about 50% of par fives in two shots, and now I find more and more par fours that I can't reach in two shots.

Anyways, quite often after playing several holes with our new playing partners, they would ask me, "What do you do for a living?" When I would reply that I was a golf pro and owned a golf course, they would more often than not start asking for help with their swings. Some would also question why I three putted or hit a bad shot. I was like a doctor at a party that had to check out rashes, lumps and other problems.

Fortunately, I came up with a much better reply to this question one round many years ago and I have used it many times since. I came up with this reply on the fly without any pre-planning or thought. When we were a few holes in and our playing partners were saying what a great golfer Jeff was, like I was a hack and must be so proud that my son could actually golf, one of them asked what I did for a living. By the way, Jeff is a terrible green reader, but he hits it well and a long way. This makes people think he shoots better than he does, and they often think I suck because I'm older and don't hit it as far as my son Jeff. Therefore, we have rounds that I beat Jeff, but our playing partners don't have any idea.

Jeff with twins at Poppy. They were our best pairing ever! They said I was the best golfer of all the retired jockeys they ever played with.

Regardless, I immediately ad-libbed my answer to the question, "I'm a retired jockey. When I retired, I got a Dunkin Donut franchise, and I just can't leave the damn things alone."

If you knew me, you would see that I meet the requirement of being short. At my peak I was barely 5'5" tall. Tall doesn't go with 5'5", so I should say "in height" instead. I am also over 225 lbs, so unless I raced Clydesdales, I certainly am too heavy. That is where the Dunkin Donuts come in. Nobody has ever doubted me, although a few have been curious about where I used to ride. I always say at smaller tracks in New Mexico, Texas, and other places in the South. Thankfully, no one has asked what tracks in particular.

I have done more trips with Jeff than with younger son Willie. Willie has lived in the Portland, OR area since he graduated from Linfield. Jeff has been our next-door neighbor and has been able to get away for golf trips. Willie is a good golfer but isn't bananas over it like Jeff is. We have done a few small golf trips and even did one golf trip to Las Vegas with Jeff, Willie, Willie's wife and me. Willie and I had also played Pebble Beach and Spyglass Hill together.

Willie and I did take a non-golf related trip in 1990. We flew to Chicago to attend the final series in Comiskey Park, the home of my favorite team, the Chicago White Sox. (Being born in Chicago I have been a White Sox fan all my life. First, because Nellie Fox was my hero and second, because Hiram liked the Cubs.) The park opened in 1910 and hosted the first ever baseball All Star Game in 1933. It also hosted the 50th anniversary All Star game in (you guessed it) 1983.

That series was against the Seattle Mariners with the final game being September 30, 1990.

We stayed in a fancy hotel downtown. I didn't rent a car so we used public transportation.

I went to the concierge to find out the best way to get to the stadium. She said to catch the EL (short for elevated train) and where to do so which was only a block away. At that location the tracks were underground.

When we descended the steps, we were in what looked like a subway station to me. My only experience of subways was seeing them in movies and an occasional news story. They were never associated with anything good. When we boarded the car, I noticed that we were the only white people. Being a "Country boy" from a small town in Washington I certainly wasn't in my comfort zone. I also had had my life threatened three times before. Once by an older Native American and twice by small groups of black kids. About a mile down the tracks the car became elevated which made it less intimidating to me. Nothing bad happened on the ride to the Stadium but for the rest of our time in Chicago we used taxies.

The games were all fun. There was even fireworks after one of them. Maybe the most interesting thing was after the final game. All through the game announcements were made telling people NOT to remove items from the stadium after the game. When the final out was made about 25 policemen on horses took the field. Police also filled every aisle way. Old Comiskey was in lockdown to keep fans from dismantling the stadium to steal souvenirs. Once we got home, I ordered and purchased two of the seats. Of course, I still have them.

Did I mention earlier that Willie was a very good soccer goalie? He was a goalkeeper for the Linfield College soccer team. Liz and I drove down and watched him play in many of their games.

It was hard for me to watch, because Willie was fearless. He did finish one game with a thumb he broke before halftime. He would dive at balls that were about to be kicked with no fear. That may have been because he hit his head on things a lot when he was young.

CHAPTER 74

Doctor Visits

L iz and I have been lucky when it comes to our health. Right now in August 2022, Liz and I have remained COVID-19 free. We have had both COVID shots and two boosters each. I am 76 and less than a month from 77. Liz is now 75.

Liz had back surgery for a ruptured disc 35 years ago and recovered well. Around the same time, she had a hysterectomy, and that surgery went smoothly as well. Just five years ago she had laparoscopic surgery to shore up some female parts. After six weeks of non-lifting of heavy things, she was fully recovered.

I already mentioned that most of my medical problems took place before I was nine years old. About twelve years ago it was discovered that I have A-fib (irregular heart rhythm). The doctor first had me take rat poison (warfarin) for six weeks. Then they performed cardioversion treatment on me. I looked at the clock in the operating room when they rolled me in there. After they electrocuted me and I woke up, it was only eleven minutes later. I laid in my bed in recovery for about 30 minutes before I walked to the desk and asked about leaving. The nurses rushed me back to bed. The nurse, who had been in the room for my procedure, was laughing because when the doctor gave me the jolt, I had taken a swing at him.

After a while longer, I got up again and put on my clothes so I could leave. When I walked to the nurses' station this time the nurses gave up and said they would get a wheelchair to haul me out to the car. They tried for about ten minutes before they gave up on finding a wheelchair, and then two of them walked me out to where Liz was waiting with our car.

Four years ago, I had surgery to repair a hernia. That went just fine also and now I am packing around some mesh that is helping keep my insides where they are supposed to be.

Now I am going to tell you about the toughest surgical experience that either Liz or I have had to endure. Going through the pre-surgical interview, the prep for surgery, the pre-operating support from friends, the actual procedure, the recovery, and the proof of success was all a long and painful experience. I know that over 50% of our population views it as nothing, but they have never experienced it.

Yes—I'm talking about my vasectomy. Liz had lost her first pregnancy with a miscarriage at about five months. That was tough on her. We then had Jeff and Willie. I say "we" because I had to do part of the procedure. They were healthy and both births went smoothly. Less than a year later, Liz miscarried what turned out to be a tubal pregnancy. Liz and I were then in agreement that it was time for Johnny G to go under the knife.

The first step was the consultation with the doctor. All sorts of scenarios were presented to us to make sure we knew what we were doing. What if Jeff or Willie died? What if we got divorced? What if Liz died? Finally, it was decided that Johnny was going through with the snipping.

I was at work at the golf course the night before I had to face the knife. Several of my buddies were hanging out telling me about what to expect. Several of them had already been neutered, so they could speak with authority about it. The description that best caught my attention pertained to the sensation when the cords were severed. They had already discussed the needles to deaden the boys and the shaving job I would have to do.

John Mowry, the big guy who we called "Lurch" said it all, "When they cut those cords, it will be like they cut the wires on a banjo, and they will snap right up and get caught in your throat!"

I couldn't wait.

The next morning, I did my best to shave the bag my boys were in, but I found out that I didn't do it well enough. Laying there on the table, naked with my feet in the stirrups, the doctor and his male assistant were checking out the area that was well lighted. Their verdict was, "You didn't shave yourself well enough!"

Unfortunately, the assistant had the solution. Out came the straight edge. I had only seen them in the movies before. With his left hand he grabbed the bag and without a hot towel or shaving cream he started scraping away. It just occurred to me that they could have shot me up first, but no such luck for me.

Once that was over, I got the Novocain shots, and then the doctor got started. I didn't feel the first incision, but when he cut the cord on the right side, I discovered that Lurch wasn't lying. By the time I caught my breath the doc was headed to the left side. For whatever reason, the left side didn't provide the banjo string effect. Once I was stitched up, I got dressed and Liz drove me home.

A couple of hours after I got home, it was like I went into shock. I didn't know what was going on and I could hardly walk. The entire area swelled up and turned black and blue. Liz called the doctor and he said things should improve. He also said to put ice on it. In about five days the swelling was going down, and I was doing better. The final step was to take in a sample after six weeks. They had to check that all I had left were blanks. No swimmers were allowed.

This final step did present a few challenges. The sample had to be delivered within 30 minutes of when I provided it. The drive from our house to the hospital was 45 minutes. The only solution I could think of was to take a magazine to the hospital and find a restroom where I could take matters into my own hands. There was a men's room just around the corner from the lab. I was able to handle things and headed for the lab, where I hoped there was a male working.

This turned out to NOT be my lucky day. Standing there to accept my sample was a beautiful young lady who couldn't have been more than 22 years of age. As I meekly handed her my little jar she said casually with a smile on her face, "Did you get this sample within the last 30 minutes?"

I immediately replied, "Is a minute and a half good enough?"

She blinked, blushed, and then turned to escape to the back room.

CHAPTER 75

Illegal Digging

Liz and I went to a home show about 25 years ago. We should have known better, because the only other home show we went to we ended up buying a house. This time we didn't buy anything, but I left my name at the Grays Harbor booth. I told the lady that I always wanted to have a house on a lake.

Within a month, the lady, who happened to be a realtor, called. With the hook set, we rushed to Ocean Shores and bought the lot on the lake. Within a year, we had a house built on the lot. We also decided we wanted privacy, so we purchased the lots on either side of the house.

I hadn't dug a razor clam since I was a kid when we had a house between Long Beach and Ocean Park. Earlier I wrote about my clam digging experience back then. Basically, the story discussed how we had dug more clams than allowed.

We seldom got down to our new house in Ocean Shores, because I was still working a great deal. Fortunately, the first low tide when razor clam digging was allowed came up when I could get away from work.

That morning we got up and dressed to go dig. When it was time to go, someone came to visit with Liz. Ocean tides happen when they happen, they don't stay low so someone can dig clams whenever they are ready. With this knowledge, I headed for the beach to start digging before I waited too long for Liz to finish visiting.

I was shocked by the number of people digging clams. As a kid when I went digging there was hardly anyone out there digging. This time it was quite different. The diggers were elbow to elbow. Trying to find a place to dig was very difficult. The parking on the beach looked more like the parking lot at a Major League Baseball game. Regardless, I found a place to park and started fighting to find clam holes to dig. When I reached the limit of 15 clams I headed to the car. The last time I dug clams the limit was 24 clams.

By the time I got back to the house, Liz was ready to go digging. I put the bucket with 15 clams in the garage and put another empty bucket in the trunk. I then drove to the beach at a location about a mile south of where I got the first limit. At this point, the tide had come in a decent amount, and most of the diggers had gone home. By the time we had dug our limits, we were the only ones left on the beach. As we headed toward the car, I stopped and dug two more clams to replace a couple of the clams that Liz had broken while digging. I left the two broken ones buried in the sand, which is technically not legal but frequently done by many diggers.

As we approached our car, a jeep drove up and parked beside us. Actually, the jeep didn't drive up by itself, the game warden was driving it. After friendly hellos and how are you doings, the warden got down to business.

It went something like this...

Warden: "Well, let me see what you got."

Me: "Sure."

He then counted the clams in each bucket and saw we had the legal amount. I was worried that he might have seen me replace the two broken ones.

Warden: "I see you have your limits."

Liz (very nervously): "So it's alright then, isn't it?"

Warden: "Well, not really. You see, what I do is randomly pick out a car and follow it when it leaves the beach. It could be anybody digging, but I just follow them to see what they are going to do. About an hour and a half ago, I followed your husband. He had been up the beach at Oyhut digging clams."

At this point I knew I was screwed. I was only thinking how unlucky I was that he picked me to follow out of the hundreds of possible other cars.

Warden (continues): "I followed him over to Bass Avenue where he pulled in the long driveway back to your blue and green house. It was hard looking through the trees, but I watched him take the bucket of clams out of the trunk and put them in the garage. I then watched him put an empty bucket back in the trunk. At that point, I figured I might as well follow him to see what he was going to do next."

Liz: "I told him he shouldn't do it."

Liz, Jeff, Kari and me on Easter Sunday when Jeff proposed marriage to Kari. She did say, "YES."

Warden: "Anyway, I just parked about 100 yards up the road and waited to see what happened. When you drove by me, I followed you here to the beach and parked back that way a bit and watched. I'm going to guess that if I came back to your house with you, I would find a limit of clams in a bucket in your garage."

Then he turned toward me and said: "Don't you think?"

Me: "Yes, I think you might be right."

Liz: "I don't like it when people break the law."

Of course, if she had been ready to go to the first outing, we would have each gotten one limit and not broken the law. Also, she was more than willing to go out to get the next two limits. We all then got in our vehicles and headed back to our house on Bass Avenue. When we got back home, I turned over my other bucket for the warden to count the clams in it.

So, I asked, "How much is this going to cost me?"

Willie, his wife Sarah, Liz and me after their wedding.

Warden: "Well, last week I caught a guy and it cost him over $2,000."

Liz: "I told him not to do it."

Me (in my head): "Shut the fk up, Liz!"

Warden: "But your husband is only one limit over, so it is $10 a clam for a total of $150."

With that he got a gunny sack out of his car and dumped my first limit from Oyhut into it. Those clams were bigger than the ones Liz and I had dug.

Me: "What are you going to do with those clams?"

Warden: "I'm taking them to the seniors center."

Me: "Oh, I bet those seniors can't get enough of those clams to eat."

Warden (a bit angry): "Are you doubting me?"

Me: "Oh, no, never. Please tell them to enjoy them."

Our two youngest grand-daughters, Cala (age 9) and Charlotte (age 3, named after my mom), plus my Dani Girl.

Inset: My granddaughter Erika created this picture of a dog on the floor of our pro shop when she was about 9 years old. She even used colored balls for the ears, eyes and nose. Erika is now 19 years old.

He then drove away leaving me with a citation in my hand and two limits of smaller clams in my trunk.

Several months later, my attorney brother Hiram called me. He asked, "What's this with the clams?"

I said, "What do you mean?"

He replied, "I see where you got a ticket for digging too many of them."

I stated, "You gotta' be kidding me! Where did you see that?"

He said, "We got a new computer at the public defender's office, and I looked you up."

Wow! Now I have a record as a clam thief.

We rarely used the house, as I seldom could sneak away from work. My golf buddies and I stayed there every year while we played in the Grays Harbor pro-am. As time went on, we realized that the privacy rewarded with the three wooded lots wasn't what we were looking for. Being wooded, there were more mosquitoes. Plus, we had trees fall and block our driveway on two different occasions. We also realized that as we grew older, we would rather have a one-level house without stairs to climb.

We looked around the area and eventually found another house on Duck Lake that had only one floor. It also had a guest house. The lot it sits on does not have a tree on it. We have neighbors on both sides of us who we enjoy. We are on a loop, so almost all of the traffic is people who live here. We loopers are sort of a community of our own.

Basically, I quit working five years ago. We bought this house six years ago, but for three years I drove the three-hour drive frequently to do payroll, pay bills and all the other bookkeeping. For over 40 years I ran the business using a calculator, paper and pencil. Instead of a computer, I had a spreadsheet, check register and payroll book. Now that prehistoric Johnny is gone, Jeff and Dave use something called a computer. I even think I have heard the name QuickBooks.

Liz has always stayed at home. She has enjoyed sewing, knitting and doll making. She even taught doll making for a number of years. A couple times a year she goes to holiday or craft fairs to sell her wares. Now at Ocean Shores she has become a regular social butterfly. She walks her pug, Toastie, at least twice a day around the loop. What would be a 15-minute walk usually takes an hour as she stops to chat with one neighbor or another. We even go to dinner with our neighbor friends.

I have been helping at the Ocean Shores Golf Course two or three days a week. I work in the pro shop and usually handle the closing shift. This allows me to still sleep in, and it isn't as busy after 1:00 PM. I volunteer my help because it gives me something to do, plus I get to meet more people and be a part of things. The golf course is seldom really busy, and this is especially true in the afternoons which keeps my stress level seldom above zero. Another reason I volunteer is that the owners, Curt and Tonya Zander, are really nice people, and they have to work long hours. Anything I can do to help makes me feel good and allows me to be part of the golf course family.

Even though I am a so-called golf professional, they let me belong to their Men's Club and play in their events. I seldom win anything, since I am what I call a reverse sandbagger. My handicap is lower than it should be rather than too high like a classic sandbagger. I am 77 years old, and my handicap is 11.8. I finally reached one of my goals on September 6th of 2019 when I shot my age of 73. I didn't think I would ever do it because I would choke. Now I have done it a total of nine times with the last time being on 5/9/22 with a 75 which was one under my age at that point. Every day I find that golf balls fly shorter and shorter distances.

While we love everything about living at Ocean Shores, we do miss living by son Jeff and his wife Kari. They have been our neighbors since they graduated from Western Washington University. We got to watch our grandchildren grow, play sports, perform in bands, and help at the golf course. Trevor is now 22 and is close to getting his Masters degree at Converse College. He had graduated from Winthrop College in South Carolina where he had a scholarship to play on their Overwatch video game team. True story, not a joke. Trevor did play some baseball and was a good pitcher. Although he rarely plays or practices golf much, he can come out of nowhere and shoot a round in the 70's.

Erika graduated from Mount Si High School this year after two years of the running start program at Bellevue Community College. In a couple weeks she will be off to Bellingham, WA to attend Western Washington University.. She has been active playing softball, soccer, basketball and golf, and running cross country. All of this in spite of having seven vertebrae fused to straighten her severe scoliosis. She is an incredibly tough young lady. She even dislocated and broke her finger in a basketball game and continued to play anyway. She then continued to play future games with the broken finger taped to the one next to it.

Kari is a wonderful mother who works full time and can't fix a bad meal. She grew up on a dairy farm and can handle anything thrown at her. From normal day to day stuff to landscaping or home remodeling, she is very talented.

Son Willie went off to Linfield College in McMinnville, Oregon and never came back. Actually, he did come back for the summers between his college years. Willie and his wife Sarah live in Milwaukie, Oregon. Willie has been a mail carrier for close to 20 years. The last 10 years or so he has been involved in Postal Union activities. In fact, he is currently the President of the Oregon Postal Union. His union activities require him to travel all over the country for union matters.

Sarah has worked for several groups to fight domestic abuse. She acted as a consultant in many of the jobs. Right now, she has her hands filled with our other two grandchildren. Cala is nine years old and very talented. She is artistic, active and very bright. Her younger sister, Charlotte, is almost four and she is more than a handful. She was named after my mother, and I wouldn't be surprised if she ends up just as talented. She gets the darndest looks on her face that express her many thoughts. She also refers to Ocean Shores by saying, "Grandpa Shores." Thankfully, Willie and his family come to visit us as much as they can.

CHAPTER 76

Remarkable Trips

S ince moving to Ocean Shores, I have done two big golf trips. One to play golf and one to watch golf.

Five of us went to the 2018 Masters Championship. I never got my wish to play Augusta, but at least I got to go there. The five included Curt Zander and Roy Eckersley, both from Ocean Shores. My son Jeff, David "Pruggy" Doty, and I rounded out the group.

Roy was the ex-pro from Ocean Shores who had been the leader of our 1988 trip to England and Scotland. He ended up being the center of most of the interesting and strange events that happened on the Augusta trip. He was our self-appointed leader and thus he scheduled flights, reserved motel rooms, and arranged the rental van. Every step of the way, Roy scheduled whatever was cheapest with no regard to comfort or individual differences.

Traveling both ways required a layover of over two hours. All of the seats were economy and could not be changed. The economy seats required that all seats were middle, no window or aisle. As a larg-er-than-average senior citizen, I absolutely hate middle seats, and so do the people stuck on either side of me. I prefer the aisle, because having to pee happens more often now that I'm over 70.

Roy reserved three rooms at a cheaper motel. Each room had one queen size bed. Of course, Roy claimed one room for himself. That left two rooms with one bed each for the remaining four of us. I will admit that I am not truly comfortable sleeping with another male. Jeff and I could have paired up as we are father and son, but that would have left one bed for Curt and David to share. At that point they knew each other, but they weren't exactly good friends. They had no desire to be-come bed partners at that point in time. Therefore, Curt and I took one room, and Jeff and David took the other. Curt did point out to me that he suffered from restless leg syndrome, and that any contact would be totally accidental. Regardless, we all managed to brave four nights

Jeff and me in front of Butler Cabin at "The Masters" at Augusta National.

together on queen beds that only had the sleeping area of a double bed because the edges collapsed off the side.

The rental van that Roy reserved was big enough and never broke down. We rented it in Atlanta where we landed, so we had a bit of a drive to Augusta. We had a definite required return time with a sizable fine for being late.

The itinerary had us watching the tournament Tuesday through Friday and flying home Saturday. Curt and I, along with others, would watch the final round Sunday back in Ocean Shores. Afterwards we did explain that even though Curt and I had slept together for four nights we didn't even spoon. Curt's wife Tonya and Liz both seemed just fine with our arrangement and explanations.

Getting back to the start of this adventure: I drove Curt and Roy to SeaTac Airport where we met Jeff and David for our flight. The first sign of trouble on this tour came on the two-hour-plus drive to SeaTac Airport. About one hour from Ocean Shores, Roy insisted we pull into a rest stop so he could use the can. Instead of using the restroom, I watched Roy pull out a pack of cigarettes and then disappear around the side of the restroom without going into it. When he returned to the car, five minutes later, he smelled of smoke. I asked him why he didn't even go into the restroom, and he claimed that he did. I told him that was crap and stated that he only got us to stop so he could sneak off to smoke. Finally, he admitted that was the truth. I soon learned that Roy wasn't as "with it" as he had been on the trip in 1988. Of course, neither am I. We were still a good match. He was fun to be with but could lose his attention and potentially get confused about his exact location.

Tuesday and Wednesday at the Masters Tournament, the three young guys walked the course to take pictures. Roy was over 80 and I was over 70 so walking the course at the speed that was necessary to see it all was out of question for us. I soon learned that Roy could wander in order to get his nicotine fix. Thursday, once the tournament started, cameras were not allowed. Keeping an eye on Roy was not easy. Roy wouldn't walk beside you; he would insist on walking 15 to 20 feet back. I think he thought it was funny to make me keep looking back, but it wasn't! I would have to turn and look back for him every few steps. If I lost him in the crowd, I'm not sure we could have ever found him again. So, it was three steps forward, and then look back for Roy. I did this over and over again anytime we changed locations. After two days of frustration, I also had a stiff neck.

Wednesday, Roy and I attended the par 3 tournament. We found a good spot to watch from. It turns out that the par 3 tournament is more like a picnic without food for the players and their families. They have their kids hitting some shots as other kids are barrel rolling down the hills. Every so often Roy would ask to go smoke. Once I was sure he would return without getting lost, I let him wander over away from the people where I could still see him. He returned from one of these smoke breaks with Gib Long, the guy who was going to line me up with a bookie over 25 years before. You remember, the guy who stiffed me for $700 and darted for Whitefish, Montana. What a small world it really is. We had a short visit, and I didn't mention the money he still owed me from years ago.

Later that afternoon I wanted to go into the huge building where you could purchase souvenirs. Roy didn't want to, but I couldn't just leave him on his own. I found a spot on a bench that had a space for him to sit. I then sat him down between two guys who assured me that they wouldn't let him get away. I told them that the day before I had put a cowbell on him, but he managed to chew it off and Roy even chuckled about that. Fortunately, when I returned about 15 minutes later they still had Roy corralled.

Augusta National is beautiful, and the Masters is probably the most prestigious tournament in golf. Just being there is a thrill, but there are several things about the tournament that are amazing. First of all, as PGA professionals we get to attend it free of charge. No reservations are necessary, just show our PGA membership cards at a booth, get our passes, and enter. Second, food and beverages for all attendees are inexpensive. Their famous pimento cheese sandwich was only $1.50. The most expensive sandwich was $3.00 for BBQ beef. A cup of beer was $3.00 and came in a nice souvenir plastic cup with "The Masters Tournament" printed on the side. The real showstopper was in the bathrooms. Attendants directed you to available urinals or toilets depending on your need. If you were going to use a toilet, they disinfected and wiped off the seat before you entered the stall. This was all pre-COVID too. Also, on the course there were banks of phones that anyone could use for no charge. I placed a call to Liz in Ocean Shores just to see if they really worked.

On Thursday and Friday, we found seats in galleries from which to view the action. We were watching on the par five 15th hole as Sergio Garcia hit four shots into the water on the way to a score of 13 on the hole. He was the defending champion from the year before too. I was totally impressed that he didn't display any fits of anger during the whole thing. He ended up shooting 81 that day and missed the cut to play the weekend.

When Jeff and I were coming back to the seats from a restroom break, I asked Jeff if anyone had a bunch of fans besides Tiger Woods and maybe Jordan Spieth. Jeff started going on about how Dustin

Johnson, Ricky Fowler, Justin Thomas, Phil Mickelson and a couple others had a big following. As we discussed who might have the biggest following, I noticed a beautiful gal with a figure to match walking in front of us wearing an outfit that showed it all off. I commented that I would bet $5 that she had a bigger following than any player at the tournament. As I said that, it turned out that her husband was passing by me on his way to catch up with her.

He gave me quite a glare and said, "That's my wife."

I said, "Nice day, isn't it."

Fortunately, he wasn't into hitting old men.

On the way back to the airport we got a late start because Roy wasn't ready to go on time. Curt was driving quite quickly in an attempt to make it back in time and Dave was looking for an easy place for us to stop and get a coffee at Starbucks. When we were only a few miles from the exit for Starbucks, Roy piped up that he needed to stop at the rest area that he saw was the next exit. We all pleaded with him, can't you wait just five more minutes until we get to Starbucks, but he insisted he had to go now. Curt stopped at the rest area, and Roy slowly walked up to the building while getting out and lighting a cigarette. He then stood outside the restroom smoking the cigarette. Finally, he went into the restroom for about 30 seconds and then came out to walk back to the van. You guessed it; it was only another bullshit smoke break.

We quickly got back on the road and to the Starbucks. Here Roy said he didn't want anything and stood outside smoking another cigarette while we all got coffee. Of course, when we came out with our drinks to get back on the road, Roy went in and ordered a coffee for himself.

Finally, we got back on the road and raced for the airport to return the car on time. Roy asked one more time for Curt to stop for a restroom break, which I am sure Roy had yet to actually take, but Curt told him no.

We got the car back almost on the exact minute it was due for return and the car rental agency was trying to charge us a massive fine for being late. Curt and Roy were both arguing with them about the fine, and whether we were actually late, when Roy abruptly left the argument. He went to his suitcase and quickly got out one of the souvenir Masters beer cups. Instantly, Jeff, Dave and I went, *Oh no, tell me this isn't what I think it is!*

Unfortunately, we were all correct. He took the cup and stood behind a half wall in this busy parking garage at the airport about 20 feet from the return counter where Curt was still arguing with the agent about the fine. He then, to all of our disbelief, proceeded to pee in the cup. He then emptied the cup into a nearby garage floor drain and finally put the cup back into the stack of souvenir cups in his suitcase.

Somehow, he pulled this off without being arrested, and Curt ended up being charged for an extra day on the van, which I helped him pay for. I will say that I don't plan on going over to Roy's house ever for drinks.

To top it all off, I had to get Roy to close his suitcase and catch the tram out to our flight in Atlanta that we would have missed if we hadn't gotten on that tram. Then again, I had to save him when it was time to catch the final flight home out of Kansas City after our layover. He was nowhere to be found and it was time to board the plane. Fortunately, I looked outside for him and found him smoking. I hauled him in just in time to catch our final flight home. Without me on the trip with him, Roy may not have ever seen his home in Ocean Shores again.

Two years ago, Jeff put together a trip for eight people to golf all over Scotland. Included in the trip was my old pal, Bill Jackson. Also joining in the trip was one of my fellow graduates from Mount Si High School, Garry Dovenberg. Garry and I had reconnected at our 50th high school reunion. Garry had moved to California shortly after graduation in 1963. You will read about Garry in the next chapter.

During this 12-day trip we would play many fantastic and famous golf courses. Between being 73 years old, pulling my left calf muscle two weeks before we left, and generally being out of shape I couldn't play every round. I had been pushing my '49 Suburban when it felt like someone hit me in the calf with a hammer. Therefore, before leaving on the trip, I had to get a handicap parking permit from the Department of Licensing to take with me, so that courses in Scotland would allow me to use a power cart.

We spent one day in Edinburgh with no golfing plans. We toured Edinburgh Castle and walked the Royal Mile. Back in 1988, we did virtually no sightseeing; this trip a full day went to seeing Edinburgh and we saw other sites along the way like Loch Ness and Castle Stuart as well as doing some touring around St. Andrews and Royal Dornoch. I also rubbed the nose of Greyfriar's Bobby for good luck. He was a Skye terrier who guarded his master's grave for 14 years between 1858 and 1872.

The first night in Scotland, I had to make up for something I had chickened out on in 1988. I ordered a hors d'oeuvre plate of haggis for the eight of us to try. Only one in our group refused to give it a try. It really wasn't bad, but I doubt I would eat it regularly.

The tour service that Jeff lined us up with was great. Shaun, our driver and guide, was fabulous. I could even understand him most of the time when he spoke. Once during the drive to North Berwick, Shaun spoke up to correct Jeff in the funniest way. Jeff was telling the guys that he had heard North Berwick was an amazing golf course that many people he knew spoke highly of it. Unfortunately for Jeff, he kept pronouncing it the way it looked as North "Bur Wick". After about the third time, Shaun in his heavy Scottish accent said, "I can't take it no more, Jeff. It's North "Bare Ick" not "Bur Wick"—which gave us all quite the laugh. Plus, now we all know how to pronounce it correctly forever more.

Unfortunately, we never got drawn in any of the many lotteries we entered to play The Old Course at St. Andrews. I was hoping to play it with Jeff, so that was a bit of a letdown. Jeff managed to play it by getting in line at 3:00 AM one day and signing up as a single to join any group they could find. By 3:00 AM he was already 17th in line. He was rewarded with his effort by getting to tee off just after 3:00 PM on that same day.

In 12 days, Jeff and two others played 11 rounds with two days of no golf. A couple others played 9 rounds; my friend Billy and his roommate Dick played 7 rounds but flew home two days early. I played 6 rounds, including walking all 18 holes at Turnberry with a little help from a caddy carrying my clubs. That was my favorite of the courses that I played. I also played Royal Troon, Royal Dornoch, Carnoustie, Kings Barns and the Kittocks Course at St. Andrews.

Years ago, I was given another nickname. Dave Gillett, a soccer player from Scotland who played defender for the Seattle Sounders, called me a "wee poison dwarf." That caught on with some of the members at Sno Falls who followed suit. Dave said there was a group in Scotland who were short, stocky and drinkers who tended to be unruly. Being proud of this nickname, I had it printed on a couple thousand golf tees. I made sure to fill my golf bag with these tees for the Scotland golf adventure as well. This worked out great, as I would give them to our caddies as well as a few others we met along the way. They all seemed to love them and thought that it was a good name for me.

All in all, it was a great trip. I managed to shoot in the 80's every round, even though it was windy every day. What we call a gale over here in the states is just a minor breeze over there in Scotland.

CHAPTER 77

2-R Garry – Wild Wet Ride

I mentioned Garry Dovenberg as a fellow golfer in our Scotland trip, and as my companion in driving my newly purchased 1949 Chevy Suburban from Sacramento, CA to Fall City, WA.

There is more to our relationship to be mentioned. First of all, he is the only two-R Garry I have ever known. I did once bowl in a league with a three B Bobb, but that's another story.

I first met Garry when I started in kindergarten. He and I continued to be classmates all the way through high school graduation.

Through grade school, Garry and I were friends and I played at his house a few times. On one of those days, Garry and his brother Jim had brought back kelp from a recent visit to the ocean. They had the whip ends. What could be more fun for 12- or 13-year-old boys than to beat each other with these 6- to 8-foot whips?

When I went back home, which was over a mile away as Garry lived right in North Bend, I hadn't looked in a mirror. I arrived home just in time for dinner and Mom and Dad were a bit taken back by the welts on my face, arms and upper body. My legs may have had some too but they didn't come under inspection.

Even though I had to listen to a lecture on safety and my lack of good sense, fortunately, Dad didn't call Garry's dad and raise hell with him.

Through high school, Garry and I remained friends, but had different interests and activities. Upon graduation, Garry immediately bolted for California and sunshine while I stayed in Washington.

Fifty years later at our 50th reunion, Garry and I hooked up and renewed our friendship.

I had attended our 10th and 20th but had missed our 25th because it took place during my trip to the British Open in 1988. I'm not even sure if Garry was at those reunions or not.

I had been on the committee to organize the 20th and 25th even though I could not attend the 25th. I was emcee for the 20th and my "brother" Dick Sparks took over that job for the 25th.

For the 50th, I was a committee member again and emcee. The reunion was a success as we had nearly 60 in attendance out of a class of 82. Classmates came from many states to attend, including California and Georgia. We had a good turnout for our 55th reunion for which I was the emcee again.

During committee meetings after the graduation to organize for the next one, it was agreed that Garry was definitely the "heart throb" of all the female committee members. I retained my position as the mutation who was funny… at times.

❧

MY FIRST VEHICLE THAT WAS mine was a 1959 Chevy Impala convertible. I was allowed to get it after my first year in college. It was mentioned earlier when I got pulled over in LaCross, WA for speeding and littering by a hayseed sheriff in a station wagon.

When I traded it in, I got $500 towards a Plymouth Barracuda. The Impala would now be worth close to $100,000. In addition, I really liked it. So over 25 years later I bought another one for only $24,500. The original was white, this one was red.

This started my search for the "ideal" old car of my dreams. The convertible was great but I was always afraid my dog might jump out of it. I did sell it after several years for a couple thousand more than I paid for it.

I then got a 1950 Chevy Pickup for $1,500. It ran OK but wasn't up for over 50 mph and I ended up giving it to a guy who then in turn built a small shed for me.

Then I bought a 1937 Chevy pickup for $3,500 that was stock. At 35 mph it felt like it was going to come apart or blow up, or shimmy off the road. Six years later and four garages later (along with many thousands of dollars), it was beautiful and could get me any speeding ticket I desired. However, it just didn't seem to be "the one" for me. I did take one hell of a bath when I sold it so at least I didn't smell.

Next up was a 1934 four-door Chevy Sedan with suicide doors in a gorgeous blue. I had learned to buy a vehicle that was already fixed up. I really liked it—BUT—it didn't have door handles. It was what they call shaved and only opened with remote clickers. That was fine, but there was also a short somewhere in the vehicle that drained the battery. I had to keep a jump starter battery with me to get in it. Fortunately, I sold that for a couple thousand more than I paid for it.

Next came a 1959 Impala two-door hardtop. My dog, Baxter, couldn't jump out of that. But somehow that didn't scratch my itch, so I got a 1950 Chevy sedan delivery. It was beautiful. The black, orange and white interior complimented the shiny black exterior. It even had a back seat and air conditioning. The only drawback to it was the road noise with it was loud and you couldn't hear the radio or carry on a conversation in it.

After a couple of years with both the '59 Impala and the sedan delivery, I had to actually think about money as our place at the ocean needed new siding. I had to sell one or the other. I sold the sedan delivery at a bit of a loss and soon regretted it, since it was more unique than the Impala.

About a year later, I decided I wanted to find a Chevy Suburban. It would have the unique qualities of the sedan delivery but be safer in that it would have windows all around for better vision. To make this purchase, I was able to sell the Impala for slightly more than I paid for it, and almost $10,000 more than I was to pay for the 1949 Suburban.

❦

So NOW WE HAVE CIRCLED back to two-R Garry. The suburban was located about an hour from where Garry lived in California. I got Garry to check it out before I paid for it. Two of my previous purchases I bought after seeing pictures and not seeing them in person for test driving them. That's how I got one with no door handles.

The plan was that I fly to Sacramento and stay one night with Garry and his beautiful wife Trish. Then I would drive to Fall City, WA in the '49 Suburban. Seldom do plans totally come together.

My flight to Sacramento got canceled until the next day. When Garry picked me up at the Sacramento Airport at 3:30 PM, he informed me that we were heading North, no overnight stay for me. His schedule did not give him time to stay in Fall City more than one night, so off we went.

We took turns driving through the night and all was fine until we hit rain in Southern Washington. The windshield wipers looked fine, but they didn't work. We stopped and got Rain X, but vision was awful in the dark and heavy rain.

Not only was the rain making vision difficulty, but it was cold and wet. There were leaks through the vents and around the windshield. The driver got soaked and the passenger only got wet. Furthermore, the heater didn't work.

However, we did make it to Fall City by 6:30 AM without crashing.

A few days later, I took the vehicle to my buddy, Joe Loranger, to have him check it out at Loranger's Automotive in Preston. Amongst things Joe discovered were:

The steering column was about to become disengaged where steering would no longer be an option.

The bolts on both front wheels weren't long enough—so if the lugs were to loosen by about a half turn, the wheels would have fallen off!

Other than that, it was a safe trip. Obviously, it has taken more than that $10,000 extra I got for the Impala to get the Suburban up to snuff. It now has power windows, rear view windows, air conditioning, no leaks, new paint job and runs great! The windshield wipers even work.

I'm pretty sure it will be my last old car—and it *is* unique!

The nine-hour drive also gave Garry and me plenty of time to catch up on the 52 years since graduation.

CHAPTER 78

Pets!

Ibelieve I mentioned my fondness of pets and dogs in particular. I know I talked about Humphrey earlier, the stray kitten I found in a tree at Snoqualmie Falls Golf. He became my buddy and the golf course cat for years.

Liz has always preferred cats and we have had many cats over the years. Many of these cats have been abandoned strays and such that we have taken into our home and loved. I did find out that smoking can cause people to acquire more cats.

I had started smoking after I found my father after his attempted suicide. The one thing he stressed to me over the years was that I should not smoke. I started smoking after that Father's Day night in 1963. Of course, I hid my smoking from him once he was released from the hospital. Over the next 30 years, he never knew I smoked, but I really showed him. I ended up hooked on smoking for many years to come. I even quit smoking during my third year of teaching but started up again 11 years later.

So, you ask, how did smoking lead to several cats? The last several years I smoked, Liz didn't know it. I know she didn't know, because if she did, she would have hounded me to quit. Also, at that time many of my employees smoked, so I was around smoke every day. My clothes smelled like smoke and my car smelled like smoke. So, during a few years span of sneaking smoke breaks, I would drive around country roads and smoke. When I bought a new car that didn't stink of smoke, I would drive to a hidden spot, park, and pound back several cigarettes.

On one of those occasions, I discovered a mother cat and six kittens in a box. When I picked up the box to bring it home, the mother cat jumped out and ran into the woods. I then put the box back and left. I planned to return and grab the mother first and then the box. Upon returning I found only four kittens left and no mother cat. I

Jeff with wife Kari, son Trevor, and daughter Erika. Trevor is now 22 and Erika is 19.

decided to take the four kittens home, since they would all die otherwise. The kitten's eyes weren't even open yet. Keith took one of the kittens once it was big enough and we kept the other three. That brought us up to six cats at the time.

Then about a year later while driving and smoking I discovered two half-grown kittens on another country road. I went home and Liz and I returned with tuna fish to lure them over. They were fairly wild. Liz grabbed the gray-colored male, and I grabbed the black-colored female. The male was tougher and bit Liz several times, but she managed to still hold onto it. We got them back home and in time they became tame.

That made our inventory of cats peak out at 8. It was time for me to quit smoking. I managed to quit because every insurance plan I

Baxter on holiday from his public relations job at Sno Falls Golf. He decided to take me to the ocean.

carried had me listed as a non-smoker. I could picture laying in a hospital bed and being told to get lost because my insurance was no good.

I had to cold turkey it, since Liz thought I didn't smoke. That meant I couldn't use the patch or chew Nicorette without indicating I had been smoking. I just gutted it out, and now have been free from smoking for over 20 years. Since then our cat population has dwindled down to zero. I won't start smoking again so we can remain cat free. Liz has her second pug, Toastie, and seems happy to go without kitty litter boxes to clean. She also can get by without scratched furniture and fur balls.

I have always loved dogs. As a kid I had Teddy. I talked about him earlier. Soon after Liz and I got married we got a couple basset hounds. When Jeff and Willie were young, we picked up two pups from people outside our local grocery store. We didn't get to keep either one of them for very long though. One of them chased the neighbors' chickens and the other one growled at people.

Then we got a little black dog from the Humane Society that the kids named Spooky. He was a wonderful little guy, but one day came home sick. Liz rushed him to the vet, but he passed away there from being poisoned. Jeff and Willie were in school that day while this all happened. I picked them up from school and headed straight to the Humane Society. On the way there, I told them that Spooky had died.

When we got there, we picked out a furry mid-sized mutt who was supposedly a mixed terrier. He was about 9 months old and already was named Charlie. When we walked in the house with Charlie, Liz took one look and laughed. She thought Charlie was funny looking.

As Charlie and the kids grew up, he was a good companion for all of us. When I was home, he gravitated to me. Every night this 55-pound fur ball would sit in my lap. I have always sweated easily, but his body heat would make me sweat that much more.

One day, when I was looking out our front window, I saw a blond-colored dog walk by. She looked lost to me. When I went to work an hour later, she was at the golf course. After work I took her home with me. When she jumped out of the cab of my pickup at home, she spotted our big orange and white cat that we called Sunny. I had already named this stray dog Angie, because I thought her hair color was the same as Angie Dickenson's. Anyway, Angie ran at Sunny. Probably because she was a dog and Sunny was a cat. Sunny, not knowing he was a cat, stood his ground and even moved toward Angie to inspect her. Angie came to a halt and then started to back away from Sunny. Sunny then pursued Angie around the yard until Angie finally got behind me for protection. That was the last time Angie ever tried to chase after a cat.

Every night Charlie would sit in my lap and Angie would lie beside our chair. Both of them would stay at home during the day while I was at work. Four years after I brought Angie home, Charlie got cancer and passed away. Angie immediately took over Charlie's place on my lap. Within a week she showed up at the golf course. She remembered where we met and I couldn't get her to stay home, so I started taking her wherever I went.

Angie lived for several years after that and upon her passing away

I just couldn't get another dog. After a couple years, I bought a book about dog breeds. Jeff and Kari were married at that time and planning to have kids. I made a list of various breeds that were good with children, and I thought I had the book and list well hidden in my office.

I was attending a PGA meeting in Portland, Oregon and got called out of it to take a phone call. Jeff was calling because he had found my list and felt I should have a dog. Wheaten Terrier was one of the breeds I listed and there was a breeder in Vancouver, Washington with a litter ready to go. Of course, Vancouver is just across the river from Portland and that was why Jeff was calling to tell me about these puppies. However, I convinced Jeff that I just wasn't ready yet even though it was over two years since Angie had passed.

About a month later, Jeff spotted an ad in the paper for puppies in Centralia, Washington that were half Wheaten Terrier and half Irish terrier. The lady who ran the kennel raised both breeds. She claimed that Mom and Dad had gotten it done through a cyclone fence. I ended up giving in and got one of the pups. I named him Baxter, but I did consider the name Cyclone instead.

Baxter became my little buddy then at 3.5 months of age, and went everywhere with me. He also took over Snoqualmie Falls Golf Course as he had the members wrapped around his little paws.

There were two ladies, in particular, that Baxter fell in love with. Each of them had about eight different people that they normally played with, including their husbands and children. When Baxter would see any one of them, he would follow them in hopes they would lead him to his girlfriends. He was a smart fella and this strategy often worked.

Baxter would also play golf with me and soon learned how to stay far enough away for his own safety. He also stayed out of the way of people when they were putting. He was a better playing partner than most people.

I appointed Baxter to the position of "Head of Public Relations" for the course. We also had a sign with our golf professionals listed and he was added to that sign as one of our golf pros.

Unfortunately, dogs just don't live long enough. When he started going downhill, I did one of the dumbest things I have ever done. I got a copy of *Marley and Me* to read. When I got towards the end of

My wonderful, smart, precious and brilliant Dani with me at the beach.

the book, Marley's age was upon her, and she was fading. As I read about all the things Marley couldn't do anymore and how she had to be carried up and down stairs I had tears running down my face. I was reading a checklist of how Baxter was fading himself.

Finally, Baxter got to where he couldn't eat, and he was therefore starving to death. He had liver failure and he was getting skinnier all the time. I had the mobile vet come to our house and I held Baxter as he was put to sleep. When I carried him out of the house in a blanket, I wanted to ask the vet if he could maybe bring him back to life, but I didn't. I had Baxter cremated and I saved his ashes. My old buddy Bill Jackson had a plaque made for me as a tribute to Baxter.

I had gone over two years between Angie's death and getting Baxter. I would have waited even longer if it hadn't been for Jeff. The day after I had Baxter put to sleep, I had my weekly bowling night.

As usual, the bowling team consumed some beer. Once I got home, I googled dog rescue and ended up on a site called Pet Finders. Soon I was staring at a little white dog that they called Oxy.

I read how Oxy went to work with the lady who was her foster parent. I then was looking at pictures of her when Liz walked in and asked what I was doing. She then looked at the pictures and read the information.

She quickly said, "Do it!"

The application required sending an attachment, which I don't know how to do. Instead, I sent a simple email expressing my interest. A lady called me the next day at the golf course to interview me.

She asked for our vet's name and phone number so she could contact him. She asked what I did to discipline a dog. There were several other questions she asked as well.

Lady: "How many people live in your home?"

Me: "Two. My wife and I."

Lady: "How old are you?"

Me: "66"

Lady: "How old is your wife?"

Me: "24"

Lady: long silence

Me: "I was just kidding. She is 64."

Lady: "Oh, that's fine, but it still would have been OK if she was 24."

Me: "Darn right it would."

In spite of the interview, I got a call the next day asking if I wanted to meet Oxy. Of course, I did, and our friends Patrick and Audrey drove me to meet her. They had been best friends with Baxter and they kind of felt like I was rushing things. We went to the catering place where Oxy helped her foster parent work. The lady handed her to me and as I sat down Oxy laid her head on my shoulder and gave me a couple kisses on my cheek and ear. That sealed the deal.

I asked the gal, "What else do I need to do?"

She asked, "Do you want to take Oxy home for good?"

Without hesitation I replied, "Well, d'uh!"

I happily paid the adoption fee and I asked her, "How many people do you normally turn down?"

She said, "About 3 out of 4."

On the way home we discussed names for Oxy. She had been Oxy for only a week. Nobody knew what name(s) she had as a stray in Stockton, California. She also had just given birth to a batch of puppies. They waited for her to finish weaning the puppies and then sent her to Seattle with about a hundred other dogs. We decided on Bailey for her name.

That night my obsessive-compulsive mind went to work, and I wasn't sure if it would be pronounced "Bale E" or "Bay Lee". Finally, I gave up and started going through the alphabet. At the letter D I decided on Dani. There is only one way to pronounce it, plus at formal occasions it could be Danielle. I ended up adding girl to it, so it became Dani Girl. I had to do that on her request. When golfers heard she was named Dani, they would say Danny Boy, and maybe even start singing it, and that would upset her. Now, she and I are both happy with Dani Girl.

Dani didn't replace Baxter because no puppy could. She helped fill the hole in my heart left by his departure. I had waited over two years after Angie passed to get Baxter. I barely waited over a day to apply to get Dani. Without a doubt, that was the way to go. When I took her home it was December 23rd, 2011. Christmas morning after presents had been opened and we had a house full of relatives, there was Dani sound asleep under the Christmas tree.

She was a skinny girl of 17 pounds with her ribs showing when I took her into our home. Now, well away from the streets of Stockton, she weighs in at about 30 pounds and she is in good shape. When I got her, they estimated her age at 1.5 years old. If they were correct, she is about 12 years old now.

Dani took over Baxter's job of running Snoqualmie Falls Golf Course, and she has most everything under control down here at Ocean Shores Golf Course as well. My life is much better with Dani in it. She and I have discussed it and we want to leave this life together. We just can't figure out the how and when.

So, Liz and I are here at Ocean Shores looking out at Duck Lake as we snuggle Toastie and Dani. We certainly wouldn't snuggle with each other or let anyone know if we did. Liz has survived just over 55 years of marriage with me and we have two sons who are both married. They have provided us with four grandchildren ranging in age from four to twenty-two and all of them are healthy and hopefully happy.

Liz sews, knits, visits with neighbors, and talks on her flip phone. She takes walks with and tends to all of Toastie's needs. She does not use a computer.

I golf, fish a little bit, read books, visit with neighbors, work and hang out at the golf course in Ocean Shores, and occasionally talk on our land-line phone. I do have a computer that I use for fantasy sports, simple emails (no attachments), buying only from eBay, and sometimes googling for information. I admit that I have spent a lot of time over the last eighteen months writing for this book. I have printed by hand the whole damn thing on wide-lined notebook paper to leave room for corrections. I have filled over 1,700 pages with my printed handwriting, of which the last 10 are on plain white copy paper because I ran out of notebook paper.

As this memoir gets ready to be published, I'm able to look back on all these stories with immense gratitude to everyone I've ever encountered. I've been one very lucky Tiny Wood/Cupcake. Or it could be Punkin/Cupcake... Captain G Spot? Or maybe Jumbo/Cupcake.

How about we sign it:

—*the Wee Poison PGA Golf Pro*

Yes, I like that one best.

The End – *For Now!*

CHAPTER 79

50th Reunion

When I wrote "The End – *For Now,*" I must have had a premonition that something else would happen that I would have to brag about. Something DID happen that made this Wee Poison PGA Golf Pro very happy!

About a month ago I was invited to the 50th High School Reunion of the class of 8th graders I taught in the 1967/68 school year. Even though I hadn't taught most of them in high school, they wanted their old 8th grade teacher to attend their high school reunion. The reunion happened a few days ago, and *YES* I attended it.

I hadn't seen more than five or six of "my kids" from that class in 55 years. I only recognized a few of them but did remember most of their names. I wore the shirt Liz made me that has a big cupcake on it.

At least 15 of them told me that I did more for them than any other teacher. Things like building their confidence and believing in themselves. Many also said that I gave them the courage to stand up and speak. Basically, they said that without my influence they never would have been able to achieve what they had done. Several of the 69-year-old girls had tears in their eyes as they spoke.

I simply attempted to teach more than just the subject matter. I tried to prepare them for life. There is the chance that those who were less pleased with me simply didn't come to the reunion.

If I ever feel depressed, I will organize another reunion for the ones I saw that night. I have been putting ice on my head the last two days so the swelling will go down and I can wear my hat again.

Today, as I sat on the sofa petting Dani and looking at Duck Lake, I did some reflecting about the reunion and my teaching days. Reflecting, for me, is a rare event that can be painful.

Earlier in this book I stated that my two years at Tolt High were the most fulfilling and enjoyable of my teaching years. But the reunion with my 8th graders made me rethink that statement. High school

Some of "my kids" from the first class I ever taught – 8th grade back in 1967/68. This is at their 50th High School Reunion. I am wearing the cupcake shirt Liz made for me, surrounded by a bunch of my 68- and 69-year-old 8th graders.

From the left: Sue Sutherland (facing away); Bev Honeywell Weller; Teddy Davis; Marlene Turple Young (kneeling in front); Elise Blomberg; Dale Rooney; Lyla Smith; Cupcake; Lou Dillinger; Sarah Eldred; Harry Whitaker; Jean Sygitowic; Mark Mills; George Gochnour; Mark Randleman.

years may have been the most enjoyable because I also coached basketball and baseball plus directed a school play. I also had more contact with parents which came from sports activities. Also, high school students were generally less troubled and easier to teach.

The "most fulfilling" part was not true. Working with 8th graders was more fulfilling for the reason stated above. I truly believe that by the time a student is in high school, his or her personality and values are fairly well established. Eighth graders are still trying to find themselves and where they fit. Life for them is more difficult. As a teacher helping them find their way, this can be very stressful, if you care, and I did.

I really can't say any era in my life hasn't been enjoyable. A few events weren't, but overall, every time period was joyful. Of course, I always looked for the fun and I almost always found it or created it.

The End – *Really, This Time.*

ACKNOWLEDGEMENTS

Many thanks to the many close friends and family who insisted for years that I should tell my life story—about tragedy & triumph, eagles & double-bogeys, hijinks & (mis-)adventures, love & enduring friendships.... I finally got off my lazy rear and handprinted it on over 1,700 pages of notebook paper. A big thanks to Audrey Nassal Johnson and son Jeff for typing my story into computers.

Paula Gratzer then pulled all of that together. She also added about six extra stories I remembered. After that she scanned and organized photos along with the captions.

Then came the amazing part: Bruce Batchelor of Agio Publishing House agreed to publish it! Bruce has tolerated having to deal with me and has put it all together with the help of his bride, Marsha.

Without all of them this memoir would never have happened.